Praise for *Python for Excel*

What can Python do for Excel? If you've ever dealt with unexpected workbook crashes, broken calculations, and tedious manual processes, you'll want to find out. Python for Excel is a comprehensive and succinct overview to getting started with Python as a spreadsheet user, and building powerful data products using both. Don't let the fear of learning to code keep you away: Felix provides an exceptional foundation for learning Python that even experienced programmers could benefit from. Moreover, he frames this information in a way that is quickly accessible and applicable to you as an Excel user. You can quickly tell reading this book that it was written by someone with years of experience teaching and working with clients on how to use Excel to its fullest extent with the help of Python programming. Felix is uniquely suited to show you the possibilities of learning Python for Excel; I hope you enjoy the master class as much as I did.

—*George Mount, Founder, Stringfest Analytics*

Python is the natural progression from Excel and it's tempting to simply discard Excel all together. Tempting, but hardly realistic. Excel is here, and here to stay, both in the corporate world and as a useful desktop tool at home and in the office. This book provides the much needed bridge between these two worlds. It explains how you can integrate Python into Excel and free yourself from the inevitable disaster of huge workbooks, thousands of formulas, and ugly VBA hacks. *Python for Excel* is probably the single most useful book on Excel that I have read and an absolute must-read for any advanced Excel user. A highly recommended book!

—*Andreas F. Clenow, CIO Acies Asset Management and author of international best-sellers* Following the Trend, Stocks on the Move, *and* Trading Evolved

Excel remains a cornerstone tool of the financial world, but a vast amount of these Excel applications are an irresponsible mess. This book does an excellent job of showing you how to build better, more robust applications with the help of xlwings.

—*Werner Brönnimann, Derivatives and DeFi practitioner and cofounder, Ubinetic AG*

Excel and Python are two of the most important tools in the Business Analytics toolbox, and together they are far greater than the sum of their parts. In this book, Felix Zumstein lays out his unparalleled mastery of the many ways to connect Python and Excel using open source, cross-platform solutions. It will be an invaluable tool for business analysts and data scientists alike, and any Python user looking to harness the power of Excel in their code.

—*Daniel Guetta, Associate Professor of Professional Practice and Director of the Business Analytics Initiative at Columbia Business School and coauthor of* Python for MBAs

Python for Excel

A Modern Environment for Automation and Data Analysis

Felix Zumstein

Beijing · Boston · Farnham · Sebastopol · Tokyo  O'REILLY®

Python for Excel

by Felix Zumstein

Published by O'Reilly Media, Inc., 1005 Gravenstein Highway North, Sebastopol, CA 95472.

O'Reilly books may be purchased for educational, business, or sales promotional use. Online editions are also available for most titles (*http://oreilly.com*). For more information, contact our corporate/institutional sales department: 800-998-9938 or *corporate@oreilly.com*.

Acquisitions Editor: Michelle Smith	**Indexer:** nSight Inc.
Development Editor: Melissa Potter	**Interior Designer:** David Futato
Production Editor: Daniel Elfanbaum	**Cover Designer:** Karen Montgomery
Copyeditor: Piper Editorial Consulting, LLC	**Illustrator:** Kate Dullea
Proofreader: nSight Inc.	

March 2021:   First Edition

Revision History for the First Edition

2021-03-04:   First Release
2022-01-14:   Second Release

See *http://oreilly.com/catalog/errata.csp?isbn=9781492081005* for release details.

978-1-492-08100-5

[LSI]

Table of Contents

Preface

Microsoft is running a feedback forum for Excel on UserVoice (*https://oreil.ly/ y1XwU*) where everybody can submit a new idea for others to vote on. The top voted feature request is "Python as an Excel scripting language," and it has roughly twice as many votes as the second most voted feature request. Though nothing really happened since the idea was added in 2015, Excel users were fueled with new hope at the end of 2020 when Guido van Rossum, the creator of Python, tweeted (*https://oreil.ly/ N1_7N*) that his "retirement was boring" and he would join Microsoft. If his move has any influence on the integration of Excel and Python, I don't know. I do know, however, what makes this combination so compelling and how you can start using Excel and Python together—today. And this is, in a nutshell, what this book is about.

The main driving force behind the *Python for Excel* story is the fact that we are living in a world of data. Nowadays, huge datasets are available to everybody and about everything. Often, these datasets are so big that they don't fit into a spreadsheet anymore. A few years ago, this may have been referred to as *big data*, but nowadays, a dataset of a few million rows is really nothing special. Excel has evolved to cope with that trend: it introduced Power Query to load and clean datasets that don't fit into a spreadsheet and Power Pivot, an add-in to perform data analysis on these datasets and present the results. Power Query is based on the Power Query M formula language (M), while Power Pivot defines formulas by using Data Analysis Expressions (DAX). If you also want to automate a few things in your Excel file, then you would use Excel's built-in automation language, Visual Basic for Applications (VBA). That is, for something fairly simple, you can end up using VBA, M, and DAX. One issue with this is that all these languages only serve you in the Microsoft world, most prominently in Excel and Power BI (I will introduce Power BI briefly in Chapter 1).

Python, on the other hand, is a general-purpose programming language that has become one of the most popular choices amongst analysts and data scientists. If you use Python with Excel, you are able to use a programming language that is good at all aspects of the story, whether that's automating Excel, accessing and preparing datasets, or performing data analysis and visualization tasks. Most importantly, you can reuse your Python skills outside of Excel: if you need to scale up your computing power, you could easily move your quantitative model, simulation, or machine learning application to the cloud, where practically unconstrained computing resources are waiting for you.

Why I Wrote This Book

Through my work on xlwings, the Excel automation package that we will meet in Part IV of this book, I am in close contact with many users who use Python for Excel —whether that's via the issue tracker (*https://oreil.ly/ZJQkB*) on GitHub, a question on StackOverflow (*https://stackoverflow.com*) or at a physical event like a meetup or a conference.

On a regular basis, I am asked to recommend resources to get started with Python. While there is certainly no shortage of Python introductions, they are often either too general (nothing about data analysis) or too specific (full scientific introductions). However, Excel users tend to be somewhere in the middle: they certainly work with data, but a full scientific introduction may be too technical. They also often have specific requirements and questions that aren't answered in any of the existing material. Some of these questions are:

- Which Python-Excel package do I need for which task?
- How do I move my Power Query database connection over to Python?
- What's the equivalent of Excel's AutoFilter or pivot table in Python?

I wrote this book to get you from zero Python knowledge to be able to automate your Excel-centric tasks and leverage Python's data analysis and scientific computing tools in Excel without any detours.

Who This Book Is For

If you are an advanced Excel user who wants to beat the limits of Excel with a modern programming language, this book is for you. Most typically, this means that you spend hours every month downloading, cleaning, and copy/pasting big amounts of data into mission-critical spreadsheets. While there are different ways to overcome Excel's limits, this book will focus on how to use Python for this task.

You should have a basic understanding of programming: it helps if you have already written a function or a for loop (no matter in which programming language) and have an idea about what an integer or a string is. You might even be able to master this book if you are used to writing complex cell formulas or have experience with tweaking recorded VBA macros. You are not expected to have any Python-specific experience, though, as there are introductions to all the tools that we will use including an introduction to Python itself.

If you are a seasoned VBA developer, you will find regular comparisons between Python and VBA that will allow you to ship around the common gotchas and hit the ground running.

This book can also be helpful if you are a Python developer and need to learn about the different ways that Python can deal with the Excel application and Excel files to be able to pick the right package given the requirements of your business users.

How This Book Is Organized

In this book, I will show you all aspects of the *Python for Excel* story split into four parts:

Part I: Introduction to Python
> This part starts by looking into the reasons why Python is such an enjoyable companion for Excel before introducing the tools we'll be using in this book: the Anaconda Python distribution, Visual Studio Code, and Jupyter notebooks. This part will also teach you enough Python to be able to master the rest of this book.

Part II: Introduction to pandas
> pandas is Python's go-to library for data analysis. We will learn how to replace Excel workbooks with a combination of Jupyter notebooks and pandas. Usually, pandas code is both easier to maintain and more efficient than an Excel workbook, and you can work with datasets that don't fit into a spreadsheet. Unlike Excel, pandas allows you to run your code wherever you want, including the cloud.

Part III: Reading and Writing Excel Files without Excel
> This part is about manipulating Excel files by using one of the following Python packages: pandas, OpenPyXL, XlsxWriter, pyxlsb, xlrd, and xlwt. These packages are able to read and write Excel workbooks directly on disk and as such replace the Excel application: as you don't require an installation of Excel, they work on any platform that Python supports, including Windows, macOS, and Linux. A typical use case for a reader package is to read in data from Excel files that you receive every morning from an external company or system and store their contents in a database. A typical use case for a writer package is to provide the functionality behind the famous "Export to Excel" button that you find in almost every application.

Part IV: Programming the Excel Application with xlwings
> In this part, we'll see how we can use Python with the xlwings package to automate the Excel application rather than reading and writing Excel files on disk.

Therefore, this part requires you to have a local installation of Excel. We will learn how to open Excel workbooks and manipulate them in front of our eyes. In addition to reading and writing files via Excel, we will build interactive Excel tools: these allow us to click a button to have Python perform something that you may have done previously with VBA macros, such as a computationally expensive calculation. We'll also learn how to write user-defined functions[1] (UDFs) in Python instead of VBA.

It's important to understand the fundamental difference between reading and writing Excel *files* (Part III) and programming the Excel *application* (Part IV) as visualized in Figure P-1.

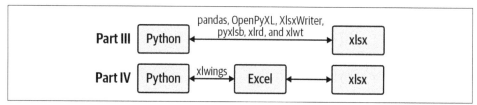

Figure P-1. Reading and writing Excel files (Part III) vs. programming Excel (Part IV)

Since Part III doesn't require an installation of Excel, everything works on all platforms that Python supports, mainly Windows, macOS, and Linux. Part IV, however, will only work on those platforms that Microsoft Excel supports, i.e., Windows and macOS, as the code relies on a local installation of Microsoft Excel.

Python and Excel Versions

This book has been tested to work with the Anaconda Python Distribution 2020.11 (which uses Python 3.8) and 2021.11 (which uses Python 3.9). If you want to use a newer version of Python such as Python 3.10, follow the instructions on the book's home page (*https://xlwings.org/book*). I will occasionally make a comment if something changes between Python 3.8 and Python 3.9.

This book also expects you to use a modern version of Excel, meaning at least Excel 2007 on Windows and Excel 2016 on macOS. The locally installed version of Excel that comes with the Microsoft 365 subscription will also work perfectly—in fact, I even recommend it, as it has the latest features that you won't find in other versions of Excel. It was also the version I used to write this book, so if you use another version of Excel, you might sometimes see a small difference in the name or location of a menu item.

---

1 Microsoft has started to use the term *custom functions* instead of UDFs. In this book, I will continue to call them UDFs.

Conventions Used in This Book

The following typographical conventions are used in this book:

Italic
: Indicates new terms, URLs, email addresses, filenames, and file extensions.

`Constant width`
: Used for program listings, as well as within paragraphs to refer to program elements such as variable or function names, databases, data types, environment variables, statements, and keywords.

`Constant width bold`
: Shows commands or other text that should be typed literally by the user.

`Constant width italic`
: Shows text that should be replaced with user-supplied values or by values determined by context.

This element signifies a tip or suggestion.

This element signifies a general note.

This element indicates a warning or caution.

Using Code Examples

I am maintaining a web page (*https://xlwings.org/book*) with additional information to help you with this book. Make sure to check it out, especially if you run into an issue.

Supplemental material (code examples, exercises, etc.) is available for download at *https://github.com/fzumstein/python-for-excel*. To download this companion repository, click on the green Code button, then select Download ZIP. Once downloaded, right-click the file on Windows and select Extract All to unzip the contained files into a folder. On macOS, simply double-click the file to unzip. If you know how to work with Git, you could also use Git to clone the repository to your local hard disk. You can put the folder anywhere you want, but I will refer to it occasionally as follows in this book:

```
C:\Users\username\python-for-excel
```

By simply downloading and unzipping the ZIP file on Windows, you'll end up with a folder structure similar to this one (note the repeated folder names):

```
C:\...\Downloads\python-for-excel-1st-edition\python-for-excel-1st-edition
```

Copying the contents of this folder into one you create under *C:\Users\<username>\python-for-excel* might make it easier for you to follow along. The same remarks are true for macOS, i.e., copy the files to */Users/<username>/python-for-excel*.

If you have a technical question or a problem using the code examples, please send an email to *bookquestions@oreilly.com*.

This book is here to help you get your job done. In general, if example code is offered with this book, you may use it in your programs and documentation. You do not need to contact us for permission unless you're reproducing a significant portion of the code. For example, writing a program that uses several chunks of code from this book does not require permission. Selling or distributing examples from O'Reilly books does require permission. Answering a question by citing this book and quoting example code does not require permission. Incorporating a significant amount of example code from this book into your product's documentation does require permission.

We appreciate, but generally do not require, attribution. An attribution usually includes the title, author, publisher, and ISBN. For example: "*Python for Excel* by Felix Zumstein (O'Reilly). Copyright 2021 Zoomer Analytics LLC, 978-1-492-08100-5."

If you feel your use of code examples falls outside fair use or the permission given above, feel free to contact us at *permissions@oreilly.com*.

O'Reilly Online Learning

 For more than 40 years, *O'Reilly Media* has provided technology and business training, knowledge, and insight to help companies succeed.

Our unique network of experts and innovators share their knowledge and expertise through books, articles, and our online learning platform. O'Reilly's online learning platform gives you on-demand access to live training courses, in-depth learning paths, interactive coding environments, and a vast collection of text and video from O'Reilly and 200+ other publishers. For more information, visit *http://oreilly.com*.

How to Contact Us

Please address comments and questions concerning this book to the publisher:

O'Reilly Media, Inc.
1005 Gravenstein Highway North
Sebastopol, CA 95472
800-998-9938 (in the United States or Canada)
707-829-0515 (international or local)
707-829-0104 (fax)

We have a web page for this book, where we list errata, examples, and any additional information. You can access this page at *https://oreil.ly/py4excel*.

Email *bookquestions@oreilly.com* to comment or ask technical questions about this book.

For more information about our books, courses, conferences, and news, see our website at *http://www.oreilly.com*.

Find us on Facebook: *http://facebook.com/oreilly*.

Follow us on Twitter: *http://twitter.com/oreillymedia*.

Watch us on YouTube: *http://www.youtube.com/oreillymedia*.

Acknowledgments

As a first-time author, I am incredibly grateful for the help I got from so many people along the way—they made this journey a lot easier for me!

At O'Reilly, I would like to thank my editor, Melissa Potter, who did a great job in keeping me motivated and on schedule and who helped me to bring this book into a readable form. I'd also like to thank Michelle Smith, who worked with me on the initial book proposal, and Daniel Elfanbaum, who never tired of answering my technical questions.

A big thank you goes to all my colleagues, friends, and clients who invested many hours in reading the earliest forms of my drafts. Their feedback was crucial to making the book easier to understand, and some of the case studies are inspired by real-world Excel problems that they shared with me. My thanks go to Adam Rodriguez, Mano Beeslar, Simon Schiegg, Rui Da Costa, Jürg Nager, and Christophe de Montrichard.

I also got helpful feedback from readers of the Early Release version that was published on the O'Reilly online learning platform. Thank you Felipe Maion, Ray Doue, Kolyu Minevski, Scott Drummond, Volker Roth, and David Ruggles!

I was very lucky that the book got reviewed by highly qualified tech reviewers and I really appreciate the hard work they put in under a lot of time pressure. Thanks for all your help, Jordan Goldmeier, George Mount, Andreas Clenow, Werner Brönnimann, and Eric Moreira!

Special thanks go to Björn Stiel, who wasn't just a tech reviewer, but from whom I also learned many of the things I am writing about in this book. I've enjoyed working with you these past few years!

Last but not least, I'd like to extend my gratitude to Eric Reynolds, who merged his ExcelPython project into the xlwings code base in 2016. He also redesigned the whole package from scratch, making my horrible API from the early days a thing of the past. Thank you very much!

## PART I

Introduction to Python

## CHAPTER 1

Why Python for Excel?

Usually, Excel users start to question their spreadsheet tools when they hit a limitation. A classic example is when Excel workbooks contain so much data and formulas that they become slow or in the worst case, crash. It does make sense, though, to question your setup before things go south: if you work on mission-critical workbooks where errors can result in financial or reputational damage or if you spend hours every day updating Excel workbooks manually, you should learn how to automate your processes with a programming language. Automation takes out the risk of human error and allows you to spend your time on more productive tasks than copy/pasting data into an Excel spreadsheet.

In this chapter, I will give you a few reasons why Python is an excellent choice in combination with Excel and what its advantages are compared to Excel's built-in automation language, VBA. After introducing Excel as a programming language and understanding its particularities, I will point out the specific features that make Python so much stronger in comparison with VBA. To start with, however, let's take a quick look at the origins of our two main characters!

In terms of computer technology, Excel and Python have both been around for a very long time: Excel was first launched in 1985 by Microsoft—and this may come as a surprise to many—it was only available for Apple Macintosh. It wasn't until 1987 that Microsoft Windows got its first version in the form of Excel 2.0. Microsoft wasn't the first player in the spreadsheet market, though: VisiCorp came out with VisiCalc in 1979, followed by Lotus Software in 1983 with Lotus 1-2-3. And Microsoft didn't lead with Excel: three years earlier, they released Multiplan, a spreadsheet program that could be used on MS-DOS and a few other operating systems, but not on Windows.

Python was born in 1991, only six years after Excel. While Excel became popular early on, it took Python a bit longer until it got adopted in certain areas like web development or system administration. In 2005, Python started to become a serious alternative for scientific computing when *NumPy*, a package for array-based computing and linear algebra, was first released. NumPy combined two predecessor packages and therefore streamlined all development efforts around scientific computing into a single project. Today, it forms the basis of countless scientific packages, including *pandas*, which came out in 2008 and which is largely responsible for the widespread adoption of Python in the world of data science and finance that started to happen after 2010. Thanks to pandas, Python, alongside R, has become one of the most commonly used languages for data science tasks like data analysis, statistics, and machine learning.

The fact that Python and Excel were both invented a long time ago isn't the only thing they have in common: Excel and Python are also both a programming language. While you are probably not surprised to hear that about Python, it may require an explanation for Excel, which I'll give you next.

Excel Is a Programming Language

This section starts by introducing Excel as a programming language, which will help you to understand why spreadsheet issues turn up in the news on a regular basis. We'll then have a look at a few best practices that have emerged in the software development community and that can save you from many typical Excel errors. We'll conclude with a brief introduction to Power Query and Power Pivot, two modern Excel tools that cover the sort of functionality for which we will use pandas instead.

If you use Excel for more than your grocery list, you are definitely using functions like =SUM(A1:A4) to sum up a range of cells. If you think for a moment about how this works, you will notice that the value of a cell usually depends on one or more other cells, which may again use functions that depend on one or more other cells, and so on. Doing such nested function calls is no different from how other programming languages work, only that you write the code in cells instead of text files. And if that didn't convince you just yet: at the end of 2020, Microsoft announced the introduction of *lambda functions*, which allow you to write reusable functions in Excel's own formula language, i.e., without having to rely on a different language like VBA. According to Brian Jones, Excel's head of product, this was the missing piece that finally makes Excel a "real" programming language.[1] This also means that Excel users should really be called Excel programmers!

There is a special thing, though, about Excel programmers: most of them are business users or domain experts without a formal education in computer science. They are traders, accountants, or engineers, to mention just a few examples. Their spreadsheet tools are designed to solve a business problem and often ignore best practices in

---

1 You can read the announcement of lambda functions on the Excel Blog (*https://oreil.ly/4-0y2*).

software development. As a consequence, these spreadsheet tools often mix inputs, calculations, and outputs on the same sheets, they may require nonobvious steps to be performed for them to work properly, and critical changes are done without any safety net. In other words, the spreadsheet tools are lacking a solid application architecture and are often undocumented and untested. Sometimes, these issues can have devastating consequences: if you forget to recalculate your trading workbook before placing a trade, you may buy or sell the wrong number of shares, which can cause you to lose money. And if it isn't just your own money you are trading, we can read about it in the news, as we'll see next.

Excel in the News

Excel is a regular guest in the news, and during the course of this writing, two new stories hit the headlines. The first one was about the HUGO Gene Nomenclature Committee, which renamed a few human genes so they wouldn't be interpreted by Excel as dates anymore. For example, to prevent that the gene MARCH1 would be turned into 1-Mar, it was renamed into MARCHF1.[2] In the second story, Excel was blamed for the delayed reporting of 16,000 COVID-19 test results in England. The issue was caused by the test results being written to the older Excel file format (*.xls*) that was limited to roughly 65,000 rows. This meant that larger datasets were simply cut off beyond that limit.[3] While these two stories show the continued importance and dominance of Excel in today's world, there is probably no other "Excel incident" that is more famous than the London Whale.

London Whale is the nickname of a trader whose trading mistakes forced JP Morgan to announce a staggering loss of $6 billion in 2012. The source of the blowup was an Excel-based value-at-risk model that was substantially underestimating the true risk of losing money in one of their portfolios. The *Report of JPMorgan Chase & Co. Management Task Force Regarding 2012 CIO Losses*[4] (2013) mentions that "the model operated through a series of Excel spreadsheets, which had to be completed manually, by a process of copying and pasting data from one spreadsheet to another." On top of these operational issues, they had a logical error: in one calculation, they were dividing by a sum instead of an average.

If you want to see more of these stories, have a look at Horror Stories (*https://oreil.ly/WLO-I*), a web page maintained by the European Spreadsheet Risks Interest Group (EuSpRIG).

---

2 James Vincent, "Scientists rename human genes to stop Microsoft Excel from misreading them as dates," *The Verge*, August 6, 2020, *https://oreil.ly/Oqo-n*.

3 Leo Kelion, "Excel: Why using Microsoft's tool caused COVID-19 results to be lost," *BBC News*, October 5, 2020, *https://oreil.ly/vvB6o*.

4 Wikipedia links to the document in one of the footnotes (*https://oreil.ly/0uUj9*) in their article about the case.

To prevent your company from ending up in the news with a similar story, let's have a look at a few best practices next that make your work with Excel massively safer.

Programming Best Practices

This section will introduce you to the most important programming best practices, including separation of concerns, the DRY principle, testing, and version control. As we will see, following them will be easier when you start using Python together with Excel.

Separation of concerns

One of the most important design principles in programming is *separation of concerns*, sometimes also referred to as *modularity*. It means that a related set of functionality should be taken care of by an independent part of the program so it can be easily replaced without affecting the rest of the application. At the highest level, an application is often divided into the following layers:[5]

- Presentation layer
- Business layer
- Data layer

To explain these layers, consider a simple currency converter like the one shown in Figure 1-1. You'll find the *currency_converter.xlsx* Excel file in the *xl* folder of the companion repository.

This is how the application works: type in the Amount and Currency into cells A4 and B4, respectively, and Excel will convert this into US dollars in cell D4. Many spreadsheet applications follow such a design and are used by businesses every day. Let me break the application down into its layers:

Presentation layer
> This is what you see and interact with, i.e., the user interface: the values of cells A4, B4, and D4 together with their labels build the presentation layer of the currency converter.

Business layer
> This layer takes care of the application-specific logic: cell D4 defines how the amount is converted into USD. The formula =A4 * VLOOKUP(B4, F4:G11, 2, FALSE) translates to Amount times Exchange rate.

---

5 The terminology is taken from *Microsoft Application Architecture Guide, 2nd Edition*, which is available online (*https://oreil.ly/8V-GS*).

Data layer

As the name suggests, this layer takes care of accessing the data: the VLOOKUP part of cell D4 is doing this job.

The data layer accesses the data from the exchange rates table that starts in cell F3 and that acts as the database of this little application. If you paid close attention, you probably noticed that cell D4 appears in all three layers: this simple application mixes the presentation, business, and data layers in a single cell.

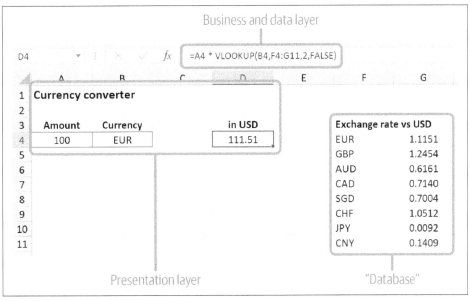

Figure 1-1. currency_converter.xlsx

This isn't necessarily an issue for this simple currency converter, but often, what starts off as a small Excel file turns soon enough into a much bigger application. How can this situation be improved? Most professional Excel developer resources advise you to use a separate sheet for each layer, in Excel's terminology usually called *inputs*, *calculations*, and *outputs*. Often, this is combined with defining a certain color code for each layer, e.g., a blue background for all input cells. In Chapter 11, we will build a real application based on these layers: Excel will be the presentation layer, while the business and data layers are moved to Python, where it's much easier to structure your code properly.

Now that you know what separation of concerns means, let's find out what the DRY principle is!

DRY principle

The Pragmatic Programmer by Hunt and Thomas (Pearson Education) popularized the DRY principle: *don't repeat yourself.* No duplicated code means fewer lines of code and fewer errors, which makes the code easier to maintain. If your business logic sits in your cell formulas, it's practically impossible to apply the DRY principle, as there is no mechanism that allows you to reuse it in another workbook. This, unfortunately, means that a common way to start a new Excel project is to copy the workbook from the previous project or from a template.

If you write VBA, the most common piece of reusable code is a function. A function gives you access to the same code block from multiple macros, for example. If you have multiple functions that you use all the time, you might want to share them between workbooks. The standard instrument to share VBA code across workbooks is add-ins, but VBA add-ins lack a robust way of distributing and updating them. While Microsoft has introduced an Excel internal add-in store to solve that issue, this only works with JavaScript-based add-ins, so it's not an option for VBA coders. This means that it is still very common to use the copy/paste approach with VBA: let's assume that you need a *cubic spline* function in Excel. The cubic spline function is a way to interpolate a curve based on a few given points in a coordinate system and is often used by fixed income traders to derive an interest rate curve for all maturities based on a few known maturity/interest rate combinations. If you search for "Cubic Spline Excel" on the internet, it won't take too long until you have a page of VBA code that does what you want. The issue with this is that most commonly, these functions were written by a single person with probably good intentions but without formal documentation or testing. Maybe they work for the majority of inputs, but what about some uncommon edge cases? If you are trading a multimillion fixed-income portfolio, you want to have something you know you can trust. At least, that is what you will hear from your internal auditors when they find out where the code is coming from.

Python makes it easy to distribute code by using a package manager, as we will see in the last section of this chapter. Before we get there, however, let's continue with testing, one of the cornerstones of solid software development.

Testing

When you tell an Excel developer to test their workbooks, they will most likely perform a few random checks: click a button and see if the macro still does what it is supposed to do or change a few inputs and check if the output looks reasonable. This is, however, a risky strategy: Excel makes it easy to introduce errors that are hard to spot. For example, you can overwrite a formula with a hardcoded value. Or you forget to adjust a formula in a hidden column.

When you tell a professional software developer to test their code, they will write *unit tests*. As the name suggests, it's a mechanism to test individual components of your program. For example, unit tests make sure that a single function of a program works properly. Most programming languages offer a way to run unit tests automatically. Running automated tests will increase the reliability of your codebase dramatically and make reasonably sure that you won't break anything that currently works when you edit your code.

If you look at the currency conversion tool in Figure 1-1, you could write a test that checks if the formula in cell D4 correctly returns USD 105 with the following inputs: 100 EUR as amount and 1.05 as the EURUSD exchange rate. Why does this help? Assume that you accidentally delete cell D4 with the conversion formula and have to rewrite it: instead of multiplying the amount with the exchange rate, you divide by it —after all, working with currencies can be confusing. When you run the above test, you will get a test failure as 100 EUR / 1.05 will not result in 105 USD anymore as the test expects. Like this, you can detect and fix the formula before you hand the spreadsheet over to your users.

Pretty much all traditional programming languages offer one or more test frameworks to write unit tests without much effort—but not Excel. Fortunately, the concept of unit tests is simple enough and by connecting Excel with Python, you get access to Python's powerful unit testing frameworks. While a more in-depth presentation of unit tests is beyond the scope of this book, I invite you to have a look at my blog post (*https://oreil.ly/crwTm*), in which I walk you through the topic with practical examples.

Unit tests are often set up to run automatically when you commit your code to your version control system. The next section explains what version control systems are and why they are hard to use with Excel files.

Version control

Another characteristic of professional programmers is that they use a system for *version control* or *source control*. A *version control system* (VCS) tracks changes in your source code over time, allowing you to see who changed what, when, and why, and allows you to revert to old versions at any point in time. The most popular version control system nowadays is Git (*https://git-scm.com*). It was originally created to manage the Linux source code and since then has conquered the programming world— even Microsoft adopted Git in 2017 to manage the Windows source code. In the Excel world, by contrast, the by far most popular version control system comes in the form of a folder where files are archived like this:

```
currency_converter_v1.xlsx
currency_converter_v2_2020_04_21.xlsx
currency_converter_final_edits_Bob.xlsx
currency_converter_final_final.xlsx
```

If, unlike in this sample, the Excel developer sticks to a certain convention in the file name, there's nothing inherently wrong with that. But keeping a version history of your files locally locks you out of important aspects of source control in the form of easier collaboration, peer reviews, sign-off processes, and audit logs. And if you want to make your workbooks more secure and stable, you don't want to miss out on these things. Most commonly, professional programmers use Git in connection with a web-based platform like GitHub, GitLab, Bitbucket, or Azure DevOps. These platforms allow you to work with so-called *pull requests* or *merge requests*. They allow developers to formally request that their changes are merged into the main codebase. A pull request offers the following information:

- Who is the author of the changes
- When were the changes made
- What is the purpose of the changes as described in the *commit message*
- What are the details of the changes as shown by the *diff view*, i.e., a view that highlights changes in green for new code and red for deleted code

This allows a coworker or a team head to review the changes and spot irregularities. Often, an extra pair of eyes will be able to spot a glitch or two or give otherwise valuable feedback to the programmer. With all these advantages, why do Excel developers prefer to use the local file system and their own naming convention instead of a professional system like Git?

- Many Excel users simply don't know about Git or give up early on, as Git has a relatively steep learning curve.
- Git allows multiple users to work on local copies of the same file in parallel. After all of them commit their work, Git can usually merge all the changes together without any manual intervention. This doesn't work for Excel files: if they are being changed in parallel on separate copies, Git doesn't know how to merge these changes back into a single file.
- Even if you manage to deal with the previous issues, Git simply doesn't deliver as much value with Excel files as it does with text files: Git isn't able to show changes between Excel files, preventing a proper peer review process.

Because of all these issues, my company has come up with xltrail (*https://xltrail.com*), a Git-based version control system that knows how to deal with Excel files. It hides away the Git complexity so that business users feel comfortable using it and also allows you to connect to external Git systems, in case you are already tracking your files with GitHub, for example. xltrail tracks the different components of a workbook, including cell formulas, named ranges, Power Queries, and VBA code, allowing you to take advantage of the classic benefits of version control including peer reviews.

Another option to make version control easier with Excel is to move your business logic from Excel into Python files, something we will do in Chapter 10. As Python files are straightforward to track with Git, you will have the most important part of your spreadsheet tool under control.

While this section is called Programming Best Practices, it is mainly pointing out why they are harder to follow with Excel than with a traditional programming language like Python. Before we turn our attention to Python, I would like to briefly introduce Power Query and Power Pivot, Microsoft's attempt at modernizing Excel.

Modern Excel

The modern era of Excel started with Excel 2007 when the ribbon menu and the new file formats (e.g., *xlsx* instead of *xls*) were introduced. However, the Excel community uses *modern Excel* to refer to the tools that were added with Excel 2010: most importantly Power Query and Power Pivot. They allow you to connect to external data sources and analyze data that is too big to fit into a spreadsheet. As their functionality overlaps with what we will do with pandas in Chapter 5, I will briefly introduce them in the first part of this section. The second part is about Power BI, which could be described as a standalone business intelligence application combining the functionality of Power Query and Power Pivot with visualization capabilities—and it has built-in support for Python!

Power Query and Power Pivot

With Excel 2010, Microsoft introduced an add-in called *Power Query*. Power Query connects to a multitude of data sources including Excel workbooks, CSV files, and SQL databases. It also offers connections to platforms like Salesforce and can even be extended to connect with systems that aren't covered out of the box. Power Query's core functionality is dealing with datasets that are too big to fit into a spreadsheet. After loading the data, you may perform additional steps to clean and manipulate it so it arrives in a usable form in Excel. You could, for example, split a column into two, merge two tables, or filter and group your data. Since Excel 2016, Power Query is not an add-in anymore but can be accessed directly on the ribbon tab Data via the Get Data button. Power Query is only partially available on macOS—however, it is being actively developed, so it should be fully supported in a future release of Excel.

Power Pivot goes hand in hand with Power Query: conceptually, it's the second step after acquiring and cleaning your data with Power Query. Power Pivot helps you to analyze and present your data in an appealing way directly in Excel. Think of it as a traditional pivot table that, like Power Query, can deal with large datasets. Power Pivot allows you to define formal data models with relationships and hierarchies, and you can add calculated columns via the DAX formula language. Power Pivot was also introduced with Excel 2010 but remains an add-in and is so far not available on macOS.

If you like to work with Power Query and Power Pivot and want to build dashboards on top of them, Power BI may be worth a look—let's see why!

Power BI

Power BI is a standalone application that was released in 2015. It is Microsoft's answer to business intelligence tools like Tableau or Qlik. Power BI Desktop is free, so if you want to play around with it, go to the Power BI home page (*https://oreil.ly/I1kGj*) and download it—note, however, that Power BI Desktop is only available for Windows. Power BI wants to make sense of large datasets by visualizing them in interactive dashboards. At its core, it is relying on the same Power Query and Power Pivot functionality as Excel. Commercial plans allow you to collaborate and share dashboards online, but these are separate from the desktop version. The main reason why Power BI is exciting in the context of this book is that it's been supporting Python scripts since 2018. Python can be used for the query part as well as the visualization part by making use of Python's plotting libraries. To me, using Python in Power BI feels a bit clunky, but the important part here is that Microsoft has recognized the importance of Python with regard to data analysis. Accordingly, the hopes are high that one day Python will find an official way into Excel, too.

So what's so great about Python that it made it into Microsoft's Power BI? The next section has a few answers!

Python for Excel

Excel is all about storing, analyzing, and visualizing data. And since Python is particularly strong in the area of scientific computing, it's a natural fit in combination with Excel. Python is also one of the very few languages that is appealing to both the professional programmer as well as the beginner user who writes a few lines of code every few weeks. Professional programmers, on the one hand, like to work with Python because it is a general-purpose programming language and therefore allows you to achieve pretty much anything without jumping through hoops. Beginners, on the other hand, like Python because it's easier to learn than other languages. As a consequence, Python is used both for ad hoc data analysis and smaller automation tasks as well as in huge production codebases like Instagram's backend.[6] This also means that when your Python-powered Excel tool becomes really popular, it's easy to add a web developer to the project who will turn your Excel-Python prototype into a fully-fledged web application. The unique advantage of Python is that the part with the

---

6 You can learn more about how Instagram uses Python on their engineering blog (*https://oreil.ly/SSnQG*).

business logic most likely doesn't need to be rewritten but can be moved as-is from the Excel prototype to the production web environment.

In this section, I'll introduce Python's core concepts and compare them with Excel and VBA. I will touch on code readability, Python's standard library and package manager, the scientific computing stack, modern language features, and cross-platform compatibility. Let's dive into readability first!

Readability and Maintainability

If your code is readable, it means that it is easy to follow and understand—especially for outsiders who haven't written the code themselves. This makes it easier to spot errors and maintain the code going forward. That's why one line in *The Zen of Python* is "readability counts." The Zen of Python is a concise summary of Python's core design principles, and we will learn how to print it in the next chapter. Let's have a look at the following code snippet in VBA:

```
If i < 5 Then
    Debug.Print "i is smaller than 5"
ElseIf i <= 10 Then
    Debug.Print "i is between 5 and 10"
Else
    Debug.Print "i is bigger than 10"
End If
```

In VBA, you can reformat the snippet into the following, which is completely equivalent:

```
If i < 5 Then
    Debug.Print "i is smaller than 5"
    ElseIf i <= 10 Then
    Debug.Print "i is between 5 and 10"
    Else
    Debug.Print "i is bigger than 10"
End If
```

In the first version, the visual indentation aligns with the logic of the code. This makes it easy to read and understand the code, which again makes it easier to spot errors. In the second version, a developer who is new to the code might not see the ElseIf and Else condition when glancing over it for the first time—this is obviously even more true if the code is part of a larger codebase.

Python doesn't accept code that is formatted like the second example: it forces you to align the visual indentation with the logic of the code, preventing readability issues. Python can do this because it relies on indentation to define code blocks as you use them in if statements or for loops. Instead of indentation, the majority of the other languages use curly braces, and VBA uses keywords such as End If, as we just saw in the code snippets. The reason behind using indentation for code blocks is that in programming, most of the time is spent on maintaining code rather than writing it in the first place. Having readable code helps new programmers (or yourself a few months after writing the code) to go back and understand what's going on.

We will learn all about Python's indentation rules in Chapter 3, but for now let's move on with the standard library: the functionality that comes with Python out of the box.

Standard Library and Package Manager

Python comes with a rich set of built-in functionality delivered by its *standard library*. The Python community likes to refer to it by saying that Python comes with "batteries included." Whether you need to uncompress a ZIP file, read the values of a CSV file, or want to fetch data from the internet, Python's standard library has you covered, and you can achieve all this in usually just a few lines of code. The same functionality in VBA would require you to write a considerable amount of code or install an add-in. And often, the solutions you find on the internet only work on Windows but not macOS.

While Python's standard library covers an impressive amount of functionality, there are still tasks that are cumbersome to program or slow when you are only relying on the standard library. This is where PyPI (*https://pypi.org*) comes in. PyPI stands for *Python Package Index* and is a giant repository where everybody (including you!) can upload open source Python packages that add additional functionality to Python.

PyPI vs. PyPy

PyPI is pronounced "pie pea eye." This is to differentiate PyPI from PyPy which is pronounced "pie pie" and which is a fast alternative implementation of Python.

For example, to make it easier to fetch data from sources on the internet, you could install the Requests package to get access to a set of commands that are powerful yet easy to use. To install it, you would use Python's package manager *pip*, which you run on a Command Prompt or Terminal. pip is a recursive acronym for *pip installs packages*. Don't worry if this sounds a bit abstract right now; I will explain how this works in detail in the next chapter. For now, it's more important to understand why package managers are so important. One of the main reasons is that any reasonable package will not just depend on Python's standard library, but again on other open source packages that are also hosted on PyPI. These dependencies might again depend on subdependencies and so forth. pip recursively checks the dependencies and subdependencies of a package and downloads and installs them. pip also makes it easy to update your packages so you can keep your dependencies up-to-date. This makes adhering to the DRY principle much easier, as you don't need to reinvent or copy/paste what's already available on PyPI. With pip and PyPI, you also have a solid mechanism to distribute and install these dependencies, something that Excel is lacking with its traditional add-ins.

Open Source Software (OSS)

At this point, I'd like to say a few words about *open source*, as I have used that word a few times in this section. If software is distributed under an open source license, it means that its source code is freely available at no cost, allowing everybody to contribute new functionality, bug fixes, or documentation. Python itself and almost all third-party Python packages are open source and most commonly maintained by developers in their spare time. This is not always an ideal state: if your company is relying on certain packages, you have an interest in the continued development and maintenance of these packages by professional programmers. Fortunately, the scientific Python community has recognized that some packages are too important to leave their fate in the hands of a few volunteers who work in the evenings and on weekends.

That's why in 2012, NumFOCUS (*https://numfocus.org*), a nonprofit organization, was created to sponsor various Python packages and projects in the area of scientific computing. The most popular Python packages sponsored by NumFOCUS are pandas, NumPy, SciPy, Matplotlib, and Project Jupyter, but nowadays they also support packages from various other languages, including R, Julia, and JavaScript. There are a few large corporate sponsors, but everybody can join NumFOCUS as a free community member—donations are tax-deductible.

With pip, you can install packages for just about anything, but for Excel users, some of the most interesting ones are certainly the packages for scientific computing. Let's learn a bit more about scientific computing with Python in the next section!

Scientific Computing

An important reason for Python's success is the fact that it was created as a general-purpose programming language. The capabilities for scientific computing were added later on in the form of third-party packages. This has the unique advantage that a data scientist can use the same language for experiments and research as a web developer, who may eventually build a production-ready application around the computational core. Being able to build scientific applications out of one language reduces friction, implementation time, and costs. Scientific packages like NumPy, SciPy, and pandas give us access to a very concise way of formulating mathematical problems. As an example, let's have a look at one of the more famous financial formulas used to calculate the portfolio variance according to Modern Portfolio Theory:

$$\sigma^2 = w^\mathsf{T} C w$$

The portfolio variance is denoted by σ^2, while w is the weight vector of the individual assets and C is the portfolio's covariance matrix. If w and C are Excel ranges, you can calculate the portfolio variance in VBA like so:

```
variance = Application.MMult(Application.MMult(Application.Transpose(w), C), w)
```

Compare this to the almost mathematical notation in Python, assuming that w and C are pandas DataFrames or NumPy arrays (I will formally introduce them in Part II):

```
variance = w.T @ C @ w
```

But it's not just about aesthetics and readability: NumPy and pandas use compiled Fortran and C code under the hood, which gives you a performance boost when working with big matrices compared to VBA.

Missing support for scientific computing is an obvious limitation in VBA. But even if you look at the core language features, VBA has fallen behind, as I will point out in the next section.

Modern Language Features

Since Excel 97, the VBA language hasn't had any major changes in terms of language features. That, however, doesn't mean that VBA isn't supported anymore: Microsoft is shipping updates with every new release of Excel to be able to automate the new Excel features introduced with that release. For example, Excel 2016 added support to auto-mate Power Query. A language that stopped evolving more than twenty years ago is missing out on modern language concepts that were introduced in all major programming languages over the years. As an example, error handling in VBA is really showing its age. If you'd like to handle an error gracefully in VBA, it goes something like this:

```
Sub PrintReciprocal(number As Variant)
    ' There will be an error if the number is 0 or a string
    On Error GoTo ErrorHandler
        result = 1 / number
    On Error GoTo 0
    Debug.Print "There was no error!"
Finally:
    ' Runs whether or not an error occurs
    If result = "" Then
        result = "N/A"
    End If
    Debug.Print "The reciprocal is: " & result
    Exit Sub
ErrorHandler:
    ' Runs only in case of an error
    Debug.Print "There was an error: " & Err.Description
    Resume Finally
End Sub
```

Please note that you probably wouldn't calculate the reciprocal like this—I only use it here as an example to make it easier to follow the code flow. VBA error handling involves the use of *labels* like `Finally` and `ErrorHandler` in the example. You instruct the code to jump to these labels via the `GoTo` or `Resume` statements. Early on, labels were recognized to be responsible for what many programmers would call *spaghetti code*: a nice way of saying that the flow of the code is hard to follow and therefore difficult to maintain. That's why pretty much all of the actively developed languages have introduced the `try/catch` mechanism—in Python called `try/except`—that I will introduce in Chapter 11. If you are a proficient VBA developer, you might also enjoy the fact that Python supports class inheritance, a feature of object-oriented programming that is missing in VBA.

Besides modern language features, there's another requirement for a modern programming language: cross-platform compatibility. Let's see why this is important!

Cross-Platform Compatibility

Even if you develop your code on a local computer that runs on Windows or macOS, it's very likely that you want to run your program on a server or in the cloud at some point. Servers allow your code to be executed on a schedule and make your application accessible from everywhere you want, with the computing power you need. In fact, I will show you how to run Python code on a server in the next chapter by introducing you to hosted Jupyter notebooks. The vast majority of servers run on Linux, as it is a stable, secure, and cost-effective operating system. And since Python programs run unchanged on all major operating systems, this will take out much of the pain when you transition from your local machine to a production setup.

In contrast, even though Excel VBA runs on Windows and macOS, it's easy to introduce functionality that only runs on Windows. In the official VBA documentation or on forums, you will often see code like this:

```
Set fso = CreateObject("Scripting.FileSystemObject")
```

Whenever you have a `CreateObject` call or are being told to go to Tools > References in the VBA editor to add a reference, you are almost always dealing with code that will only run on Windows. Another prominent area where you need to watch out if you want your Excel files to work across Windows and macOS are *ActiveX controls*. ActiveX controls are elements like buttons and dropdowns that you can place on your sheets, but they work only on Windows. Make sure to avoid them if you want your workbook to run on macOS too!

Conclusion

In this chapter, we met Python and Excel, two very popular technologies that have been around for multiple decades—a long time compared to many other technologies that we use today. The London Whale served as an example of how much can go wrong (in dollar terms) when you don't use Excel properly with mission-critical workbooks. This was our motivation to look into a minimal set of programming best practices: applying separation of concerns, following the DRY principle, and making use of automated testing and version control. We then had a look at Power Query and Power Pivot, Microsoft's approach at dealing with data that is bigger than your spreadsheet. I, however, feel that they are often not the right solution, as they lock you into the Microsoft world and prevent you from taking advantage of the flexibility and power of modern cloud-based solutions.

Python comes with convincing features that are missing in Excel: the standard library, the package manager, libraries for scientific computing, and cross-platform compatibility. By learning how to combine Excel with Python, you can have the best of both worlds and will save time through automation, commit fewer errors as it's easier to follow programming best practices, and you will be able to take your application and scale it up outside of Excel if you ever need to.

Now that you know why Python is such a powerful companion for Excel, it's time to set up your development environment to be able to write your first lines of Python code!

## CHAPTER 2

Development Environment

You probably can't wait to learn the basics of Python but before we get there, you first need to set up your computer accordingly. To write VBA code or Power Queries, it's enough to fire up Excel and open the VBA or Power Query editor, respectively. With Python, it's a bit more work.

We will start this chapter by installing the Anaconda Python distribution. Besides installing Python, Anaconda will also give us access to the Anaconda Prompt and Jupyter notebooks, two essential tools that we will use throughout this book. The *Anaconda Prompt* is a special Command Prompt (Windows) or Terminal (macOS); it allows us to run Python scripts and other command line tools that we will meet in this book. *Jupyter notebooks* allow us to work with data, code, and charts in an interactive way, which makes them a serious competitor to Excel workbooks. After playing around with Jupyter notebooks, we will install *Visual Studio Code* (VS Code), a powerful text editor. VS Code works great for writing, running, and debugging Python scripts and comes with an integrated Terminal. Figure 2-1 summarizes what's included in Anaconda and VS Code.

As this book is about Excel, I am focusing on Windows and macOS in this chapter. However, everything up to and including Part III runs on Linux as well. Let's get started by installing Anaconda!

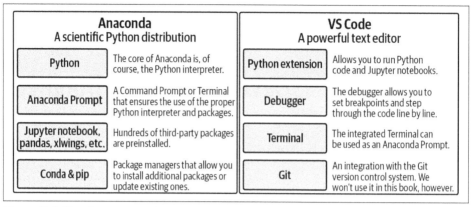

Figure 2-1. Development environment

The Anaconda Python Distribution

Anaconda is arguably the most popular Python distribution used for data science and comes with hundreds of third-party packages preinstalled: it includes Jupyter note-books and most of the other packages that this book will use extensively, including pandas, OpenPyXL, and xlwings. The Anaconda Individual Edition is free for private use and guarantees that all the included packages are compatible with each other. It installs into a single folder and can easily be uninstalled again. After installing it, we will learn a few basic commands on the Anaconda Prompt and run an interactive Python session. We'll then meet the package managers Conda and pip before wrapping this section up with Conda environments. Let's get started by downloading and installing Anaconda!

Installation

Go to the Anaconda home page (*https://oreil.ly/QV7Na*) and download the latest version of the Anaconda installer (Individual Edition). Make sure to download the 64-bit graphical installer for the Python 3.x version.[1] Once downloaded, double-click the installer to start the installation process and make sure to accept all the defaults. For more detailed installation instructions, follow the official documentation (*https://oreil.ly/r01wn*).

---

1 32-bit systems only exist with Windows and have become rare. An easy way to find out which Windows version you have is by going to the *C:* drive in the File Explorer. If you can see both the *Program Files* and *Program Files (x86)* folders, you are on a 64-bit version of Windows. If you can only see the *Program Files* folder, you are on a 32-bit system.

Other Python Distributions

While the instructions in this book assume that you have the Anaconda Individual Edition installed, the code and concepts shown will work with any other Python installation, too. In this case, however, you will have to install the required dependencies by following the instructions included in *requirements.txt* in the companion repository.

With Anaconda installed, we can now start using the Anaconda Prompt. Let's see what this is and how it works!

Anaconda Prompt

The *Anaconda Prompt* is really just a Command Prompt on Windows and a Terminal on macOS that have been set up to run with the correct Python interpreter and third-party packages. The Anaconda Prompt is the most basic tool to run Python code, and we will make extensive use of it in this book to run Python scripts and all sorts of command line tools that are offered by various packages.

Anaconda Prompt without Anaconda

If you don't use the Anaconda Python distribution, you will have to use the *Command Prompt* on Windows and the *Terminal* on macOS whenever I instruct you to use the Anaconda Prompt.

If you have never used a Command Prompt on Windows or a Terminal on macOS, don't worry: you only need to know a handful of commands that will already give you a lot of power. Once you get used to it, using the Anaconda Prompt is often faster and more convenient than clicking your way through graphical user menus. Let's get started:

Windows

Click on the Start menu button and start typing **Anaconda Prompt**. In the appearing entries, choose Anaconda Prompt, not Anaconda Powershell Prompt. Either select it with the arrow keys and hit Enter or use your mouse to click on it. If you prefer to open it via the Start menu, you will find it under Anaconda3. It is a good idea to pin the Anaconda Prompt to your Windows taskbar as you will use it regularly throughout this book. The input line of the Anaconda Prompt will start with (base):

```
(base) C:\Users\felix>
```

macOS

On macOS, you won't find an application called Anaconda Prompt. Instead, by Anaconda Prompt, I am referring to the Terminal that has been set up by the Anaconda installer to automatically activate a Conda environment (I will say more about Conda environments in a moment): press Command-Space bar or open the Launchpad, then type in **Terminal** and hit Enter. Alternatively, open the Finder and navigate to *Applications > Utilities*, where you will find the Terminal app that you can double-click. Once the Terminal appears, it should look something like this, i.e., the input line has to start with (base):

```
(base) felix@MacBook-Pro ~ %
```

If you are on an older version of macOS, it looks rather like this:

```
(base) MacBook-Pro:~ felix$
```

Unlike the Command Prompt on Windows, the Terminal on macOS doesn't show the full path of the current directory. Instead, the tilde stands for the home directory, which is usually */Users/<username>*. To see the full path of your current directory, type **pwd** followed by Enter. pwd stands for *print working directory*.

If the input line in your Terminal doesn't start with (base) after the installation of Anaconda, here is a common reason: if you had the Terminal running during the Anaconda installation, you will need to restart it. Note that clicking on the red cross on the top left of the Terminal window will only hide it but not quit it. Instead, right-click on the Terminal in the dock and select Quit or hit Command-Q while the Terminal is your active window. When you start it again and the Terminal shows (base) at the beginning of a new line, you are all set. It's a good idea to keep the Terminal in your dock, as you will use it regularly throughout this book.

Having the Anaconda Prompt up and running, try out the commands outlined in Table 2-1. I am explaining each command in more detail after the table.

Table 2-1. Commands for the Anaconda Prompt

Command	Windows	macOS
List files in current directory	dir	ls -la
Change directory (relative)	cd path\to\dir	cd path/to/dir
Change directory (absolute)	cd C:\path\to\dir	cd /path/to/dir
Change to D drive	D:	(doesn't exist)
Change to parent directory	cd ..	cd ..
Scroll through previous commands	↑ (up-arrow)	↑ (up-arrow)

List files in current directory

On Windows, type in **dir** for *directory*, then hit Enter. This will print the content of the directory you are currently in.

On macOS, type in **ls -la** followed by Enter. ls is short for *list directory contents*, and -la will print the output in the *long listing* format and include *all* files, including hidden ones.

Change directory

Type **cd Down** and hit the Tab key. cd stands for *change directory*. If you are in your home folder, the Anaconda Prompt should most likely be able to autocomplete it to cd Downloads. If you are in a different folder or don't have a folder called *Downloads*, simply start to type the beginning of one of the directory names you saw with the previous command (dir or ls -la) before hitting the Tab key to autocomplete. Then hit Enter to change into the autocompleted directory. If you are on Windows and need to change your drive, you first need to type in the drive name before you can change into the correct directory:

```
C:\Users\felix> D:
D:\> cd data
D:\data>
```

Note that by starting your path with a directory or file name that is within your current directory, you are using a *relative path*, e.g., cd Downloads. If you would like to go outside of your current directory, you can type in an *absolute path*, e.g., cd C:\Users on Windows or cd /Users on macOS (mind the forward slash at the beginning).

Change to parent directory

To go to your parent directory, i.e., one level up in your directory hierarchy, type **cd ..** followed by Enter (make sure that there is a space between cd and the dots). You can combine this with a directory name, for example, if you want to go up one level, and then to change to the *Desktop*, enter **cd ..\Desktop**. On macOS, replace the backslash with a forward slash.

Scroll through previous commands

Use the up-arrow key to scroll through the previous commands. This will save you many keystrokes if you need to run the same commands over and over again. If you scroll too far, use the down-arrow key to scroll back.

File Extensions

Unfortunately, Windows and macOS hide file extensions by default in the Windows Explorer or macOS Finder, respectively. This can make it harder to work with Python scripts and the Anaconda Prompt, as they will require you to refer to files including their extensions. When working with Excel, showing file extensions also helps you understand whether you're dealing with the default *xlsx* file, a macro-enabled *xlsm* file, or any of the other Excel file formats. Here is how you make the file extensions visible:

Windows

Open a File Explorer and click on the View tab. Under the Show/Hide group, activate the "File name extensions" checkbox.

macOS

Open the Finder and go to Preferences by hitting Command-, (Command-comma). On the Advanced tab, check the box next to "Show all filename extensions."

And that's already it! You are now able to fire up the Anaconda Prompt and run commands in the desired directory. You'll be using this right away in the next section, where I'll show you how to start an interactive Python session.

Python REPL: An Interactive Python Session

You can start an interactive Python session by running the `python` command on an Anaconda Prompt:

```
(base) C:\Users\felix>python
Python 3.8.5 (default, Sep 3 2020, 21:29:08) [...] :: Anaconda, Inc. on win32
Type "help", "copyright", "credits" or "license" for more information.
>>>
```

The text that gets printed in a Terminal on macOS will slightly differ, but otherwise, it works the same. This book is based on Python 3.8—if you would like to use a newer version of Python, make sure to consult the book's home page (*https://xlwings.org/ book*) for instructions.

Anaconda Prompt Notation

Going forward, I will start lines of code with `(base)>` to denote that they are typed into an Anaconda Prompt. For example, to launch an interactive Python interpreter, I will write:

```
(base)> python
```

which on Windows will look similar to this:

```
(base) C:\Users\felix> python
```

and on macOS similar to this (remember, on macOS, the Terminal is your Anaconda Prompt):

```
(base) felix@MacBook-Pro ~ % python
```

Let's play around a bit! Note that >>> in an interactive session means that Python expects your input; you don't have to type this in. Follow along by typing in each line that starts with >>> and confirm with the Enter key:

```
>>> 3 + 4
7
>>> "python " * 3
'python python python '
```

This interactive Python session is also referred to as Python *REPL*, which stands for *read-eval-print loop*: Python reads your input, evaluates it, and prints the result instantly while waiting for your next input. Remember the Zen of Python that I mentioned in the previous chapter? You can now read the full version to get some insight into the guiding principles of Python (smile included). Simply run this line by hitting Enter after typing it in:

```
>>> import this
```

To exit out of your Python session, type **quit()** followed by the Enter key. Alternatively, hit Ctrl+Z on Windows, then hit the Enter key. On macOS, simply hit Ctrl-D— no need to press Enter.

Having exited the Python REPL, it's a good moment to play around with Conda and pip, the package managers that come with the Anaconda installation.

Package Managers: Conda and pip

I already said a few words about pip, Python's package manager in the previous chapter: pip takes care of downloading, installing, updating, and uninstalling Python packages as well as their dependencies and subdependencies. While Anaconda works with pip, it has a built-in alternative package manager called Conda. One advantage of Conda is that it can install more than just Python packages, including additional versions of the Python interpreter. As a short recap: packages add additional functionality to your Python installation that is not covered by the standard library. pandas, which I will properly introduce in Chapter 5, is an example of such a package. Since it comes preinstalled in Anaconda's Python installation, you don't have to install it manually.

Conda vs. pip

With Anaconda, you should install everything you can via Conda and only use pip to install those packages that Conda can't find. Otherwise, Conda may overwrite files that were previously installed with pip.

Table 2-2 gives you an overview of the commands that you will use most often. These commands have to be typed into an Anaconda Prompt and will allow you to install, update, and uninstall your third-party packages.

Table 2-2. Conda and pip commands

Action	Conda	pip
List all installed packages	`conda list`	`pip freeze`
Install the latest package version	`conda install` *package*	`pip install` *package*
Install a specific package version	`conda install` *package=1.0.0*	`pip install` *package==1.0.0*
Update a package	`conda update` *package*	`pip install --upgrade` *package*
Uninstall a package	`conda remove` *package*	`pip uninstall` *package*

For example, to see what packages are already available in your Anaconda distribution, type:

```
(base)> conda list
```

Whenever this book requires a package that is not included in the Anaconda installation, I will point this out explicitly and show you how to install it. However, it may be a good idea to take care of installing the missing packages now so that you won't need to deal with it later on. Let's first install plotly and xlutils, the packages that are available via Conda:

```
(base)> conda install plotly xlutils
```

After running this command, Conda will show you what it's going to do and requires you to confirm by typing **y** and hitting Enter. Once done, you can install pyxlsb and pytrends with pip, as these packages are not available via Conda:

```
(base)> pip install pyxlsb pytrends
```

Unlike Conda, pip will install the packages right away when you hit Enter without the need to confirm.

Package Versions

Many Python packages are updated often and sometimes introduce changes that aren't backward compatible. This will likely break some of the examples in this book. I will try to keep up with these changes and post fixes on the book's home page (*https:// xlwings.org/book*), but you could also create a Conda environment that uses the same versions of the packages that I was using when writing this book. I will introduce Conda environments in the next section, and you will find detailed instructions on how to create a Conda environment with the specific packages in Appendix A.

You know now how to use the Anaconda Prompt to start a Python interpreter and install additional packages. In the next section, I'll explain what (`base`) at the beginning of your Anaconda Prompt means.

Conda Environments

You may have been wondering why the Anaconda Prompt shows (`base`) at the beginning of each input line. It's the name of the active *Conda environment*. A Conda environment is a separate "Python world" with a specific version of Python and a set of installed packages with specific versions. Why is this necessary? When you start to work on different projects in parallel, they will have different requirements: one project may use Python 3.8 with pandas 0.25.0, while another project may use Python 3.9 with pandas 1.0.0. Code that is written for pandas 0.25.0 will often require changes to run with pandas 1.0.0, so you can't just upgrade your Python and pandas versions without making changes to your code. Using a Conda environment for each project makes sure that every project runs with the correct dependencies. While Conda environments are specific to the Anaconda distribution, the concept exists with every Python installation under the name *virtual environment*. Conda environments are more powerful because they make it easier to deal with different versions of Python itself, not just packages.

While you work through this book, you will not have to change your Conda environment, as we'll always be using the default `base` environment. However, when you start building real projects, it's good practice to use one Conda or virtual environment for each project to avoid any potential conflicts between their dependencies. Everything you need to know about dealing with multiple Conda environments is explained in Appendix A. There you will also find instructions on creating a Conda environment with the exact versions of the packages that I used to write this book. This will allow you to run the examples in this book as-is for many years to come. The other option is to watch the book's home page (*https://xlwings.org/book*) for potential changes required for newer versions of Python and the packages.

Having resolved the mystery around Conda environments, it's time to introduce the next tool, one that we will use intensely in this book: Jupyter notebooks!

Jupyter Notebooks

In the previous section, I showed you how to start an interactive Python session from an Anaconda Prompt. This is useful if you want a bare-bones environment to test out something simple. For the majority of your work, however, you want an environment that is easier to use. For example, going back to previous commands and displaying charts is hard with a Python REPL running in an Anaconda Prompt. Fortunately, Anaconda comes with much more than just the Python interpreter: it also includes *Jupyter notebooks*, which have emerged as one of the most popular ways to run

Python code in a data science context. Jupyter notebooks allow you to tell a story by combining executable Python code with formatted text, pictures, and charts into an interactive notebook that runs in your browser. They are beginner-friendly and thus especially useful for the first steps of your Python journey. They are, however, also hugely popular for teaching, prototyping, and researching, as they facilitate reproducible research.

Jupyter notebooks have become a serious competitor to Excel as they cover roughly the same use case as a workbook: you can quickly prepare, analyze, and visualize data. The difference to Excel is that all of it happens by writing Python code instead of clicking around in Excel with your mouse. Another advantage is that Jupyter notebooks don't mix data and business logic: the Jupyter notebook holds your code and charts, whereas you typically consume data from an external CSV file or a database. Having Python code visible in your notebook makes it easy to see what's going on compared to Excel, where the formulas are hidden away behind a cell's value. Jupyter notebooks are also easy to run both locally and on a remote server. Servers usually have more power than your local machine and can run your code fully unattended, something that is hard to do with Excel.

In this section, I'll show you the very basics of how you run and navigate a Jupyter notebook: we will learn about notebook cells and see what the difference is between the edit and command mode. We'll then understand why the run order of cells matters before we wrap this section up by learning how to properly shut down notebooks. Let's get started with our first notebook!

Running Jupyter Notebooks

On your Anaconda Prompt, change to the directory of your companion repository, then launch a Jupyter notebook server:

```
(base)> cd C:\Users\username\python-for-excel
(base)> jupyter notebook
```

This will automatically open your browser and show the Jupyter dashboard with the files in the directory from where you were running the command. On the top right of the Jupyter dashboard, click on New, then select Python 3 from the dropdown list (see Figure 2-2).

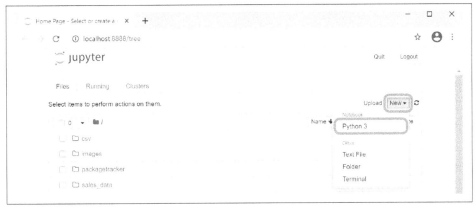

Figure 2-2. The Jupyter dashboard

This will open a new browser tab with your first empty Jupyter notebook as shown in Figure 2-3.

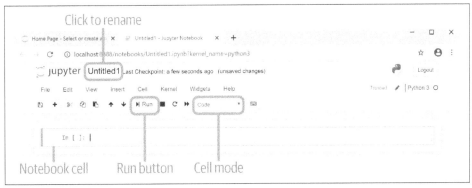

Figure 2-3. An empty Jupyter notebook

It's a good habit to click on Untitled1 next to the Jupyter logo to rename your workbook into something more meaningful, e.g., *first_notebook*. The lower part of Figure 2-3 shows a notebook cell—move on to the next section to learn more about them!

Notebook Cells

In Figure 2-3, you see an empty cell with a blinking cursor. If the cursor doesn't blink, click into the cell with your mouse, i.e., to the right of In [ ]. Now repeat the exercise from the last section: type in **3 + 4** and run the cell by either clicking on the Run button in the menu bar at the top or—much easier—by hitting Shift+Enter. This will run the code in the cell, print the result below the cell and jump to the next cell. In this case, it inserts an empty cell below as we only have one cell so far. Going into a bit more detail: while a cell is calculating, it shows In [*] and when it's done, the asterisk turns into a number, e.g., In [1]. Below the cell you will have the corresponding output labeled with the same number: Out [1]. Every time you run a cell, the counter increases by one, which helps you to see in which order the cells were executed. Going forward, I will show the code samples in this format, e.g., the REPL example from before looks like this:

```
In [1]: 3 + 4

Out[1]: 7
```

This notation allows you to follow along easily by typing **3 + 4** into a notebook cell. When running it by hitting Shift+Enter, you will get what I show as output under Out[1]. If you read this book in an electronic format supporting colors, you will notice that the input cell formats strings, numbers, and so on with different colors to make it easier to read. This is called *syntax highlighting*.

 Cell Output

If the last line in a cell returns a value, it is automatically printed by the Jupyter notebook under Out [ ]. However, when you use the print function or when you get an exception, it is printed directly below the In cell without the Out [ ] label. The code samples in this book are formatted to reflect this behavior.

Cells can have different types, two of which are of interest to us:

Code

This is the default type. Use it whenever you want to run Python code.

Markdown

Markdown is a syntax that uses standard text characters for formatting and can be used to include nicely formatted explanations and instructions in your notebook.

To change a cell's type to Markdown, select the cell, then choose Markdown in the cell mode dropdown (see Figure 2-3). I'll show you a keyboard shortcut to change the cell mode in Table 2-3. After changing an empty cell into a Markdown cell, type in the following text, which explains a few Markdown rules:

```
# This is a first-level heading

## This is a second-level heading

You can make your text *italic* or **bold** or `monospaced`.

* This is a bullet point
* This is another bullet point
```

After hitting Shift+Enter, the text will be rendered into nicely formatted HTML. At this point, your notebook should look like what's in Figure 2-4. Markdown cells also allow you to include images, videos, or formulas; see the Jupyter notebook docs (*https://oreil.ly/elGTF*).

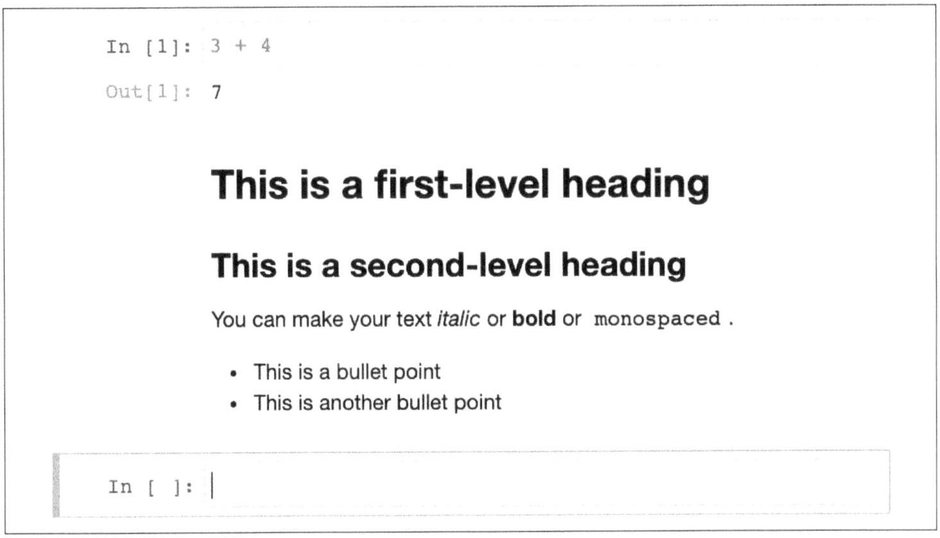

```
In [1]: 3 + 4

Out[1]: 7
```

This is a first-level heading

This is a second-level heading

You can make your text *italic* or **bold** or `monospaced` .

- This is a bullet point
- This is another bullet point

```
In [ ]: |
```

Figure 2-4. The notebook after running a code cell and a Markdown cell

Now that you know about the code and Markdown cell types, it's time to learn an easier way to navigate between cells: the next section introduces the edit and command mode along with a few keyboard shortcuts.

Edit vs. Command Mode

When you interact with cells in a Jupyter notebook, you are either in the *edit mode* or in the *command mode*:

Edit mode
> Clicking into a cell starts the edit mode: the border around the selected cell turns green, and the cursor in the cell is blinking. Instead of clicking into a cell, you can also hit Enter when the cell is selected.

Command mode
> To switch into command mode, hit the Escape key; the border around the selected cell will be blue, and there won't be any blinking cursor. The most important keyboard shortcuts that you can use while being in command mode are shown in Table 2-3.

Table 2-3. Keyboard shortcuts (command mode)

Shortcut	Action
Shift+Enter	Run the cell (works also in edit mode)
↑ (up-arrow)	Move cell selector up
↓ (down-arrow)	Move cell selector down
b	Insert a new cell *below* the current cell
a	Insert a new cell *above* the current cell
dd	Delete the current cell (type two times the letter d)
m	Change cell type to Markdown
y	Change cell type to code

Knowing these keyboard shortcuts will allow you to work with notebooks efficiently without having to switch between keyboard and mouse all the time. In the next section, I'll show you a common gotcha that you need to be aware of when using Jupyter notebooks: the importance of running cells in order.

Run Order Matters

As easy and user-friendly notebooks are to get started, they also make it easy to get into confusing states if you don't run cells sequentially. Assume you have the following notebook cells that are run from top to bottom:

```
In [2]: a = 1
In [3]: a
Out[3]: 1
In [4]: a = 2
```

Cell Out[3] prints the value 1 as expected. However, if you now go back and run In[3] again, you will end up in this situation:

```
In [2]: a = 1
In [5]: a
Out[5]: 2
In [4]: a = 2
```

Out[5] shows now the value 2, which is probably not what you would expect when you read the notebook from the top, especially if cell In[4] would be farther away, requiring you to scroll down. To prevent such cases, I would recommend that you rerun not just a single cell, but all of its previous cells, too. Jupyter notebooks offer you an easy way to accomplish this under the menu Cell > Run all above. After these words of caution, let's see how you shut down a notebook properly!

Shutting Down Jupyter Notebooks

Every notebook runs in a separate *Jupyter kernel*. A kernel is the "engine" that runs the Python code you type into a notebook cell. Every kernel uses resources from your operating system in the form of CPU and RAM. Therefore, when you close a notebook, you should also shut down its kernel so that the resources can be used again by other tasks—this will prevent your system from slowing down. The easiest way to accomplish this is by closing a notebook via File > Close and Halt. If you would just close the browser tab, the kernel will not be shut down automatically. Alternatively, on the Jupyter dashboard, you can close running notebooks from the tab Running.

To shut down the whole Jupyter server, click the Quit button at the top right of the Jupyter dashboard. If you have already closed your browser, you can type Ctrl+C twice in the Anaconda Prompt where the notebook server is running or close the Anaconda Prompt altogether.

Jupyter Notebooks in the Cloud

Jupyter notebooks have become so popular that they are offered as a hosted solution by various cloud providers. I am introducing three services here that are all free to use. The advantage of these services is that they run instantly and everywhere you can access a browser, without the need to install anything locally. You could, for example, run the samples on a tablet while reading the first three parts. Since Part IV requires a local installation of Excel, this won't work there, though.

Binder
> Binder (*https://mybinder.org*) is a service provided by Project Jupyter, the organization behind Jupyter notebooks. Binder is meant to try out the Jupyter notebooks from public Git repositories—you don't store anything on Binder itself and hence you don't need to sign up or log in to use it.

Kaggle Notebooks
> Kaggle (*https://kaggle.com*) is a platform for data science. As it hosts data science competitions, you get easy access to a huge collection of datasets. Kaggle has been part of Google since 2017.

Google Colab
> Google Colab (*https://oreil.ly/4PLcS*) (short for Colaboratory) is Google's notebook platform. Unfortunately, the majority of the Jupyter notebook keyboard shortcuts don't work, but you can access files on your Google Drive, including Google Sheets.

The easiest way to run the Jupyter notebooks of the companion repository in the cloud is by going to its Binder URL (*https://oreil.ly/MAjJK*). You will be working on a copy of the companion repository, so feel free to edit and break stuff as you like!

Now that know how to work with Jupyter notebooks, let's move on and learn about how to write and run standard Python scripts. To do this, we'll use Visual Studio Code, a powerful text editor with great Python support.

Visual Studio Code

In this section, we'll install and configure *Visual Studio Code* (VS Code), a free and open source text editor from Microsoft. After introducing its most important components, we'll write a first Python script and run it in a few different ways. To begin with, however, I will explain when we'll use Jupyter notebooks as opposed to running Python scripts and why I chose VS Code for this book.

While Jupyter notebooks are amazing for interactive workflows like researching, teaching, and experimenting, they are less ideal if you want to write Python scripts geared toward a production environment that do not need the visualization capabilities of notebooks. Also, more complex projects that involve many files and developers are hard to manage with Jupyter notebooks. In this case, you want to use a proper text editor to write and run classic Python files. In theory, you could use just about any text editor (even Notepad would work), but in reality, you want one that "understands" Python. That is, a text editor that supports at least the following features:

Syntax highlighting
> The editor colors words differently based on whether they represent a function, a string, a number, etc. This makes it much easier to read and understand the code.

Autocomplete
> Autocomplete or *IntelliSense*, as Microsoft calls it, automatically suggests text components so that you have to type less, which leads to fewer errors.

And soon enough, you have other needs that you would like to access directly from within the editor:

Run code
> Switching back and forth between the text editor and an external Anaconda Prompt (i.e., Command Prompt or Terminal) to run your code can be a hassle.

Debugger
> A debugger allows you to step through the code line by line to see what's going on.

Version control
> If you use Git to version control your files, it makes sense to handle the Git-related stuff directly in the editor so you don't have to switch back and forth between two applications.

There is a wide spectrum of tools that can help you with all that, and as usual, every developer has different needs and preferences. Some may indeed want to use a no-frills text editor together with an external Command Prompt. Others may prefer an *integrated development environment* (IDE): IDEs try to put everything you'll ever need into a single tool, which can make them bloated.

I chose VS Code for this book as it has quickly become one of the most popular code editors among developers after its initial release in 2015: in the StackOverflow Developer Survey 2019 (*https://oreil.ly/savHe*), it came out as the most popular development environment. What makes VS Code such a popular tool? In essence, it's the right mix between a bare-bones text editor and a full-blown IDE: VS Code is a mini IDE that comes with everything you need for programming out of the box, but not more:

Cross-platform
>   VS Code runs on Windows, macOS, and Linux. There are also cloud-hosted versions like GitHub Codespaces (*https://oreil.ly/bDGWE*).

Integrated tools
>   VS Code comes with a debugger, support for Git version control, and has an integrated Terminal that you can use as Anaconda Prompt.

Extensions
>   Everything else, e.g., Python support, is added via extensions that can be installed with a single click.

Lightweight
>   Depending on your operating system, the VS Code installer is just 50–100 MB.

Visual Studio Code vs. Visual Studio

Don't confuse Visual Studio Code with Visual Studio, the IDE! While you could use Visual Studio for Python development (it comes with PTVS, the *Python Tools for Visual Studio*), it's a really heavy installation and is traditionally used to work with .NET languages like C#.

To find out if you agree with my praise for VS Code, there is no better way than installing it and trying it out yourself. The next section gets you started!

Installation and Configuration

Download the installer from the VS Code home page (*https://oreil.ly/26Jfa*). For the latest installation instructions, please always refer to the official docs.

Windows
Double-click the installer and accept all defaults. Then open VS Code via Windows Start menu, where you will find it under Visual Studio Code.

macOS
Double-click the ZIP file to unpack the app. Then drag and drop *Visual Studio Code.app* into the *Applications* folder: you can now start it from the Launchpad. If the application doesn't start, go to System Preferences > Security & Privacy > General and choose Open Anyway.

When you open VS Code for the first time, it looks like Figure 2-5. Note that I have switched from the default dark theme to a light theme to make the screenshots easier to read.

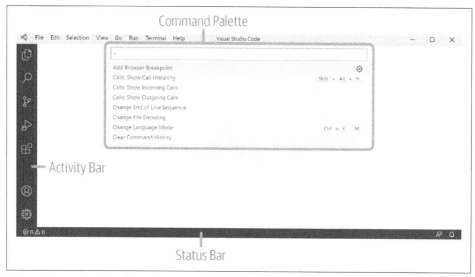

Figure 2-5. Visual Studio Code

Activity Bar
On the lefthand side, you see the Activity Bar with the following icons from top to bottom:

- Explorer
- Search
- Source Control

- Run

- Extensions

Status Bar

At the bottom of the editor, you have the Status Bar. Once you have the configuration complete and edit a Python file, you will see the Python interpreter show up there.

Command Palette

You can show the Command Palette via F1 or with the keyboard shortcut Ctrl +Shift+P (Windows) or Command-Shift-P (macOS). If you are unsure about something, your first stop should always be the Command Palette, as it gives you easy access to almost everything you can do with VS Code. For example, if you are looking for keyboard shortcuts, type in **keyboard shortcuts**, select the entry "Help: Keyboard Shortcuts Reference," and hit Enter.

VS Code is a great text editor out of the box, but to make it work nicely with Python, there are a few more things to configure: click on the Extensions icon on the Activity Bar and search for Python. Install the official Python extension that shows Microsoft as the author. It will take a moment to install and once done, you may need to click the Reload Required button to finish—alternatively, you could also restart VS Code completely. Finalize the configuration according to your platform:

Windows

Open the Command Palette and type **default profile**. Select the entry that reads "Terminal: Select Default Profile" and hit Enter. In the dropdown menu, select Command Prompt and confirm by hitting Enter. This is required because otherwise VS Code can't properly activate Conda environments.

macOS

Open the Command Palette and type **shell command**. Select the entry that reads "Shell Command: Install 'code' command in PATH" and hit Enter. This is required so that you can start VS Code conveniently from the Anaconda Prompt (i.e., the Terminal).

Now that VS Code is installed and configured, let's use it to write and run our first Python script!

Running a Python Script

While you can open VS Code via the Start menu on Windows or Launchpad on macOS, it's often faster to open VS Code from the Anaconda Prompt, where you are able to launch it via the code command. Therefore, open a new Anaconda Prompt and change into the directory where you want to work by using the cd command, then instruct VS Code to open the current directory (represented by the dot):

```
(base)> cd C:\Users\username\python-for-excel
(base)> code .
```

Starting VS Code this way will cause the Explorer on the Activity Bar to automatically show the contents of the directory you were in when you ran the code command. Note that VS Code will ask "Do you trust the authors of the files in this folder?" Confirm this dialog by clicking the "Yes, I trust the authors" button.

Alternatively, you could also open a directory via File > Open Folder (on macOS: File > Open), but this might cause permission errors on macOS when we start using xlwings in Part IV. When you hover over the file list in the Explorer on the Activity Bar, you will see the New File button appear as shown in Figure 2-6. Click on New File and call your file *hello_world.py*, then hit Enter. Once it opens in the editor, write the following line of code:

```
print("hello world!")
```

Remember that Jupyter notebooks conveniently print the return value of the last line automatically? When you run a traditional Python script, you need to tell Python explicitly what to print, which is why you need to use the print function here. In the Status Bar, you should now see your Python version, e.g., "Python 3.8.5 64-bit (conda)." If you click on it, the Command Palette will open and allow you to select a different Python interpreter if you have more than one (this includes Conda environments). Your set up should now look like the one in Figure 2-6.

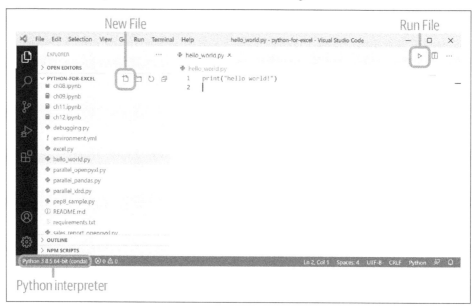

Figure 2-6. VS Code with hello_world.py open

Before we can run the script, make sure to save it by hitting Ctrl+S on Windows or Command-S on macOS. With Jupyter notebooks, we could simply select a cell and hit Shift+Enter to run that cell. With VS Code, you can run your code from either the Anaconda Prompt or by clicking the Run button. Running Python code from the Anaconda Prompt is how you most likely run scripts that are on a server, so it's important to know how this works.

Anaconda Prompt

Open an Anaconda Prompt, cd into the directory with the script, then run the script like so:

```
(base)> cd C:\Users\username\python-for-excel
(base)> python hello_world.py
hello world!
```

The last line is the output that is printed by the script. Note that if you are not in the same directory as your Python file, you need to use the full path to your Python file:

```
(base)> python C:\Users\username\python-for-excel\hello_world.py
hello world!
```

Long File Paths on the Anaconda Prompt

A convenient way to deal with long file paths is to drag and drop the file onto your Anaconda Prompt. This will write the full path wherever the cursor is.

Anaconda Prompt in VS Code

You don't need to switch away from VS Code to work with the Anaconda Prompt: VS Code has an integrated Terminal that you can show via the keyboard shortcut Ctrl+` or via View > Terminal. Since it opens in the project folder, you don't need to change the directory first:

```
(base)> python hello_world.py
hello world!
```

Run Button in VS Code

In VS code, there is an easy way to run your code without having to use the Anaconda Prompt: when you edit a Python file, you will see a green Play icon at the top right—this is the Run File button, as shown in Figure 2-6. Clicking it will open the Terminal at the bottom automatically and run the code there.

Opening Files in VS Code

VS Code has an unconventional default behavior when you single-click a file in the Explorer (Activity Bar): the file is opened in preview mode, which means that the next file that you single-click will replace it in the tab unless you have made some changes to the file. If you want to switch off the single-click behavior (so a single-click will select a file and a double-click will open it), go to Preferences > Settings (Ctrl+, on Windows or Command-, on macOS) and set the dropdown under Workbench > "List: Open Mode" to "doubleClick."

At this point, you know how to create, edit, and run Python scripts in VS Code. VS Code can do quite a bit more, though: in Appendix B, I explain how to use the debugger and how you can run Jupyter notebooks with VS Code.

Alternative Text Editors and IDEs

Tools are something individual, and just because this book is based on Jupyter notebooks and VS Code doesn't mean you shouldn't have a look at other options.

Some popular text editors include:

Sublime Text
Sublime (*https://oreil.ly/9FVLD*) is a fast commercial text editor.

Notepad++
Notepad++ (*https://oreil.ly/7Ksk9*) is free and has been around for a very long time but is Windows-only.

Vim or Emacs
Vim (*https://vim.org*) or Emacs (*https://oreil.ly/z__Kz*) may not be the best options for beginner programmers due to their steep learning curve, but they are very popular among professionals. The rivalry between the two free editors is so big that Wikipedia describes it as the "editor war."

Popular IDEs include:

PyCharm
The PyCharm (*https://oreil.ly/OrIj-*) community edition is free and very powerful, while the professional edition is commercial and adds support for scientific tools and web development.

Spyder
Spyder (*https://spyder-ide.org*) is similar to MATLAB's IDE and comes with a variable explorer. Since it's included in the Anaconda distribution, you can give it a try by running the following on an Anaconda Prompt: (base)> **spyder**.

JupyterLab

JupyterLab (*https://jupyter.org*) is a web-based IDE developed by the team behind Jupyter notebooks and can, of course, run Jupyter notebooks. Other than that, it tries to integrate everything else you need for your data science tasks into a single tool.

Wing Python IDE

Wing Python IDE (*https://wingware.com*) is an IDE that has been around for a long time. There are free simplified versions and a commercial version called Wing Pro.

Komodo IDE

Komodo IDE (*https://oreil.ly/Cdtab*) is a commercial IDE developed by Active-State and supports many other languages apart from Python.

PyDev

PyDev (*https://pydev.org*) is a Python IDE based on the popular Eclipse IDE.

Conclusion

In this chapter, I showed you how to install and use the tools we will work with: the Anaconda Prompt, Jupyter notebooks, and VS Code. We also ran a tiny bit of Python code in a Python REPL, in a Jupyter notebook, and as script in VS Code.

I do recommend you get comfortable with the Anaconda Prompt, as it will give you a lot of power once you get used to it. The ability to work with Jupyter notebooks in the cloud is also very comfortable, as it allows you to run the code samples of the first three parts of this book in your browser.

With a working development environment, you are now ready to tackle the next chapter, where you'll learn enough Python to be able to follow the rest of the book.

CHAPTER 3

Getting Started with Python

With Anaconda installed and Jupyter notebooks up and running, you have everything in place to get started with Python. Although this chapter doesn't go much further than the basics, it still covers a lot of ground. If you are at the beginning of your coding career, there may be a lot to digest. However, most concepts will get clearer once you use them in later chapters as part of a practical example, so there's no need to worry if you don't understand something fully the first time around. Whenever Python and VBA differ significantly, I will point this out to make sure you can transition from VBA to Python smoothly and are aware of the obvious traps. If you haven't done any VBA before, feel free to ignore these parts.

I will start this chapter with Python's basic data types, such as integers and strings. After that, I will introduce indexing and slicing, a core concept in Python that gives you access to specific elements of a sequence. Up next are data structures like lists and dictionaries that can hold multiple objects. I'll continue with the `if` statement and the `for` and `while` loops before getting to an introduction of functions and modules that allow you to organize and structure your code. To wrap this chapter up, I will show you how to format your Python code properly. As you have probably guessed by now, this chapter is as technical as it can get. Running the examples for yourself in a Jupyter notebook is therefore a good idea to make everything a bit more interactive and playful. Either type the examples yourself or run them by using the provided notebooks in the companion repository.

Data Types

Python, like every other programming language, treats numbers, text, booleans, etc. differently by assigning them a different *data type*. The data types that we will use most often are integers, floats, booleans, and strings. In this section, I am going to introduce them one after another with a few examples. To be able to understand data types, though, I first need to explain what an object is.

Objects

In Python, *everything* is an object, including numbers, strings, functions, and everything else that we'll meet in this chapter. Objects can make complex things easy and intuitive by giving you access to a set of variables and functions. So before anything else, let me say a few words about variables and functions!

Variables

In Python, a *variable* is a name that you assign to an object by using the equal sign. In the first line of the following example, the name a is assigned to the object 3:

```
In [1]: a = 3
        b = 4
        a + b

Out[1]: 7
```

This works the same for all objects, which is simpler compared to VBA, where you use the equal sign for data types like numbers and strings and the Set statement for objects like workbooks or worksheets. In Python, you change a variable's type simply by assigning it to a new object. This is referred to as *dynamic typing*:

```
In [2]: a = 3
        print(a)
        a = "three"
        print(a)

3
three
```

Unlike VBA, Python is case-sensitive, so a and A are two different variables. Variable names must follow certain rules:

- They must start with either a letter or an underscore
- They must consist of letters, numbers, and underscores

After this short introduction to variables, let's see how we can make function calls!

Functions

I will introduce functions with a lot more detail later in this chapter. For now, you should simply know how to call built-in functions like print that we used in the previous code sample. To call a function, you add parentheses to the function name and provide the arguments within the parentheses, which is pretty much equivalent to the mathematical notation:

```
function_name(argument1, argument2, ...)
```

Let's now look at how variables and functions work in the context of objects!

Attributes and methods

In the context of objects, variables are called *attributes* and functions are called *methods*: attributes give you access to the data of an object, and methods allow you to perform an action. To access attributes and methods, you use the dot notation like this: `myobject.attribute` and `myobject.method()`.

Let's make this a bit more tangible: if you write a car racing game, you would most likely use an object that represents a car. The `car` object could have a `speed` attribute that allows you to get the current speed via `car.speed`, and you might be able to accelerate the car by calling the accelerate method `car.accelerate(10)`, which would increase the speed by ten miles per hour.

The type of an object and with that its behavior is defined by a *class*, so the previous example would require you to write a `Car` class. The process of getting a `car` object out of a `Car` class is called *instantiation*, and you instantiate an object by calling the class in the same way as you call a function: `car = Car()`. We won't write our own classes in this book, but if you are interested in how this works, have a look at Appendix C.

We will use a first object method in the next section to make a text string uppercase, and we will get back to the topic of objects and classes when we talk about `datetime` objects toward the end of this chapter. Now, however, let's move on with those objects that have a numeric data type!

Numeric Types

The data types `int` and `float` represent *integers* and *floating-point numbers*, respectively. To find out the data type of a given object, use the built-in `type`:

```
In [3]: type(4)

Out[3]: int

In [4]: type(4.4)

Out[4]: float
```

If you want to force a number to be a `float` instead of an `int`, it's good enough to use a trailing decimal point or the `float` constructor:

```
In [5]: type(4.)

Out[5]: float

In [6]: float(4)
```

```
Out[6]: 4.0
```

The last example can also be turned around: using the `int` constructor, you can turn a `float` into an `int`. If the fractional part is not zero, it will be truncated:

```
In [7]: int(4.9)
```

```
Out[7]: 4
```

 Excel Cells Always Store Floats

You may need to convert a `float` to an `int` when you read in a number from an Excel cell and provide it as an argument to a Python function that expects an integer. The reason is that numbers in Excel cells are always stored as floats behind the scenes, even if Excel shows you what looks like an integer.

Python has a few more numeric types that I won't use or discuss in this book: there are the `decimal`, `fraction`, and `complex` data types. If floating-point inaccuracies are an issue (see sidebar), use the `decimal` type for exact results. These cases are very rare, though. As a rule of thumb: if Excel would be good enough for the calculations, use floats.

Floating-point Inaccuracies

By default, Excel often shows rounded numbers: type **=1.125-1.1** into a cell, and you will see 0.025. While this might be what you expect, it is not what Excel stores internally. Change the display format to show at least 16 decimals, and it will change to 0.0249999999999999. This is the effect of *floating-point inaccuracy*: computers live in a binary world, i.e., they calculate only with zeros and ones. Certain decimal fractions like 0.1 can't be stored as a finite binary floating-point number, which explains the result from the subtraction. In Python, you will see the same effect, but Python doesn't hide the decimals from you:

```
In [8]: 1.125 - 1.1
```

```
Out[8]: 0.02499999999999991
```

Mathematical operators

Calculating with numbers requires the use of mathematical operators like the plus or minus sign. Except for the power operator, there shouldn't be any surprise if you come from Excel:

```
In [9]: 3 + 4  # Sum
```

```
Out[9]: 7
```

```
In [10]: 3 - 4  # Subtraction
Out[10]: -1
In [11]: 3 / 4  # Division
Out[11]: 0.75
In [12]: 3 * 4  # Multiplication
Out[12]: 12
In [13]: 3**4  # The power operator (Excel uses 3^4)
Out[13]: 81
In [14]: 3 * (3 + 4)  # Use of parentheses
Out[14]: 21
```

Comments

In the previous examples, I was describing the operation of the example by using *comments* (e.g., # Sum). Comments help other people (and yourself a few weeks after writing the code) to understand what's going on in your program. It is good practice to only comment those things that are not already evident from reading the code: when in doubt, it's better to have no comment than an outdated comment that contradicts the code. Anything starting with a hash sign is a comment in Python and is ignored when you run the code:

```
In [15]: # This is a sample we've seen before.
         # Every comment line has to start with a #
         3 + 4
Out[15]: 7
In [16]: 3 + 4  # This is an inline comment
Out[16]: 7
```

Most editors have a keyboard shortcut to comment/uncomment lines. In Jupyter notebooks and VS Code, it is Ctrl+/ (Windows) or Command-/ (macOS). Note that Markdown cells in Jupyter notebooks won't accept comments—if you start a line with a # there, Markdown will interpret this as a heading.

Having integers and floats covered, let's move straight to the next section about booleans!

Booleans

The boolean types in Python are True or False, exactly like in VBA. The boolean operators and, or, and not, however, are all lowercase, while VBA shows them capitalized. Boolean expressions are similar to how they work in Excel, except for equality and inequality operators:

```
In [17]: 3 == 4  # Equality (Excel uses 3 = 4)

Out[17]: False

In [18]: 3 != 4  # Inequality (Excel uses 3 <> 4)

Out[18]: True

In [19]: 3 < 4  # Smaller than. Use > for bigger than.

Out[19]: True

In [20]: 3 <= 4  # Smaller or equal. Use >= for bigger or equal.

Out[20]: True

In [21]: # You can chain logical expressions
         # In VBA, this would be: 10 < 12 And 12 < 17
         # In Excel formulas, this would be: =AND(10 < 12, 12 < 17)
         10 < 12 < 17

Out[21]: True

In [22]: not True  # "not" operator

Out[22]: False

In [23]: False and True  # "and" operator

Out[23]: False

In [24]: False or True  # "or" operator

Out[24]: True
```

Every Python object evaluates to either `True` or `False`. The majority of objects are `True`, but there are some that evaluate to `False` including None (see sidebar), `False`, 0 or empty data types, e.g., an empty string (I'll introduce strings in the next section).

None

None is a built-in constant and represents "the absence of a value" according to the official docs. For example, if a function does not explicitly return anything, it returns None. It is also a good choice to represent empty cells in Excel as we will see in Part III and Part IV.

To double-check if an object is `True` or `False`, use the `bool` constructor:

```
In [25]: bool(2)

Out[25]: True

In [26]: bool(0)
```

```
Out[26]: False

In [27]: bool("some text")  # We'll get to strings in a moment

Out[27]: True

In [28]: bool("")

Out[28]: False

In [29]: bool(None)

Out[29]: False
```

With booleans in our pocket, there is one more basic data type left: textual data, better known as *strings*.

Strings

If you have ever worked with strings in VBA that are longer than one line and contain variables and literal quotes, you probably wished it was easier. Fortunately, this is an area where Python is particularly strong. Strings can be expressed by using either double quotes (") or single quotes ('). The only condition is that you have to start and end the string with the same type of quotes. You can use + to concatenate strings or * to repeat strings. Since I showed you the repeating case already when trying out the Python REPL in the previous chapter, here is a sample using the plus sign:

```
In [30]: "A double quote string. " + 'A single quote string.'

Out[30]: 'A double quote string. A single quote string.'
```

Depending on what you want to write, using single or double quotes can help you to easily print literal quotes without the need to escape them. If you still need to escape a character, you precede it with a backslash:

```
In [31]: print("Don't wait! " + 'Learn how to "speak" Python.')

Don't wait! Learn how to "speak" Python.

In [32]: print("It's easy to \"escape\" characters with a leading \\.")

It's easy to "escape" characters with a leading \.
```

When you are mixing strings with variables, you usually work with *f-strings*, short for *formatted string literal*. Simply put an f in front of your string and use variables in between curly braces:

```
In [33]: # Note how Python allows you to conveniently assign multiple
         # values to multiple variables in a single line
         first_adjective, second_adjective = "free", "open source"
         f"Python is {first_adjective} and {second_adjective}."

Out[33]: 'Python is free and open source.'
```

As I mentioned at the beginning of this section, strings are objects like everything else, and they offer a few methods (i.e., functions) to perform an action on that string. For example, this is how you transform between upper and lowercase letters:

```
In [34]: "PYTHON".lower()

Out[34]: 'python'

In [35]: "python".upper()

Out[35]: 'PYTHON'
```

Getting Help

How do you know what attributes certain objects like strings offer and what arguments their methods accept? The answer depends a bit on the tool you use: with Jupyter notebooks, hit the Tab key after typing the dot that follows an object, for example `"python".`**`<Tab>`**. This will make a dropdown appear with all the attributes and methods that this object offers. If your cursor is in a method, for example within the parentheses of `"python".upper()`, hit Shift+Tab to get the description of that function. VS Code will display this information automatically as a tooltip. If you run a Python REPL on the Anaconda Prompt, use `dir("python")` to get the available attributes and `help("python".upper)` to print the description of the `upper` method. Other than that, it's always a good idea to get back to Python's online documentation (*https://docs.python.org*). If you are looking for the documentation of third-party packages like pandas, it's helpful to search for them on PyPI (*https://pypi.org*), Python's package index, where you will find the links to the respective home pages and documentation.

When working with strings, a regular task is to select parts of a string: for example, you may want to get the USD part out of the EURUSD exchange rate notation. The next section shows you Python's powerful indexing and slicing mechanism that allows you to do exactly this.

Indexing and Slicing

Indexing and slicing give you access to specific elements of a sequence. Since strings are sequences of characters, we can use them to learn how it works. In the next section, we will meet additional sequences like lists and tuples that support indexing and slicing too.

Indexing

Figure 3-1 introduces the concept of *indexing*. Python is zero-based, which means that the first element in a sequence is referred to by index 0. Negative indices from -1 allow you to refer to elements from the end of the sequence.

Figure 3-1. Indexing from the beginning and end of a sequence

Common Error Traps for VBA Developers

If you are coming from VBA, indexing is a common error trap. VBA uses one-based indexing for most collections like sheets (`Sheets(1)`) but uses zero-based indexing for arrays (`MyArray(0)`), although that default can be changed. Another difference is that VBA uses parentheses for indexing while Python uses square brackets.

The syntax for indexing is as follows:

```
sequence[index]
```

Accordingly, you access specific elements from a string like this:

```
In [36]: language = "PYTHON"

In [37]: language[0]

Out[37]: 'P'

In [38]: language[1]

Out[38]: 'Y'

In [39]: language[-1]

Out[39]: 'N'

In [40]: language[-2]

Out[40]: 'O'
```

You will often want to extract more than just a single character—this is where slicing comes in.

Slicing

If you want to get more than one element from a sequence, you use the *slicing* syntax, which works as follows:

```
sequence[start:stop:step]
```

Python uses half-open intervals: the `start` index is included while the `stop` index is not. If you leave the `start` or `stop` arguments away, it will include everything from the beginning or to the end of the sequence, respectively. `step` determines the direction and the step size: for example, 2 will return every second element from left to right and -3 will return every third element from right to left. The default step size is one:

```
In [41]: language[:3]  # Same as language[0:3]

Out[41]: 'PYT'

In [42]: language[1:3]

Out[42]: 'YT'

In [43]: language[-3:]  # Same as language[-3:6]

Out[43]: 'HON'

In [44]: language[-3:-1]

Out[44]: 'HO'

In [45]: language[::2]  # Every second element

Out[45]: 'PTO'

In [46]: language[-1:-4:-1]  # Negative step goes from right to left

Out[46]: 'NOH'
```

So far we've looked at just a single index or slice operation, but Python also allows you to *chain* multiple index and slice operations together. For example, if you want to get the second character out of the last three characters, you could do it like this:

```
In [47]: language[-3:][1]

Out[47]: 'O'
```

This is the same as `language[-2]` so in this case, it wouldn't make much sense to use chaining, but it will make more sense when we use indexing and slicing with lists, one of the data structures that I am going to introduce in the next section.

Data Structures

Python offers powerful data structures that make working with a collection of objects really easy. In this section, I am going to introduce lists, dictionaries, tuples, and sets. While each of these data structures has slightly different characteristics, they are all

---

able to hold multiple objects. In VBA, you may have used collections or arrays to hold multiple values. VBA even offers a data structure called dictionary that works conceptually the same as Python's dictionary. It is, however, only available on the Windows version of Excel out of the box. Let's get started with lists, the data structure that you will probably use most.

Lists

Lists are capable of holding multiple objects of different data types. They are so versatile that you will use them all the time. You create a list as follows:

```
[element1, element2, ...]
```

Here are two lists, one with the names of Excel files and the other one with a few numbers:

```
In [48]: file_names = ["one.xlsx", "two.xlsx", "three.xlsx"]
         numbers = [1, 2, 3]
```

Like strings, lists can easily be concatenated with the plus sign. This also shows you that lists can hold different types of objects:

```
In [49]: file_names + numbers
```

```
Out[49]: ['one.xlsx', 'two.xlsx', 'three.xlsx', 1, 2, 3]
```

As lists are objects like everything else, lists can also have other lists as their elements. I will refer to them as *nested lists*:

```
In [50]: nested_list = [[1, 2, 3], [4, 5, 6], [7, 8, 9]]
```

If you rearrange this to span over multiple lines, you can easily recognize that this is a very nice representation of a matrix, or a range of spreadsheet cells. Note that the square brackets implicitly allow you to break the lines (see sidebar). Via indexing and slicing, you get the elements you want:

```
In [51]: cells = [[1, 2, 3],
                  [4, 5, 6],
                  [7, 8, 9]]
```

```
In [52]: cells[1]  # Second row
```

```
Out[52]: [4, 5, 6]
```

```
In [53]: cells[1][1:]  # Second row, second and third column
```

```
Out[53]: [5, 6]
```

Line Continuation

Sometimes, a line of code can get so long that you will need to break it up into two or more lines to keep your code readable. Technically, you can either use parentheses or a backslash to break up the line:

```
In [54]: a = (1 + 2
              + 3)
In [55]: a = 1 + 2 \
             + 3
```

Python's style guide, however, prefers that you use *implicit line breaks* if possible: whenever you are using an expression that contains parentheses, square brackets, or curly braces, use them to introduce a line break without having to introduce an additional character. I will say more about Python's style guide toward the end of this chapter.

You can change elements in lists:

```
In [56]: users = ["Linda", "Brian"]

In [57]: users.append("Jennifer")  # Most commonly you add to the end
         users

Out[57]: ['Linda', 'Brian', 'Jennifer']

In [58]: users.insert(0, "Kim")  # Insert "Kim" at index 0
         users

Out[58]: ['Kim', 'Linda', 'Brian', 'Jennifer']
```

To delete an element, use either `pop` or `del`. While `pop` is a method, `del` is implemented as a statement in Python:

```
In [59]: users.pop()  # Removes and returns the last element by default

Out[59]: 'Jennifer'

In [60]: users

Out[60]: ['Kim', 'Linda', 'Brian']

In [61]: del users[0]  # del removes an element at the given index
```

Some other useful things you can do with lists are:

```
In [62]: len(users)  # Length

Out[62]: 2

In [63]: "Linda" in users  # Check if users contains "Linda"

Out[63]: True
```

```
In [64]: print(sorted(users))  # Returns a new sorted list
         print(users)  # The original list is unchanged

['Brian', 'Linda']
['Linda', 'Brian']

In [65]: users.sort()  # Sorts the original list
         users

Out[65]: ['Brian', 'Linda']
```

Note that you can use len and in with strings as well:

```
In [66]: len("Python")

Out[66]: 6

In [67]: "free" in "Python is free and open source."

Out[67]: True
```

To get access to elements in a list, you refer to them by their position or index—that's not always practical. Dictionaries, the topic of the next section, allow you to get access to elements via a key (often a name).

Dictionaries

Dictionaries map keys to values. You will come across key/value combinations all the time. The easiest way to create a dictionary is as follows:

```
{key1: value1, key2: value2, ...}
```

While lists allow you to access elements by index, i.e., position, dictionaries allow you to access elements by key. As with indices, keys are accessed via square brackets. The following code samples will use a currency pair (key) that maps to the exchange rate (value):

```
In [68]: exchange_rates = {"EURUSD": 1.1152,
                           "GBPUSD": 1.2454,
                           "AUDUSD": 0.6161}

In [69]: exchange_rates["EURUSD"]  # Access the EURUSD exchange rate

Out[69]: 1.1152
```

The following samples show you how to change existing values and add new key/value pairs:

```
In [70]: exchange_rates["EURUSD"] = 1.2  # Change an existing value
         exchange_rates

Out[70]: {'EURUSD': 1.2, 'GBPUSD': 1.2454, 'AUDUSD': 0.6161}

In [71]: exchange_rates["CADUSD"] = 0.714  # Add a new key/value pair
         exchange_rates

Out[71]: {'EURUSD': 1.2, 'GBPUSD': 1.2454, 'AUDUSD': 0.6161, 'CADUSD': 0.714}
```

The easiest way to merge two or more dictionaries is by *unpacking* them into a new one. You unpack a dictionary by using two leading asterisks. If the second dictionary contains keys from the first one, the values from the first will be overridden. You can see this happening by looking at the GBPUSD exchange rate:

```
In [72]: {**exchange_rates, **{"SGDUSD": 0.7004, "GBPUSD": 1.2222}}

Out[72]: {'EURUSD': 1.2,
          'GBPUSD': 1.2222,
          'AUDUSD': 0.6161,
          'CADUSD': 0.714,
          'SGDUSD': 0.7004}
```

Python 3.9 introduced the pipe character as a dedicated merge operator for dictionaries, which allows you to simplify the previous expression to this:

```
exchange_rates | {"SGDUSD": 0.7004, "GBPUSD": 1.2222}
```

Many objects can serve as keys; the following is an example with integers:

```
In [73]: currencies = {1: "EUR", 2: "USD", 3: "AUD"}

In [74]: currencies[1]

Out[74]: 'EUR'
```

By using the get method, dictionaries allow you to use a default value in case the key doesn't exist:

```
In [75]: # currencies[100] would raise an exception. Instead of 100,
         # you could use any other non-existing key, too.
         currencies.get(100, "N/A")

Out[75]: 'N/A'
```

Dictionaries can often be used when you would use a Case statement in VBA. The previous example could be written like this in VBA:

```
Select Case x
Case 1
    Debug.Print "EUR"
Case 2
    Debug.Print "USD"
Case 3
    Debug.Print "AUD"
Case Else
    Debug.Print "N/A"
End Select
```

Now that you know how to work with dictionaries, let's move on to the next data structure: tuples. They are similar to lists with one big difference, as we will see in the next section.

Tuples

Tuples are similar to lists with the difference that they are *immutable*: once created, their elements can't be changed. While you can often use tuples and lists interchangeably, tuples are the obvious choice for a collection that never changes throughout the program. Tuples are created by separating values with commas:

```
mytuple = element1, element2, ...
```

Using parentheses often makes it easier to read:

```
In [76]: currencies = ("EUR", "GBP", "AUD")
```

Tuples allow you to access elements the same way as lists, but they won't allow you to change elements. Instead, concatenating tuples will create a new tuple behind the scenes, then bind your variable to this new tuple:

```
In [77]: currencies[0]  # Accessing the first element

Out[77]: 'EUR'

In [78]: # Concatenating tuples will return a new tuple.
         currencies + ("SGD",)

Out[78]: ('EUR', 'GBP', 'AUD', 'SGD')
```

I explain the difference between *mutable* vs. *immutable* objects in detail in Appendix C, but for now, let's have a look at the last data structure of this section: sets.

Sets

Sets are collections that have no duplicate elements. While you can use them for set theory operations, in practice they often help you to get the unique values of a list or a tuple. You create sets by using curly braces:

```
{element1, element2, ...}
```

To get the unique objects in a list or a tuple, use the set constructor like so:

```
In [79]: set(["USD", "USD", "SGD", "EUR", "USD", "EUR"])

Out[79]: {'EUR', 'SGD', 'USD'}
```

Other than that, you can apply set theory operations like intersection and union:

```
In [80]: portfolio1 = {"USD", "EUR", "SGD", "CHF"}
         portfolio2 = {"EUR", "SGD", "CAD"}

In [81]: # Same as portfolio2.union(portfolio1)
         portfolio1.union(portfolio2)

Out[81]: {'CAD', 'CHF', 'EUR', 'SGD', 'USD'}

In [82]: # Same as portfolio2.intersection(portfolio1)
         portfolio1.intersection(portfolio2)
```

```
Out[82]: {'EUR', 'SGD'}
```

For a full overview of set operations, see the official docs (*https://oreil.ly/ju4ed*). Before moving on, let's quickly revise the four data structures we just met in Table 3-1. It shows a sample for each data structure in the notation I used in the previous paragraphs, the so-called *literals*. Additionally, I am also listing their constructors that offer an alternative to using the literals and are often used to convert from one data structure to another. For example, to convert a tuple to a list, do:

```
In [83]: currencies = "USD", "EUR", "CHF"
         currencies

Out[83]: ('USD', 'EUR', 'CHF')

In [84]: list(currencies)

Out[84]: ['USD', 'EUR', 'CHF']
```

Table 3-1. Data structures

Data Structure	Literals	Constructor
List	`[1, 2, 3]`	`list((1, 2, 3))`
Dictionary	`{"a": 1, "b": 2}`	`dict(a=1, b=2)`
Tuple	`(1, 2, 3)`	`tuple([1, 2, 3])`
Set	`{1, 2, 3}`	`set((1, 2, 3))`

At this point, you know all important data types including basic ones like floats and strings, and data structures like lists and dictionaries. In the next section, we move on to control flow.

Control Flow

This section presents the `if` statement as well as the `for` and `while` loops. The `if` statement allows you to execute certain lines of code only if a condition is met, and the `for` and `while` loops will execute a block of code repeatedly. At the end of the section, I will also introduce list comprehensions, which are a way to construct lists that can serve as an alternative to `for` loops. I will start this section with the definition of code blocks, for which I also need to introduce one of Python's most noteworthy particularities: significant white space.

Code Blocks and the pass Statement

A *code block* defines a section in your source code that is used for something special. For example, you use a code block to define the lines over which your program is looping or it makes up the definition of a function. In Python, you define code blocks by indenting them, not by using keywords like in VBA or curly braces like in most other languages. This is referred to as *significant white space*. The Python community has settled on four spaces as indentation, but you usually type them in by hitting the Tab key: both Jupyter notebooks and VS Code will automatically convert your Tab key into four spaces. Let me show you how code blocks are formally defined by using the `if` statement:

```
if condition:
    pass  # Do nothing
```

The line preceding the code block always terminates with a colon. Since the end of the code block is reached when you no longer indent the line, you need to use the `pass` statement if you want to create a dummy code block that does nothing. In VBA, this would correspond to the following:

```
If condition Then
    ' Do nothing
End If
```

Note that "Do nothing" is a comment in both versions, and could be left out. Now that you know how to define code blocks, let's start using them in the next section, where I will properly introduce the `if` statement.

The if Statement and Conditional Expressions

To introduce the `if` statement, let me reproduce the example from "Readability and Maintainability" on page 13 in Chapter 1, but this time in Python:

```
In [85]: i = 20
         if i < 5:
             print("i is smaller than 5")
         elif i <= 10:
             print("i is between 5 and 10")
         else:
             print("i is bigger than 10")

i is bigger than 10
```

If you would do the same as we did in Chapter 1, i.e., indent the `elif` and `else` statements, you would get a `SyntaxError`. Python won't let you indent your code differently from the logic. Compared to VBA, the keywords are lowercase and instead of `ElseIf` in VBA, Python uses `elif`. `if` statements are an easy way to tell if a programmer is new to Python or if they have already adopted a *Pythonic* style: in Python, a simple `if` statement doesn't require any parentheses around it and to test if a value is `True`, you don't need to do that explicitly.

Here is what I mean by that:

```
In [86]: is_important = True
         if is_important:
             print("This is important.")
```

```
else:
    print("This is not important.")
```

```
This is important.
```

The same works if you want to check if a sequence like a list is empty or not:

```
In [87]: values = []
         if values:
             print(f"The following values were provided: {values}")
         else:
             print("There were no values provided.")
```

```
There were no values provided.
```

Programmers coming from other languages would often write something like `if (is_important == True)` or `if len(values) > 0` instead.

Conditional expressions, also called *ternary operators*, allow you to use a more compact style for simple `if/else` statements:

```
In [88]: is_important = False
         print("important") if is_important else print("not important")
```

```
not important
```

With `if` statements and conditional expressions in our pocket, let's turn our attention to `for` and `while` loops in the next section.

The for and while Loops

If you need to do something repeatedly like printing the value of ten different variables, you are doing yourself a big favor by not copy/pasting the print statement ten times. Instead, use a `for` loop to do the work for you. `for` loops iterate over the items of a sequence like a list, a tuple, or a string (remember, strings are sequences of characters). As an introductory example, let's create a `for` loop that takes each element of the `currencies` list, assigns it to the variable `currency` and prints it—one after another until there are no more elements in the list:

```
In [89]: currencies = ["USD", "HKD", "AUD"]

         for currency in currencies:
             print(currency)
```

```
USD
HKD
AUD
```

As a side note, VBA's `For Each` statement is close to how Python's `for` loop works. The previous example could be written like this in VBA:

```
Dim currencies As Variant
Dim curr As Variant   'currency is a reserved word in VBA
```

```
currencies = Array("USD", "HKD", "AUD")

For Each curr In currencies
    Debug.Print curr
Next
```

In Python, if you need a counter variable in a for loop, the range or enumerate built-ins can help you with that. Let's first look at range, which provides a sequence of numbers: you call it by either providing a single stop argument or by providing a start and stop argument, with an optional step argument. Like with slicing, start is inclusive, stop is exclusive, and step determines the step size, with 1 being the default:

```
range(stop)
range(start, stop, step)
```

range evaluates lazily, which means that without explicitly asking for it, you won't see the sequence it generates:

```
In [90]: range(5)

Out[90]: range(0, 5)
```

Converting the range to a list solves this issue:

```
In [91]: list(range(5))  # stop argument

Out[91]: [0, 1, 2, 3, 4]

In [92]: list(range(2, 5, 2))  # start, stop, step arguments

Out[92]: [2, 4]
```

Most of the time, there's no need to wrap range with a list, though:

```
In [93]: for i in range(3):
             print(i)

0
1
2
```

If you need a counter variable while looping over a sequence, use enumerate. It returns a sequence of (index, element) tuples. By default, the index starts at zero and increments by one. You can use enumerate in a loop like this:

```
In [94]: for i, currency in enumerate(currencies):
             print(i, currency)

0 USD
1 HKD
2 AUD
```

Looping over tuples and sets works the same as with lists. When you loop over dictionaries, Python will loop over the keys:

```
In [95]: exchange_rates = {"EURUSD": 1.1152,
                           "GBPUSD": 1.2454,
                           "AUDUSD": 0.6161}
         for currency_pair in exchange_rates:
             print(currency_pair)

EURUSD
GBPUSD
AUDUSD
```

By using the items method, you get the key and the value at the same time as tuple:

```
In [96]: for currency_pair, exchange_rate in exchange_rates.items():
             print(currency_pair, exchange_rate)

EURUSD 1.1152
GBPUSD 1.2454
AUDUSD 0.6161
```

To exit a loop, use the break statement:

```
In [97]: for i in range(15):
             if i == 2:
                 break
             else:
                 print(i)

0
1
```

You skip the remainder of an iteration with the continue statement, which means that the loop continues with the next element i:

```
In [98]: for i in range(4):
             if i == 2:
                 continue
             else:
                 print(i)

0
1
3
```

When comparing for loops in VBA with Python, there is a subtle difference: in VBA, the counter variable increases beyond your upper limit after finishing the loop:

```
For i = 1 To 3
    Debug.Print i
Next i
Debug.Print i
```

This prints:

```
1
2
3
4
```

In Python, it behaves like you would probably expect it to:

```
In [99]: for i in range(1, 4):
             print(i)
         print(i)

1
2
3
3
```

Instead of looping over a sequence, you can also use *while loops* to run a loop while a certain condition is true:

```
In [100]: n = 0
          while n <= 2:
              print(n)
              n += 1

0
1
2
```

Augmented Assignment

I have used the *augmented assignment* notation in the last example: n += 1. This is the same as if you would write n = n + 1. It also works with all the other mathematical operators that I've introduced earlier on; for example, for minus you could write n -= -1.

Quite often, you will need to collect certain elements in a list for further processing. In this case, Python offers an alternative to writing loops: list, dictionary, and set comprehensions.

List, Dictionary, and Set Comprehensions

List, dictionary, and set comprehensions are technically a way to create the respective data structure, but they often replace a for loop, which is why I am introducing them here. Assume that in the following list of USD currency pairs, you'd like to pick out those currencies where USD is quoted as the second currency. You could write the following for loop:

```
In [101]: currency_pairs = ["USDJPY", "USDGBP", "USDCHF",
                            "USDCAD", "AUDUSD", "NZDUSD"]
```

```
In [102]: usd_quote = []
          for pair in currency_pairs:
              if pair[3:] == "USD":
                  usd_quote.append(pair[:3])
          usd_quote

Out[102]: ['AUD', 'NZD']
```

This is often easier to write with a *list comprehension*. A list comprehension is a concise way of creating a list. You can grab its syntax from this example, which does the same as the previous for loop:

```
In [103]: [pair[:3] for pair in currency_pairs if pair[3:] == "USD"]

Out[103]: ['AUD', 'NZD']
```

If you don't have any condition to satisfy, simply leave the if part away. For example, to invert all the currency pairs so that the first currency comes second and vice versa, you would do:

```
In [104]: [pair[3:] + pair[:3] for pair in currency_pairs]

Out[104]: ['JPYUSD', 'GBPUSD', 'CHFUSD', 'CADUSD', 'USDAUD', 'USDNZD']
```

With dictionaries, there are dictionary comprehensions:

```
In [105]: exchange_rates = {"EURUSD": 1.1152,
                            "GBPUSD": 1.2454,
                            "AUDUSD": 0.6161}
          {k: v * 100 for (k, v) in exchange_rates.items()}

Out[105]: {'EURUSD': 111.52, 'GBPUSD': 124.54, 'AUDUSD': 61.61}
```

And with sets, there are set comprehensions:

```
In [106]: {s + "USD" for s in ["EUR", "GBP", "EUR", "HKD", "HKD"]}

Out[106]: {'EURUSD', 'GBPUSD', 'HKDUSD'}
```

At this point, you are already able to write simple scripts, as you know most of the basic building blocks of Python. In the next section, you will learn how to organize your code to keep it maintainable when your scripts start to get bigger.

Code Organization

In this section, we'll look into how to bring code into a maintainable structure: I'll start by introducing functions with all the details that you will commonly need before I'll show you how to split your code into different Python modules. The knowledge about modules will allow us to finish this section by looking into the datetime module that is part of the standard library.

Functions

Even if you will use Python for simple scripts only, you are still going to write functions regularly: they are one of the most important constructs of every programming language and allow you to reuse the same lines of code from anywhere in your program. We'll start this section by defining a function before we see how to call it!

Defining functions

To write your own function in Python, you have to use the keyword `def`, which stands for function *definition*. Unlike VBA, Python doesn't differentiate between a function and a Sub procedure. In Python, the equivalent of a Sub procedure is simply a function that doesn't return anything. Functions in Python follow the syntax for code blocks, i.e., you end the first line with a colon and indent the body of the function:

```
def function_name(required_argument, optional_argument=default_value, ...):
    return value1, value2, ...
```

Required arguments

Required arguments do not have a default value. Multiple arguments are separated by commas.

Optional arguments

You make an argument optional by supplying a default value. `None` is often used to make an argument optional if there is no meaningful default.

Return value

The `return` statement defines the value that the function returns. If you leave it away, the function automatically returns `None`. Python conveniently allows you to return multiple values separated by commas.

To be able to play around with a function, let's define one that is able to convert the temperature from Fahrenheit or Kelvin to degrees Celsius:

```
In [107]: def convert_to_celsius(degrees, source="fahrenheit"):
              if source.lower() == "fahrenheit":
                  return (degrees-32) * (5/9)
              elif source.lower() == "kelvin":
                  return degrees - 273.15
              else:
                  return f"Don't know how to convert from {source}"
```

I am using the string method `lower`, which transforms the provided strings to lowercase. This allows us to accept the `source` string with any capitalization while the comparison will still work. With the `convert_to_celsius` function defined, let's see how we can call it!

Calling functions

As briefly mentioned at the beginning of this chapter, you call a function by adding parentheses to the function name, enclosing the function arguments:

```
value1, value2, ... = function_name(positional_arg, arg_name=value, ...)
```

Positional arguments
> If you provide a value as a positional argument (`positional_arg`), the values are matched to the arguments according to their position in the function definition.

Keyword arguments
> By providing the argument in the form `arg_name=value`, you're providing a keyword argument. This has the advantage that you can provide the arguments in any order. It is also more explicit to the reader and can make it easier to understand. For example, if the function is defined as `f(a, b)`, you could call the function like this: `f(b=1, a=2)`. This concept also exists in VBA, where you could use keyword arguments by calling a function like this: `f(b:=1, a:=1)`. In VBA, however, they are referred to as *named arguments*.

Let's play around with the `convert_to_celsius` function to see how this all works in practice:

```
In [108]: convert_to_celsius(100, "fahrenheit")  # Positional arguments

Out[108]: 37.77777777777778

In [109]: convert_to_celsius(50)  # Will use the default source (fahrenheit)

Out[109]: 10.0

In [110]: convert_to_celsius(source="kelvin", degrees=0)  # Keyword arguments

Out[110]: -273.15
```

Now that you know how to define and call functions, let's see how to organize them with the help of modules.

Modules and the import Statement

When you write code for bigger projects, you will have to split it into different files at some point to be able to bring it into a maintainable structure. As we have already seen in the previous chapter, Python files have the extension *.py* and you usually refer to your main file as a *script*. If you now want your main script to access functionality from other files, you need to *import* that functionality first. In this context, Python source files are called *modules*. To get a better feeling for how this works and what the different import options are, have a look at the file *temperature.py* in the companion repository by opening it with VS Code (Example 3-1). If you need a refresher on how to open files in VS Code, have another look at Chapter 2.

Example 3-1. temperature.py

```python
TEMPERATURE_SCALES = ("fahrenheit", "kelvin", "celsius")


def convert_to_celsius(degrees, source="fahrenheit"):
    if source.lower() == "fahrenheit":
        return (degrees-32) * (5/9)
    elif source.lower() == "kelvin":
        return degrees - 273.15
    else:
        return f"Don't know how to convert from {source}"


print("This is the temperature module.")
```

To be able to import the `temperature` module from your Jupyter notebook, you will need the Jupyter notebook and the `temperature` module to be in the same directory —as it is in the case of the companion repository. To import, you only use the name of the module, without the *.py* ending. After running the `import` statement, you will have access to all the objects in that Python module via the dot notation. For example, use `temperature.convert_to_celsius()` to perform your conversion:

```
In [111]: import temperature

This is the temperature module.

In [112]: temperature.TEMPERATURE_SCALES

Out[112]: ('fahrenheit', 'kelvin', 'celsius')

In [113]: temperature.convert_to_celsius(120, "fahrenheit")

Out[113]: 48.88888888888889
```

Note that I used uppercase letters for `TEMPERATURE_SCALES` to express that it is a constant—I will say more about that toward the end of this chapter. When you execute the cell with `import temperature`, Python will run the *temperature.py* file from top to bottom. You can easily see this happening since importing the module will fire the print function at the bottom of *temperature.py*.

Modules Are Only Imported Once

If you run the `import temperature` cell again, you will notice that it does not print anything anymore. This is because Python modules are only imported once per session. If you change code in a module that you import, you need to restart your Python interpreter to pick up all the changes, i.e., in a Jupyter notebook, you'd have to click on Kernel > Restart.

In reality, you usually don't print anything in modules. This was only to show you the effect of importing a module more than once. Most commonly, you put functions and classes in your modules (for more on classes, see Appendix C). If you don't want to type `temperature` every time you use an object from the temperature module, change the `import` statement like this:

```
In [114]: import temperature as tp

In [115]: tp.TEMPERATURE_SCALES

Out[115]: ('fahrenheit', 'kelvin', 'celsius')
```

Assigning a short alias `tp` to your module can make it easier to use while it's still always clear where an object comes from. Many third-party packages suggest a specific convention when using an alias. For example, pandas is using `import pandas as pd`. There is one more option to import objects from another module:

```
In [116]: from temperature import TEMPERATURE_SCALES, convert_to_celsius

In [117]: TEMPERATURE_SCALES

Out[117]: ('fahrenheit', 'kelvin', 'celsius')
```

The __pycache__ Folder

When you import the `temperature` module, you will see that Python creates a folder called *__pycache__* with files that have the *.pyc* extension. These are bytecode-compiled files that the Python interpreter creates when you import a module. For our purposes, we can simply ignore this folder, as it is a technical detail of how Python runs your code.

When using the `from x import y` syntax, you import specific objects only. By doing this, you are importing them directly into the *namespace* of your main script: that is, without looking at the `import` statements, you won't be able to tell whether the imported objects were defined in your current Python script or Jupyter notebook or if they come from another module. This could cause conflicts: if your main script has a function called `convert_to_celsius`, it would override the one that you are importing from the `temperature` module. If, however, you use one of the two previous methods, your local function and the one from the imported module could live next to each other as `convert_to_celsius` and `temperature.convert_to_celsius`.

Don't Name Your Scripts Like Existing Packages

A common source for errors is to name your Python file the same as an existing Python package or module. If you create a file to test out some pandas functionality, don't call that file *pandas.py*, as this can cause conflicts.

Now that you know how the import mechanism works, let's use it right away to import the `datetime` module! This will also allow you to learn a few more things about objects and classes.

The datetime Class

Working with date and time is a common operation in Excel, but it comes with limitations: for example, Excel's cell format for time doesn't support smaller units than milliseconds and time zones are not supported at all. In Excel, date and time are stored as a simple float called the *date serial number*. The Excel cell is then formatted to display it as date and/or time. For example, January 1, 1900 has the date serial number of 1, which means that this is also the earliest date that you can work with in Excel. Time gets translated into the decimal part of the float, e.g., `01/01/1900 10:10:00` is represented by `1.4236111111`.

In Python, to work with date and time, you import the `datetime` module, which is part of the standard library. The `datetime` module contains a class with the same name that allows us to create `datetime` objects. Since having the same name for the module and the class can be confusing, I will use the following import convention throughout this book: `import datetime as dt`. This makes it easy to differentiate between the module (`dt`) and the class (`datetime`).

Up to this point, we were most of the time using *literals* to create objects like lists or dictionaries. Literals refer to the syntax that Python recognizes as a specific object type—in the case of a list, this would be something like `[1, 2, 3]`. However, most of the objects have to be created by calling their class: this process is called *instantiation*, and objects are therefore also called *class instances*. Calling a class works the same way as calling a function, i.e., you add parentheses to the class name and provide the arguments in the same way we did with functions. To instantiate a `datetime` object, you need to call the class like this:

```
import datetime as dt
dt.datetime(year, month, day, hour, minute, second, microsecond, timezone)
```

Let's go through a couple of examples to see how you work with `datetime` objects in Python. For the purpose of this introduction, let's ignore time zones and work with time-zone-naive `datetime` objects:

```
In [118]: # Import the datetime module as "dt"
          import datetime as dt

In [119]: # Instantiate a datetime object called "timestamp"
          timestamp = dt.datetime(2020, 1, 31, 14, 30)
          timestamp

Out[119]: datetime.datetime(2020, 1, 31, 14, 30)
```

```
In [120]: # Datetime objects offer various attributes, e.g., to get the day
          timestamp.day

Out[120]: 31

In [121]: # The difference of two datetime objects returns a timedelta object
          timestamp - dt.datetime(2020, 1, 14, 12, 0)

Out[121]: datetime.timedelta(days=17, seconds=9000)

In [122]: # Accordingly, you can also work with timedelta objects
          timestamp + dt.timedelta(days=1, hours=4, minutes=11)

Out[122]: datetime.datetime(2020, 2, 1, 18, 41)
```

To *format* datetime objects into strings, use the strftime method, and to *parse* a string and convert it into a datetime object, use the strptime function (you can find an overview of the accepted format codes in the datetime docs (*https://oreil.ly/gXOts*)):

```
In [123]: # Format a datetime object in a specific way
          # You could also use an f-string: f"{timestamp:%d/%m/%Y %H:%M}"
          timestamp.strftime("%d/%m/%Y %H:%M")

Out[123]: '31/01/2020 14:30'

In [124]: # Parse a string into a datetime object
          dt.datetime.strptime("12.1.2020", "%d.%m.%Y")

Out[124]: datetime.datetime(2020, 1, 12, 0, 0)
```

After this short introduction to the datetime module, let's move on to the last topic of this chapter, which is about formatting your code properly.

PEP 8: Style Guide for Python Code

You may have been wondering why I was sometimes using variable names with underscores or in all caps. This section will explain my formatting choices by introducing you to Python's official style guide. Python uses so-called Python Enhancement Proposals (PEP) to discuss the introduction of new language features. One of these, the Style Guide for Python Code, is usually referred to by its number: PEP 8. PEP 8 is a set of style recommendations for the Python community; if everybody who works on the same code adheres to the same style guide, the code becomes much more readable. This is especially important in the world of open source where many programmers work on the same project, often without knowing each other personally. Example 3-2 shows a short Python file that introduces the most important conventions.

Example 3-2. pep8_sample.py

```
"""This script shows a few PEP 8 rules. ❶
"""

import datetime as dt ❷


TEMPERATURE_SCALES = ("fahrenheit", "kelvin",
                      "celsius") ❸
❹

class TemperatureConverter: ❺
    pass  # Doesn't do anything at the moment ❻


def convert_to_celsius(degrees, source="fahrenheit"): ❼
    """This function converts degrees Fahrenheit or Kelvin
    into degrees Celsius. ❽
    """
    if source.lower() == "fahrenheit": ❾
        return (degrees-32) * (5/9) ❿
    elif source.lower() == "kelvin":
        return degrees - 273.15
    else:
        return f"Don't know how to convert from {source}"


celsius = convert_to_celsius(44, source="fahrenheit") ⓫
non_celsius_scales = TEMPERATURE_SCALES[:-1] ⓬

print("Current time: " + dt.datetime.now().isoformat())
print(f"The temperature in Celsius is: {celsius}")
```

❶ Explain what the script/module does with a *docstring* at the top. A docstring is a special type of string, enclosed with triple quotes. Apart from serving as a string for documenting your code, a docstring also makes it easy to write strings over multiple lines and is useful if your text contains a lot of double-quotes or single-quotes, as you won't need to escape them. They are also useful to write multiline SQL queries, as we will see in Chapter 11.

❷ All imports are at the top of the file, one per line. List the imports of the standard library first, then those of third-party packages, and finally those from your own modules. This sample only makes use of the standard library.

❸ Use capital letters with underscores for constants. Use a maximum line length of 79 characters. If possible, take advantage of parentheses, square brackets, or curly braces for implicit line breaks.

❹ Separate classes and functions with two empty lines from the rest of the code.

❺ Despite the fact that many classes like `datetime` are all lowercase, your own classes should use `CapitalizedWords` as names. For more on classes, see Appendix C.

❻ Inline comments should be separated by at least two spaces from the code. Code blocks should be indented by four spaces.

❼ Functions and function arguments should use lowercase names with underscores if they improve readability. Don't use spaces between the argument name and its default value.

❽ A function's docstring should also list and explain the function arguments. I haven't done this here to keep the sample short, but you will find complete docstrings in the *excel.py* file that is included in the companion repository and that we will meet in Chapter 8.

❾ Don't use spaces around the colon.

❿ Use spaces around mathematical operators. If operators with different priorities are used, you may consider adding spaces around those with the lowest priority only. Since the multiplication in this example has the lowest priority, I have added spaces around it.

⓫ Use lowercase names for variables. Make use of underscores if they improve readability. When assigning a variable name, use spaces around the equal sign. However, when calling a function, don't use spaces around the equal sign used with keyword arguments.

⓬ With indexing and slicing, don't use spaces around the square brackets.

This is a simplified summary of PEP 8, so it's a good idea to have a look at the original PEP 8 (*https://oreil.ly/3fTTZ*) once you start to get more serious with Python. PEP 8 clearly states that it is a recommendation and that your own style guides will take precedence. After all, consistency is the most important factor. If you are interested in other publicly available guidelines, you may want to have a look at Google's style guide for Python (*https://oreil.ly/6sYSa*), which is reasonably close to PEP 8. In practice, most Python programmers loosely adhere to PEP 8, and ignoring the maximum line length of 79 characters is probably the most common sin.

Since it might be difficult to format your code properly while writing it, you can have your style checked automatically. The next section shows you how this works with VS Code.

PEP 8 and VS Code

When working with VS Code, there is an easy way to make sure your code sticks to PEP 8: use a *linter*. A linter checks your source code for syntax and style errors. Fire up the command palette (Ctrl+Shift+P on Windows or Command-Shift-P on macOS) and search for Python: Select Linter. A popular option is *flake8*, a package that comes preinstalled with Anaconda. If enabled, VS Code will underline issues with squiggly lines every time you save your file. Hovering over such a squiggly line will give you an explanation in a tooltip. You switch a linter off again by searching for "Python: Enable Linting" in the command palette and choosing "Disable Linting." If you prefer, you can also run `flake8` on an Anaconda Prompt to have a report printed (the command only prints something if there is a violation of PEP 8, so running this on *pep8_sample.py* won't print anything unless you introduce a violation):

```
(base)> cd C:\Users\username\python-for-excel
(base)> flake8 pep8_sample.py
```

Python has recently taken static code analysis a step further by adding support for *type hints*. The next section explains how they work.

Type Hints

In VBA, you often see code that prefixes each variable with an abbreviation for the data type, like `strEmployeeName` or `wbWorkbookName`. While nobody will stop you from doing this in Python, it isn't commonly done. You also won't find an equivalent to VBA's `Option Explicit` or `Dim` statement to declare the type of a variable. Instead, Python 3.5 introduced a feature called *type hints*. Type hints are also referred to as *type annotations* and allow you to declare the data type of a variable. They are completely optional and have no effect on how the code is run by the Python interpreter (there are, however, third-party packages like pydantic (*https://oreil.ly/J9W8h*) that can enforce type hints at runtime). The main purpose of type hints is to allow text editors like VS Code to catch more errors before running the code, but they can also improve code autocompletion of VS Code and other editors. The most popular type checker for type annotated code is mypy, which VS Code offers as a linter. To get a feeling of how type annotations work in Python, here is a short sample without type hints:

```
x = 1

def hello(name):
    return f"Hello {name}!"
```

And again with type hints:

```
x: int = 1
```

```
def hello(name: str) -> str:
    return f"Hello {name}!"
```

As type hints generally make more sense in bigger codebases, I am not going to use them in the remainder of this book.

Conclusion

This chapter was a packed introduction to Python. We met the most important building blocks of the language, including data structures, functions, and modules. We also touched on some of Python's particularities like meaningful white space and code formatting guidelines, better known as PEP 8. To continue with this book, you won't need to know all the details: as a beginner, just knowing about lists and dictionaries, indexing and slicing, as well as how to work with functions, modules, for loops, and if statements will get you far already.

Compared to VBA, I find Python more consistent and powerful but at the same time easier to learn. If you are a VBA die-hard fan and this chapter didn't convince you just yet, I am pretty sure the next part will: there, I will give you an introduction to array-based calculations before starting our data analysis journey with the pandas library. Let's get started with Part II by learning a few basics about NumPy!

PART II

Introduction to pandas

## CHAPTER 4

NumPy Foundations

As you may recall from Chapter 1, NumPy is the core package for scientific computing in Python, providing support for array-based calculations and linear algebra. As NumPy is the backbone of pandas, I am going to introduce its basics in this chapter: after explaining what a NumPy array is, we will look into vectorization and broadcasting, two important concepts that allow you to write concise mathematical code and that you will find again in pandas. After that, we're going to see why NumPy offers special functions called universal functions before we wrap this chapter up by learning how to get and set values of an array and by explaining the difference between a view and a copy of a NumPy array. Even if we will hardly use NumPy directly in this book, knowing its basics will make it easier to learn pandas in the next chapter.

Getting Started with NumPy

In this section, we'll learn about one- and two-dimensional NumPy arrays and what's behind the technical terms *vectorization*, *broadcasting*, and *universal function*.

NumPy Array

To perform array-based calculations with nested lists, as we met them in the last chapter, you would have to write some sort of loop. For example, to add a number to every element in a nested list, you can use the following nested list comprehension:

```
In [1]: matrix = [[1, 2, 3],
                  [4, 5, 6],
                  [7, 8, 9]]

In [2]: [[i + 1 for i in row] for row in matrix]

Out[2]: [[2, 3, 4], [5, 6, 7], [8, 9, 10]]
```

This isn't very readable and more importantly, if you do this with big arrays, looping through each element becomes very slow. Depending on your use case and the size of the arrays, calculating with NumPy arrays instead of Python lists can make your calculations from a couple of times to around a hundred times faster. NumPy achieves this performance by making use of code that was written in C or Fortran—these are compiled programming languages that are much faster than Python. A NumPy array is an N-dimensional array for *homogenous data*. Homogenous means that all elements in the array need to be of the same data type. Most commonly, you are dealing with one- and two-dimensional arrays of floats as schematically displayed in Figure 4-1.

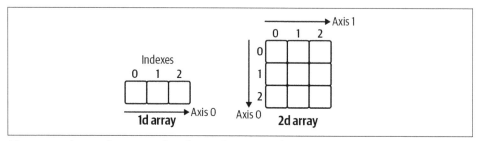

Figure 4-1. A one-dimensional and two-dimensional NumPy array

Let's create a one- and two-dimensional array to work with throughout this chapter:

```
In [3]: # First, let's import NumPy
        import numpy as np

In [4]: # Constructing an array with a simple list results in a 1d array
        array1 = np.array([10, 100, 1000.])

In [5]: # Constructing an array with a nested list results in a 2d array
        array2 = np.array([[1., 2., 3.],
                           [4., 5., 6.]])
```

Array Dimension

It's important to note the difference between a one- and two-dimensional array: a one-dimensional array has only one axis and hence does not have an explicit column or row orientation. While this behaves like arrays in VBA, you may have to get used to it if you come from a language like MATLAB, where one-dimensional arrays always have a column or row orientation.

Even if `array1` consists of integers except for the last element (which is a float), the homogeneity of NumPy arrays forces the data type of the array to be `float64`, which is capable of accommodating all elements. To learn about an array's data type, access its `dtype` attribute:

```
In [6]: array1.dtype
```

```
Out[6]: dtype('float64')
```

Since `dtype` gives you back `float64` instead of `float` which we met in the last chapter, you may have guessed that NumPy uses its own numerical data types, which are more granular than Python's data types. This usually isn't an issue though, as most of the time, conversion between the different data types in Python and NumPy happens automatically. If you ever need to explicitly convert a NumPy data type to one of Python's basic data types, simply use the corresponding constructor (I will say more about accessing an element from an array shortly):

```
In [7]: float(array1[0])
```

```
Out[7]: 10.0
```

For a full list of NumPy's data types, see the NumPy docs (*https://oreil.ly/irDyH*). With NumPy arrays, you can write simple code to perform array-based calculations, as we will see next.

Vectorization and Broadcasting

If you build the sum of a scalar and a NumPy array, NumPy will perform an element-wise operation, which means that you don't have to loop through the elements yourself. The NumPy community refers to this as *vectorization*. It allows you to write concise code, practically representing the mathematical notation:

```
In [8]: array2 + 1
```

```
Out[8]: array([[2., 3., 4.],
               [5., 6., 7.]])
```

Scalar

Scalar refers to a basic Python data type like a float or a string. This is to differentiate them from data structures with multiple elements like lists and dictionaries or one- and two-dimensional NumPy arrays.

The same principle applies when you work with two arrays: NumPy performs the operation element-wise:

```
In [9]: array2 * array2
```

```
Out[9]: array([[ 1.,  4.,  9.],
               [16., 25., 36.]])
```

If you use two arrays with different shapes in an arithmetic operation, NumPy extends—if possible—the smaller array automatically across the larger array so that their shapes become compatible. This is called *broadcasting*:

```
In [10]: array2 * array1

Out[10]: array([[  10.,  200., 3000.],
                [  40.,  500., 6000.]])
```

To perform matrix multiplications or dot products, use the @ operator:[1]

```
In [11]: array2 @ array2.T  # array2.T is a shortcut for array2.transpose()

Out[11]: array([[14., 32.],
                [32., 77.]])
```

Don't be intimidated by the terminology I've introduced in this section such as scalar, vectorization, or broadcasting! If you have ever worked with arrays in Excel, this should all feel very natural as shown in Figure 4-2. The screenshot is taken from *array_calculations.xlsx*, which you will find in the *xl* directory of the companion repository.

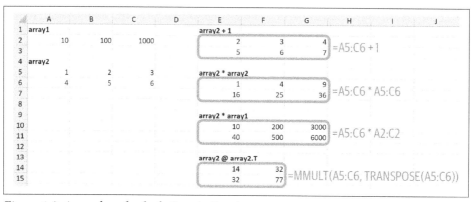

Figure 4-2. Array-based calculations in Excel

You know now that arrays perform arithmetic operations element-wise, but how can you apply a function on every element in an array? This is what universal functions are here for.

Universal Functions (ufunc)

Universal functions (ufunc) work on every element in a NumPy array. For example, if you use Python's standard square root function from the math module on a NumPy array, you will get an error:

```
In [12]: import math

In [13]: math.sqrt(array2)  # This will raise en Error
```

---

1 If it's been a while since your last linear algebra class, you can skip this example—matrix multiplication is not something this book builds upon.

```
--------------------------------------------------------------------
TypeError                                 Traceback (most recent call last)
<ipython-input-13-5c37e8f41094> in <module>
----> 1 math.sqrt(array2)  # This will raise en Error

TypeError: only size-1 arrays can be converted to Python scalars
```

You could, of course, write a nested loop to get the square root of every element, then build a NumPy array again from the result:

```
In [14]: np.array([[math.sqrt(i) for i in row] for row in array2])

Out[14]: array([[1.        , 1.41421356, 1.73205081],
                [2.        , 2.23606798, 2.44948974]])
```

This will work in cases where NumPy doesn't offer a ufunc and the array is small enough. However, if NumPy has a ufunc, use it, as it will be much faster with big arrays—apart from being easier to type and read:

```
In [15]: np.sqrt(array2)

Out[15]: array([[1.        , 1.41421356, 1.73205081],
                [2.        , 2.23606798, 2.44948974]])
```

Some of NumPy's ufuncs, like sum, are additionally available as array methods: if you want the sum of each column, do the following:

```
In [16]: array2.sum(axis=0)  # Returns a 1d array

Out[16]: array([5., 7., 9.])
```

The argument axis=0 refers to the axis along the rows while axis=1 refers to the axis along the columns, as depicted in Figure 4-1. Leaving the axis argument away sums up the whole array:

```
In [17]: array2.sum()

Out[17]: 21.0
```

You will meet more NumPy ufuncs throughout this book, as they can be used with pandas DataFrames.

So far, we've always worked with the entire array. The next section shows you how to manipulate parts of an array and introduces a few helpful array constructors.

Creating and Manipulating Arrays

I'll start this section by getting and setting specific elements of an array before introducing a few useful array constructors, including one to create pseudorandom numbers that you could use for a Monte Carlo simulation. I'll wrap this section up by explaining the difference between a view and a copy of an array.

Getting and Setting Array Elements

In the last chapter, I showed you how to index and slice lists to get access to specific elements. When you work with nested lists like matrix from the first example in this chapter, you can use *chained indexing*: matrix[0][0] will get you the first element of the first row. With NumPy arrays, however, you provide the index and slice arguments for both dimensions in a single pair of square brackets:

```
numpy_array[row_selection, column_selection]
```

For one-dimensional arrays, this simplifies to numpy_array[selection]. When you select a single element, you will get back a scalar; otherwise, you will get back a one- or two-dimensional array. Remember that slice notation uses a start index (included) and an end index (excluded) with a colon in between, as in start:end. By leaving away the start and end index, you are left with a colon, which therefore stands for all rows or all columns in a two-dimensional array. I have visualized a few examples in Figure 4-3, but you may also want to give Figure 4-1 another look, as the indices and axes are labeled there. Remember, by slicing a column or row of a two-dimensional array, you end up with a one-dimensional array, not with a two-dimensional column or row vector!

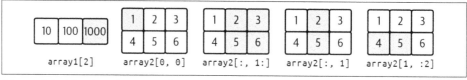

Figure 4-3. Selecting elements of a NumPy array

Play around with the examples shown in Figure 4-3 by running the following code:

```
In [18]: array1[2]  # Returns a scalar

Out[18]: 1000.0

In [19]: array2[0, 0]  # Returns a scalar

Out[19]: 1.0

In [20]: array2[:, 1:]  # Returns a 2d array

Out[20]: array([[2., 3.],
                [5., 6.]])

In [21]: array2[:, 1]  # Returns a 1d array

Out[21]: array([2., 5.])

In [22]: array2[1, :2]  # Returns a 1d array

Out[22]: array([4., 5.])
```

So far, I have constructed the sample arrays by hand, i.e., by providing numbers in a list. But NumPy also offers a few useful functions to construct arrays.

Useful Array Constructors

NumPy offers a few ways to construct arrays that will also be helpful to create pandas DataFrames, as we will see in Chapter 5. One way to easily create arrays is to use the `arange` function. This stands for *array range* and is similar to the built-in `range` that we met in the previous chapter—with the difference that `arange` returns a NumPy array. Combining it with `reshape` allows us to quickly generate an array with the desired dimensions:

```
In [23]: np.arange(2 * 5).reshape(2, 5)  # 2 rows, 5 columns

Out[23]: array([[0, 1, 2, 3, 4],
                [5, 6, 7, 8, 9]])
```

Another common need, for example for Monte Carlo simulations, is to generate arrays of normally distributed pseudorandom numbers. NumPy makes this easy:

```
In [24]: np.random.randn(2, 3)  # 2 rows, 3 columns

Out[24]: array([[-0.30047275, -1.19614685, -0.13652283],
                [ 1.05769357,  0.03347978, -1.2153504 ]])
```

Other helpful constructors worth exploring are `np.ones` and `np.zeros` to create arrays with ones and zeros, respectively, and `np.eye` to create an identity matrix. We'll come across some of these constructors again in the next chapter, but for now, let's learn about the difference between a view and a copy of a NumPy array.

View vs. Copy

NumPy arrays return *views* when you slice them. This means that you are working with a subset of the original array without copying the data. Setting a value on a view will therefore also change the original array:

```
In [25]: array2

Out[25]: array([[1., 2., 3.],
                [4., 5., 6.]])

In [26]: subset = array2[:, :2]
         subset

Out[26]: array([[1., 2.],
                [4., 5.]])

In [27]: subset[0, 0] = 1000

In [28]: subset

Out[28]: array([[1000.,    2.],
                [   4.,    5.]])
```

```
In [29]: array2
Out[29]: array([[1000.,    2.,    3.],
                [   4.,    5.,    6.]])
```

If that's not what you want, you would have to change `In [26]` as follows:

```
subset = array2[:, :2].copy()
```

Working on a copy will leave the original array unchanged.

Conclusion

In this chapter, I showed you how to work with NumPy arrays and what's behind expressions such as vectorization and broadcasting. Putting these technical terms aside, working with arrays should feel quite intuitive given that they follow the mathematical notation very closely. While NumPy is an incredibly powerful library, there are two main issues when you want to use it for data analysis:

- The whole NumPy array needs to be of the same data type. This, for example, means that you can't perform any of the arithmetic operations we did in this chapter when your array contains a mix of text and numbers. As soon as text is involved, the array will have the data type `object`, which will not allow mathematical operations.

- Using NumPy arrays for data analysis makes it hard to know what each column or row refers to because you typically select columns via their position, such as in `array2[:, 1]`.

pandas has solved these issues by providing smarter data structures on top of NumPy arrays. What they are and how they work is the topic of the next chapter.

## CHAPTER 5

Data Analysis with pandas

This chapter will introduce you to pandas, the *Python Data Analysis Library* or—how I like to put it—the Python-based spreadsheet with superpowers. It's so powerful that some of the companies that I worked with have managed to get rid of Excel completely by replacing it with a combination of Jupyter notebooks and pandas. As a reader of this book, however, I assume you will keep Excel, in which case pandas will serve as an interface for getting data in and out of spreadsheets. pandas makes tasks that are particularly painful in Excel easier, faster, and less error-prone. Some of these tasks include getting big datasets from external sources and working with statistics, time series, and interactive charts. pandas' most important superpowers are vectorization and data alignment. As we've already seen in the previous chapter with NumPy arrays, vectorization allows you to write concise, array-based code while data alignment makes sure that there is no data mismatch when you work with multiple datasets.

This chapter covers the whole data analysis journey: it starts with cleaning and preparing data before it shows you how to make sense out of bigger datasets via aggregation, descriptive statistics, and visualization. At the end of the chapter, we'll see how we can import and export data with pandas. But first things first—let's get started with an introduction to pandas' main data structures: DataFrame and Series!

DataFrame and Series

DataFrame and Series are the core data structures in pandas. In this section, I am introducing them with a focus on the main components of a DataFrame: index, columns, and data. A *DataFrame* is similar to a two-dimensional NumPy array, but it comes with column and row labels and each column can hold different data types. By extracting a single column or row from a DataFrame, you get a one-dimensional Series. Again, a *Series* is similar to a one-dimensional NumPy array with labels. When you look at the structure of a DataFrame in Figure 5-1, it won't take a lot of imagination to see that DataFrames are going to be your Python-based spreadsheets.

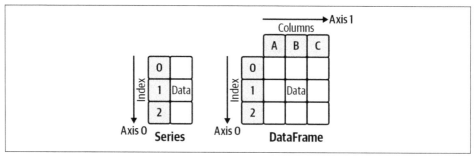

Figure 5-1. A pandas Series and DataFrame

To show you how easy it is to transition from a spreadsheet to a DataFrame, consider the following Excel table in Figure 5-2, which shows participants of an online course with their score. You will find the corresponding file *course_participants.xlsx* in the *xl* folder of the companion repo.

	A	B	C	D	E	F
1	user_id	name	age	country	score	continent
2	1001	Mark		55 Italy		4.5 Europe
3	1000	John		33 USA		6.7 America
4	1002	Tim		41 USA		3.9 America
5	1003	Jenny		12 Germany		9 Europe

Figure 5-2. course_participants.xlsx

To make this Excel table available in Python, start by importing pandas, then use its `read_excel` function, which returns a DataFrame:

```
In [1]: import pandas as pd

In [2]: pd.read_excel("xl/course_participants.xlsx")

Out[2]:    user_id   name  age  country  score continent
        0     1001   Mark   55    Italy    4.5    Europe
        1     1000   John   33      USA    6.7   America
        2     1002    Tim   41      USA    3.9   America
        3     1003  Jenny   12  Germany    9.0    Europe
```

The read_excel Function with Python 3.9

If you are running `pd.read_excel` with Python 3.9 or above, make sure to use at least pandas 1.2 or you will get an error when reading *xlsx* files.

If you run this in a Jupyter notebook, the DataFrame will be nicely formatted as an HTML table, which makes it even closer to how the table looks in Excel. I will spend the whole of Chapter 7 on reading and writing Excel files with pandas, so this was only an introductory example to show you that spreadsheets and DataFrames are, indeed, very similar. Let's now re-create this DataFrame from scratch without reading it from the Excel file: one way of creating a DataFrame is to provide the data as a nested list, along with values for `columns` and `index`:

```
In [3]: data = [["Mark", 55, "Italy", 4.5, "Europe"],
                ["John", 33, "USA", 6.7, "America"],
                ["Tim", 41, "USA", 3.9, "America"],
                ["Jenny", 12, "Germany", 9.0, "Europe"]]
        df = pd.DataFrame(data=data,
                          columns=["name", "age", "country",
                                   "score", "continent"],
                          index=[1001, 1000, 1002, 1003])
        df

Out[3]:       name  age  country  score continent
        1001  Mark   55    Italy    4.5    Europe
        1000  John   33      USA    6.7   America
        1002   Tim   41      USA    3.9   America
        1003 Jenny   12  Germany    9.0    Europe
```

Keyword Argument vs. Variable Name

In the previous example, I am calling the `DataFrame` class with `data=data`. While you will see this often in Python code, it may look a bit confusing at first sight: the part on the left of the equal sign is the name of the function parameter, while the part on the right of the equal sign is the name of the variable that you pass into the function as argument. If you don't like this, you can change the variable name to something like `source_data` on the previous line, so that calling the DataFrame class would read `pd.Data Frame(data=source_data, ...)`. For a refresher about keyword arguments, see Chapter 3.

By calling the `info` method, you will get some basic information, most importantly the number of data points and the data types for each column:

```
In [4]: df.info()

<class 'pandas.core.frame.DataFrame'>
Int64Index: 4 entries, 1001 to 1003
Data columns (total 5 columns):
 #   Column   Non-Null Count  Dtype
---  ------   --------------  -----
 0   name     4 non-null      object
 1   age      4 non-null      int64
```

```
 2   country    4 non-null    object
 3   score      4 non-null    float64
 4   continent  4 non-null    object
dtypes: float64(1), int64(1), object(3)
memory usage: 192.0+ bytes
```

If you are just interested in the data type of your columns, run `df.dtypes` instead. Columns with strings or mixed data types will have the data type `object`. [1] Let us now have a closer look at the index and columns of a DataFrame.

Index

The row labels of a DataFrame are called *index*. If you don't have a meaningful index, leave it away when constructing a DataFrame. pandas will then automatically create an integer index starting at zero. We saw this in the very first example when we read the DataFrame from the Excel file. An index will allow pandas to look up data faster and is essential for many common operations, e.g., combining two DataFrames. You access the index object like the following:

```
In [5]: df.index

Out[5]: Int64Index([1001, 1000, 1002, 1003], dtype='int64')
```

If it makes sense, give the index a name. Let's follow the table in Excel, and give it the name `user_id`:

```
In [6]: df.index.name = "user_id"
        df

Out[6]:          name  age  country  score continent
        user_id
        1001     Mark   55    Italy    4.5    Europe
        1000     John   33      USA    6.7   America
        1002      Tim   41      USA    3.9   America
        1003    Jenny   12  Germany    9.0    Europe
```

Unlike the primary key of a database, a DataFrame index can have duplicates, but looking up values may be slower in that case. To turn an index into a regular column use `reset_index`, and to set a new index use `set_index`. If you don't want to lose your existing index when setting a new one, make sure to reset it first:

```
In [7]: # "reset_index" turns the index into a column, replacing the
        # index with the default index. This corresponds to the DataFrame
        # from the beginning that we loaded from Excel.
        df.reset_index()
```

---

1 pandas 1.0.0 introduced a dedicated `string` data type to make some operations easier and more consistent with text. As it is still experimental, I am not going to make use of it in this book.

```
Out[7]:    user_id    name  age  country  score continent
        0     1001    Mark   55    Italy    4.5    Europe
        1     1000    John   33      USA    6.7   America
        2     1002     Tim   41      USA    3.9   America
        3     1003   Jenny   12  Germany    9.0    Europe
```

```
In [8]: # "reset_index" turns "user_id" into a regular column and
        # "set_index" turns the column "name" into the index
        df.reset_index().set_index("name")
```

```
Out[8]:        user_id  age  country  score continent
       name
       Mark       1001   55    Italy    4.5    Europe
       John       1000   33      USA    6.7   America
       Tim        1002   41      USA    3.9   America
       Jenny      1003   12  Germany    9.0    Europe
```

By doing df.reset_index().set_index("name"), you are using *method chaining*: since reset_index() returns a DataFrame, you can directly call another DataFrame method without having to write out the intermediate result first.

DataFrame Methods Return Copies

Whenever you call a method on a DataFrame in the form df.method_name(), you will get back a copy of the DataFrame with that method applied, leaving the original DataFrame untouched. We have just done that by calling df.reset_index(). If you wanted to change the original DataFrame, you would have to assign the return value back to the original variable like the following:

df = df.reset_index()

Since we are not doing this, it means that our variable df is still holding its original data. The next samples also call DataFrame methods, i.e., don't change the original DataFrame.

To change the index, use the reindex method:

```
In [9]: df.reindex([999, 1000, 1001, 1004])
```

```
Out[9]:          name   age country  score continent
       user_id
       999        NaN   NaN     NaN    NaN       NaN
       1000      John  33.0     USA    6.7   America
       1001      Mark  55.0   Italy    4.5    Europe
       1004       NaN   NaN     NaN    NaN       NaN
```

This is a first example of data alignment at work: reindex will take over all rows that match the new index and will introduce rows with missing values (NaN) where no information exists. Index elements that you leave away will be dropped. I will introduce NaN properly a bit later in this chapter. Finally, to sort an index, use the sort_index method:

```
In [10]: df.sort_index()

Out[10]:          name  age  country  score continent
         user_id
         1000      John   33      USA    6.7   America
         1001      Mark   55    Italy    4.5    Europe
         1002       Tim   41      USA    3.9   America
         1003     Jenny   12  Germany    9.0    Europe
```

If, instead, you want to sort the rows by one or more columns, use sort_values:

```
In [11]: df.sort_values(["continent", "age"])

Out[11]:          name  age  country  score continent
         user_id
         1000      John   33      USA    6.7   America
         1002       Tim   41      USA    3.9   America
         1003     Jenny   12  Germany    9.0    Europe
         1001      Mark   55    Italy    4.5    Europe
```

The sample shows how to sort first by continent, then by age. If you wanted to sort by only one column, you could also provide the column name as a string:

```
df.sort_values("continent")
```

This has covered the basics of how indices work. Let's now turn our attention to its horizontal equivalent, the DataFrame columns!

Columns

To get information about the columns of a DataFrame, run the following code:

```
In [12]: df.columns

Out[12]: Index(['name', 'age', 'country', 'score', 'continent'], dtype='object')
```

If you don't provide any column names when constructing a DataFrame, pandas will number the columns with integers starting at zero. With columns, however, this is almost never a good idea as columns represent variables and are therefore easy to name. You assign a name to the column headers in the same way we did it with the index:

```
In [13]: df.columns.name = "properties"
         df

Out[13]: properties  name  age  country  score continent
         user_id
         1001         Mark   55    Italy    4.5    Europe
         1000         John   33      USA    6.7   America
         1002          Tim   41      USA    3.9   America
         1003        Jenny   12  Germany    9.0    Europe
```

If you don't like the column names, rename them:

```
In [14]: df.rename(columns={"name": "First Name", "age": "Age"})

Out[14]: properties First Name  Age  country  score continent
         user_id
         1001             Mark   55    Italy    4.5    Europe
         1000             John   33      USA    6.7   America
         1002              Tim   41      USA    3.9   America
         1003            Jenny   12  Germany    9.0    Europe
```

If you want to delete columns, use the following syntax (the sample shows you how to drop columns and indices at the same time):

```
In [15]: df.drop(columns=["name", "country"],
             index=[1000, 1003])

Out[15]: properties  age  score continent
         user_id
         1001          55    4.5    Europe
         1002          41    3.9   America
```

The columns and the index of a DataFrame are both represented by an Index object, so you can change your columns into rows and vice versa by transposing your DataFrame:

```
In [16]: df.T  # Shortcut for df.transpose()

Out[16]: user_id       1001     1000     1002      1003
         properties
         name          Mark     John      Tim     Jenny
         age             55       33       41        12
         country      Italy      USA      USA   Germany
         score          4.5      6.7      3.9         9
         continent   Europe  America  America    Europe
```

It's worth remembering here that our DataFrame df is still unchanged, as we have never reassigned the returning DataFrame from the method calls back to the original df variable. If you would like to reorder the columns of a DataFrame, you could use the reindex method that we used with the index, but selecting the columns in the desired order is often more intuitive:

```
In [17]: df.loc[:, ["continent", "country", "name", "age", "score"]]

Out[17]: properties continent  country   name  age  score
         user_id
         1001          Europe    Italy   Mark   55    4.5
         1000         America      USA   John   33    6.7
         1002         America      USA    Tim   41    3.9
         1003          Europe  Germany  Jenny   12    9.0
```

This last example needs quite a few explanations: everything about loc and how data selection works is the topic of the next section.

Data Manipulation

Real-world data hardly gets served on a silver platter, so before working with it, you need to clean it and bring it into a digestible form. We'll begin this section by looking at how to select data from a DataFrame, how to change it, and how to deal with missing and duplicate data. We'll then perform a few calculations with DataFrames and see how you work with text data. To wrap this section up, we'll find out when pandas returns a view vs. a copy of the data. Quite a few concepts in this section are related to what we have already seen with NumPy arrays in the last chapter.

Selecting Data

Let's start with accessing data by label and position before looking at other methods, including boolean indexing and selecting data by using a MultiIndex.

Selecting by label

The most common way of accessing the data of a DataFrame is by referring to its labels. Use the attribute loc, which stands for *location*, to specify which rows and columns you want to retrieve:

```
df.loc[row_selection, column_selection]
```

loc supports the slice notation and therefore accepts a colon to select all rows or columns, respectively. Additionally, you can provide lists with labels as well as a single column or row name. Have a look at Table 5-1 to see a few examples of how you select different parts from our sample DataFrame df.

Table 5-1. Data selection by label

Selection	Return Data Type	Example
Single value	Scalar	df.loc[1000, "country"]
One column (1d)	Series	df.loc[:, "country"]
One column (2d)	DataFrame	df.loc[:, ["country"]]
Multiple columns	DataFrame	df.loc[:, ["country", "age"]]
Range of columns	DataFrame	df.loc[:, "name":"country"]
One row (1d)	Series	df.loc[1000, :]
One row (2d)	DataFrame	df.loc[[1000], :]
Multiple rows	DataFrame	df.loc[[1003, 1000], :]
Range of rows	DataFrame	df.loc[1000:1002, :]

Label Slicing Has Closed Intervals

Using slice notation with labels is inconsistent with respect to how everything else in Python and pandas works: they *include* the upper end.

Applying our knowledge from Table 5-1, let's use `loc` to select scalars, Series, and DataFrames:

```
In [18]: # Using scalars for both row and column selection returns a scalar
         df.loc[1001, "name"]

Out[18]: 'Mark'

In [19]: # Using a scalar on either the row or column selection returns a Series
         df.loc[[1001, 1002], "age"]

Out[19]: user_id
         1001    55
         1002    41
         Name: age, dtype: int64

In [20]: # Selecting multiple rows and columns returns a DataFrame
         df.loc[:1002, ["name", "country"]]

Out[20]: properties   name country
         user_id
         1001         Mark   Italy
         1000         John     USA
         1002          Tim     USA
```

It's important for you to understand the difference between a DataFrame with one or more columns and a Series: even with a single column, DataFrames are two-dimensional, while Series are one-dimensional. Both DataFrame and Series have an index, but only the DataFrame has column headers. When you select a column as Series, the column header becomes the name of the Series. Many functions or methods will work on both Series and DataFrame, but when you perform arithmetic calculations, the behavior differs: with DataFrames, pandas aligns the data according to the column headers—more about that a little later in this chapter.

Shortcut for Column Selection

Since selecting columns is such a common operation, pandas offers a shortcut. Instead of:

```
df.loc[:, column_selection]
```

you can write:

```
df[column_selection]
```

For example, `df["country"]` returns a Series from our sample DataFrame and `df[["name", "country"]]` returns a DataFrame with two columns.

Selecting by position

Selecting a subset of a DataFrame by position corresponds to what we did at the beginning of this chapter with NumPy arrays. With DataFrames, however, you have to use the `iloc` attribute, which stands for *integer location*:

```
df.iloc[row_selection, column_selection]
```

When using slices, you deal with the standard half-open intervals. Table 5-2 gives you the same cases we looked at previously in Table 5-1.

Table 5-2. Data selection by position

Selection	Return Data Type	Example
Single value	Scalar	`df.iloc[1, 2]`
One column (1d)	Series	`df.iloc[:, 2]`
One column (2d)	DataFrame	`df.iloc[:, [2]]`
Multiple columns	DataFrame	`df.iloc[:, [2, 1]]`
Range of columns	DataFrame	`df.iloc[:, :3]`
One row (1d)	Series	`df.iloc[1, :]`
One row (2d)	DataFrame	`df.iloc[[1], :]`
Multiple rows	DataFrame	`df.iloc[[3, 1], :]`
Range of rows	DataFrame	`df.iloc[1:3, :]`

Here is how you use `iloc`—again with the same samples that we used with `loc` before:

```
In [21]: df.iloc[0, 0]  # Returns a Scalar

Out[21]: 'Mark'

In [22]: df.iloc[[0, 2], 1]  # Returns a Series

Out[22]: user_id
         1001    55
         1002    41
         Name: age, dtype: int64

In [23]: df.iloc[:3, [0, 2]]  # Returns a DataFrame

Out[23]: properties  name country
         user_id
         1001        Mark  Italy
         1000        John   USA
         1002         Tim   USA
```

Selecting data by label or position is not the only means to access a subset of your DataFrame. Another important way is to use boolean indexing; let's see how it works!

Selecting by boolean indexing

Boolean indexing refers to selecting subsets of a DataFrame with the help of a Series or a DataFrame whose data consists of only `True` or `False`. Boolean Series are used to select specific columns and rows of a DataFrame, while boolean DataFrames are used to select specific values across a whole DataFrame. Most commonly, you will use boolean indexing to filter the rows of a DataFrame. Think of it as the AutoFilter functionality in Excel. For example, this is how you filter your DataFrame so it only shows people who live in the USA and are older than 40 years:

```
In [24]: tf = (df["age"] > 40) & (df["country"] == "USA")
         tf  # This is a Series with only True/False

Out[24]: user_id
         1001    False
         1000    False
         1002     True
         1003    False
         dtype: bool

In [25]: df.loc[tf, :]

Out[25]: properties name  age country  score continent
         user_id
         1002         Tim   41     USA    3.9   America
```

There are two things I need to explain here. First, due to technical limitations, you can't use Python's boolean operators from Chapter 3 with DataFrames. Instead, you need to use the symbols as shown in Table 5-3.

Table 5-3. Boolean operators

Basic Python Data Types	DataFrames and Series
and	&
or		
not	~

Second, if you have more than one condition, make sure to put every boolean expression in between parentheses so operator precedence doesn't get in your way: for example, & has higher operator precedence than ==. Therefore, without parentheses, the expression from the sample would be interpreted as:

```
df["age"] > (40 & df["country"]) == "USA"
```

If you want to filter the index, you can refer to it as `df.index`:

```
In [26]: df.loc[df.index > 1001, :]

Out[26]: properties  name  age  country  score continent
         user_id
```

```
1002              Tim    41     USA    3.9    America
1003            Jenny    12  Germany   9.0    Europe
```

For what you would use the in operator with basic Python data structures like lists, use isin with a Series. This is how you filter your DataFrame to participants from Italy and Germany:

```
In [27]: df.loc[df["country"].isin(["Italy", "Germany"]), :]

Out[27]: properties   name  age  country  score continent
         user_id
         1001         Mark  55    Italy    4.5    Europe
         1003        Jenny  12  Germany    9.0    Europe
```

While you use loc to provide a boolean Series, DataFrames offer a special syntax without loc to select values given the full DataFrame of booleans:

```
df[boolean_df]
```

This is especially helpful if you have DataFrames that consist of only numbers. Providing a DataFrame of booleans returns the DataFrame with NaN wherever the boolean DataFrame is False. Again, a more detailed discussion of NaN will follow shortly. Let's start by creating a new sample DataFrame called rainfall that consists of only numbers:

```
In [28]: # This could be the yearly rainfall in millimeters
         rainfall = pd.DataFrame(data={"City 1": [300.1, 100.2],
                                       "City 2": [400.3, 300.4],
                                       "City 3": [1000.5, 1100.6]})
         rainfall

Out[28]:    City 1  City 2  City 3
         0   300.1   400.3  1000.5
         1   100.2   300.4  1100.6

In [29]: rainfall < 400

Out[29]:    City 1  City 2  City 3
         0    True   False   False
         1    True    True   False

In [30]: rainfall[rainfall < 400]

Out[30]:    City 1  City 2  City 3
         0   300.1     NaN     NaN
         1   100.2   300.4     NaN
```

Note that in this example, I have used a dictionary to construct a new DataFrame—this is often convenient if the data already exists in that form. Working with booleans in this way is most commonly used to filter out specific values such as outliers.

To wrap up the data selection part, I will introduce a special type of index called the MultiIndex.

Selecting by using a MultiIndex

A *MultiIndex* is an index with more than one level. It allows you to hierarchically group your data and gives you easy access to subsets. For example, if you set the index of our sample DataFrame df to a combination of continent and country, you can easily select all rows with a certain continent:

```
In [31]: # A MultiIndex needs to be sorted
         df_multi = df.reset_index().set_index(["continent", "country"])
         df_multi = df_multi.sort_index()
         df_multi

Out[31]: properties          user_id   name   age  score
         continent country
         America   USA          1000   John    33    6.7
                   USA          1002    Tim    41    3.9
         Europe    Germany      1003  Jenny    12    9.0
                   Italy        1001   Mark    55    4.5

In [32]: df_multi.loc["Europe", :]

Out[32]: properties  user_id   name   age  score
         country
         Germany        1003  Jenny    12    9.0
         Italy          1001   Mark    55    4.5
```

Note that pandas prettifies the output of a MultiIndex by not repeating the leftmost index level (the continents) for each row. Instead, it only prints the continent when it changes. Selecting over multiple index levels is done by providing a tuple:

```
In [33]: df_multi.loc[("Europe", "Italy"), :]

Out[33]: properties          user_id  name  age  score
         continent country
         Europe    Italy        1001  Mark   55    4.5
```

If you want to selectively reset part of a MultiIndex, provide the level as an argument. Zero is the first column from the left:

```
In [34]: df_multi.reset_index(level=0)

Out[34]: properties continent  user_id   name   age  score
         country
         USA         America      1000   John    33    6.7
         USA         America      1002    Tim    41    3.9
         Germany     Europe       1003  Jenny    12    9.0
         Italy       Europe       1001   Mark    55    4.5
```

While we won't manually create a MultiIndex in this book, there are certain operations like groupby, which will cause pandas to return a DataFrame with a MultiIndex, so it's good to know what it is. We will meet groupby later in this chapter.

Now that you know various ways to *select* data, it's time to learn how you *change* data.

Setting Data

The easiest way to change the data of a DataFrame is by assigning values to certain elements using the loc or iloc attributes. This is the starting point of this section before we turn to other ways of manipulating existing DataFrames: replacing values and adding new columns.

Setting data by label or position

As pointed out earlier in this chapter, when you call DataFrame methods like df.reset_index(), the method will always be applied to a copy, leaving the original DataFrame untouched. However, assigning values via the loc and iloc attributes changes the original DataFrame. Since I want to leave our DataFrame df untouched, I am working with a copy here that I am calling df2. If you want to change a single value, do the following:

```
In [35]: # Copy the DataFrame first to leave the original untouched
         df2 = df.copy()

In [36]: df2.loc[1000, "name"] = "JOHN"
         df2

Out[36]: properties   name  age  country  score continent
         user_id
         1001         Mark   55    Italy    4.5    Europe
         1000         JOHN   33      USA    6.7   America
         1002          Tim   41      USA    3.9   America
         1003        Jenny   12  Germany    9.0    Europe
```

You can also change multiple values at the same time. One way to change the score of the users with ID 1000 and 1001 is to use a list:

```
In [37]: df2.loc[[1000, 1001], "score"] = [3, 4]
         df2

Out[37]: properties   name  age  country  score continent
         user_id
         1001         Mark   55    Italy    4.0    Europe
         1000         JOHN   33      USA    3.0   America
         1002          Tim   41      USA    3.9   America
         1003        Jenny   12  Germany    9.0    Europe
```

Changing data by position via iloc works the same way. Let's now move on to see how you change the data by using boolean indexing.

Setting data by boolean indexing

Boolean indexing, which we used to filter rows, can also be used to assign values in a DataFrame. Imagine that you need to anonymize all names of people who are below 20 years old or from the USA:

```
In [38]: tf = (df2["age"] < 20) | (df2["country"] == "USA")
         df2.loc[tf, "name"] = "xxx"
         df2

Out[38]: properties  name  age  country  score  continent
         user_id
         1001         Mark   55    Italy    4.0     Europe
         1000          xxx   33      USA    3.0    America
         1002          xxx   41      USA    3.9    America
         1003          xxx   12  Germany    9.0     Europe
```

Sometimes, you have a dataset where you need to replace certain values across the board, i.e., not specific to certain columns. In that case, make use of the special syntax again and provide the whole DataFrame with booleans like this (the sample makes use again of the `rainfall` DataFrame):

```
In [39]: # Copy the DataFrame first to leave the original untouched
         rainfall2 = rainfall.copy()
         rainfall2

Out[39]:    City 1  City 2  City 3
         0   300.1   400.3  1000.5
         1   100.2   300.4  1100.6

In [40]: # Set the values to 0 wherever they are below 400
         rainfall2[rainfall2 < 400] = 0
         rainfall2

Out[40]:    City 1  City 2  City 3
         0     0.0   400.3  1000.5
         1     0.0     0.0  1100.6
```

If you just want to replace a value with another one, there is an easier way to do it, as I will show you next.

Setting data by replacing values

If you want to replace a certain value across your entire DataFrame or selected columns, use the `replace` method:

```
In [41]: df2.replace("USA", "U.S.")

Out[41]: properties  name  age  country  score  continent
         user_id
         1001         Mark   55    Italy    4.0     Europe
         1000          xxx   33     U.S.    3.0    America
         1002          xxx   41     U.S.    3.9    America
         1003          xxx   12  Germany    9.0     Europe
```

If, instead, you only wanted to act on the `country` column, you could use this syntax instead:

```
df2.replace({"country": {"USA": "U.S."}})
```

In this case, since USA only turns up in the country column, it yields the same result as the previous sample. To wrap this section up, let's see how you can add additional columns to a DataFrame.

Setting data by adding a new column

To add a new column to a DataFrame, assign values to a new column name. For example, you could add a new column to a DataFrame by using a scalar or list:

```
In [42]: df2.loc[:, "discount"] = 0
         df2.loc[:, "price"] = [49.9, 49.9, 99.9, 99.9]
         df2

Out[42]: properties  name  age  country  score continent  discount  price
         user_id
         1001         Mark   55    Italy    4.0    Europe         0   49.9
         1000          xxx   33      USA    3.0   America         0   49.9
         1002          xxx   41      USA    3.9   America         0   99.9
         1003          xxx   12  Germany    9.0    Europe         0   99.9
```

Adding a new column often involves vectorized calculations:

```
In [43]: df2 = df.copy()  # Let's start with a fresh copy
         df2.loc[:, "birth year"] = 2021 - df2["age"]
         df2

Out[43]: properties  name  age  country  score continent  birth year
         user_id
         1001         Mark   55    Italy    4.5    Europe        1966
         1000         John   33      USA    6.7   America        1988
         1002          Tim   41      USA    3.9   America        1980
         1003        Jenny   12  Germany    9.0    Europe        2009
```

I will show you more about calculating with DataFrames in a moment, but before we get there, do you remember that I have used NaN a few times already? The next section will finally give you more context around the topic of missing data.

Missing Data

Missing data can be a problem as it has the potential to bias the results of your data analysis, thereby making your conclusions less robust. Nevertheless, it's very common to have gaps in your datasets that you will have to deal with. In Excel, you usually have to deal with empty cells or #N/A errors, but pandas uses NumPy's np.nan for missing data, displayed as NaN. NaN is the floating-point standard for *Not-a-Number*. For timestamps, pd.NaT is used instead, and for text, pandas uses None. Using None or np.nan, you can introduce missing values:

```
In [44]: df2 = df.copy()  # Let's start with a fresh copy
         df2.loc[1000, "score"] = None
         df2.loc[1003, :] = None
         df2
```

```
Out[44]: properties  name   age country  score continent
         user_id
         1001        Mark  55.0   Italy    4.5    Europe
         1000        John  33.0     USA    NaN   America
         1002         Tim  41.0     USA    3.9   America
         1003        None   NaN    None    NaN      None
```

To clean a DataFrame, you often want to remove rows with missing data. This is as simple as:

```
In [45]: df2.dropna()
```

```
Out[45]: properties  name   age country  score continent
         user_id
         1001        Mark  55.0   Italy    4.5    Europe
         1002         Tim  41.0     USA    3.9   America
```

If, however, you only want to remove rows where *all* values are missing, use the how parameter:

```
In [46]: df2.dropna(how="all")
```

```
Out[46]: properties  name   age country  score continent
         user_id
         1001        Mark  55.0   Italy    4.5    Europe
         1000        John  33.0     USA    NaN   America
         1002         Tim  41.0     USA    3.9   America
```

To get a boolean DataFrame or Series depending on whether there is NaN or not, use isna:

```
In [47]: df2.isna()
```

```
Out[47]: properties   name    age country  score continent
         user_id
         1001        False  False    False  False     False
         1000        False  False    False   True     False
         1002        False  False    False  False     False
         1003         True   True     True   True      True
```

To fill missing values, use fillna. For example, to replace NaN in the score column with its mean (I will introduce descriptive statistics like mean shortly):

```
In [48]: df2.fillna({"score": df2["score"].mean()})
```

```
Out[48]: properties  name   age country  score continent
         user_id
         1001        Mark  55.0   Italy    4.5    Europe
         1000        John  33.0     USA    4.2   America
         1002         Tim  41.0     USA    3.9   America
         1003        None   NaN    None    4.2      None
```

Missing data isn't the only condition that requires us to clean our dataset. The same is true for duplicate data, so let's see what our options are!

Duplicate Data

Like missing data, duplicates negatively impact the reliability of your analysis. To get rid of duplicate rows, use the drop_duplicates method. Optionally, you can provide a subset of the columns as argument:

```
In [49]: df.drop_duplicates(["country", "continent"])

Out[49]: properties   name  age  country  score continent
         user_id
         1001         Mark   55    Italy    4.5    Europe
         1000         John   33      USA    6.7   America
         1003        Jenny   12  Germany    9.0    Europe
```

By default, this will leave the first occurrence. To find out if a certain column contains duplicates or to get its unique values, use the following two commands (use df.index instead of df["country"] if you wanted to run this on the index instead):

```
In [50]: df["country"].is_unique

Out[50]: False

In [51]: df["country"].unique()

Out[51]: array(['Italy', 'USA', 'Germany'], dtype=object)
```

And finally, to understand which rows are duplicates, use the duplicated method, which returns a boolean Series: by default, it uses the parameter keep="first", which keeps the first occurrence and marks only duplicates with True. By setting the parameter keep=False, it will return True for all rows, including its first occurrence, making it easy to get a DataFrame with all duplicate rows. In the following example, we look at the country column for duplicates, but in reality, you often look at the index or entire rows. In this case, you'd have to use df.index.duplicated() or df.duplicated() instead:

```
In [52]: # By default, it marks only duplicates as True, i.e.
         # without the first occurrence
         df["country"].duplicated()

Out[52]: user_id
         1001     False
         1000     False
         1002      True
         1003     False
         Name: country, dtype: bool

In [53]: # To get all rows where "country" is duplicated, use
         # keep=False
         df.loc[df["country"].duplicated(keep=False), :]

Out[53]: properties   name  age country  score continent
         user_id
```

```
1000       John   33    USA    6.7    America
1002        Tim   41    USA    3.9    America
```

Once you have cleaned your DataFrames by removing missing and duplicate data, you might want to perform some arithmetic operations—the next section gives you an introduction to how this works.

Arithmetic Operations

Like NumPy arrays, DataFrames and Series make use of vectorization. For example, to add a number to every value in the `rainfall` DataFrame, simply do the following:

```
In [54]: rainfall

Out[54]:    City 1  City 2  City 3
         0   300.1   400.3  1000.5
         1   100.2   300.4  1100.6

In [55]: rainfall + 100

Out[55]:    City 1  City 2  City 3
         0   400.1   500.3  1100.5
         1   200.2   400.4  1200.6
```

However, the true power of pandas is its automatic *data alignment* mechanism: when you use arithmetic operators with more than one DataFrame, pandas automatically aligns them by their columns and row indices. Let's create a second DataFrame with some of the same row and column labels. We then build the sum:

```
In [56]: more_rainfall = pd.DataFrame(data=[[100, 200], [300, 400]],
                                       index=[1, 2],
                                       columns=["City 1", "City 4"])

         more_rainfall

Out[56]:    City 1  City 4
         1     100     200
         2     300     400

In [57]: rainfall + more_rainfall

Out[57]:    City 1  City 2  City 3  City 4
         0     NaN     NaN     NaN     NaN
         1   200.2     NaN     NaN     NaN
         2     NaN     NaN     NaN     NaN
```

The index and columns of the resulting DataFrame are the union of the indices and columns of the two DataFrames: the fields that have a value in both DataFrames show the sum, while the rest of the DataFrame shows NaN. This may be something you have to get used to if you come from Excel, where empty cells are automatically turned into zeros when you use them in arithmetic operations. To get the same behavior as in Excel, use the `add` method with a `fill_value` to replace NaN values with zeros:

```
In [58]: rainfall.add(more_rainfall, fill_value=0)
```

```
Out[58]:    City 1  City 2  City 3  City 4
         0   300.1   400.3  1000.5     NaN
         1   200.2   300.4  1100.6   200.0
         2   300.0     NaN     NaN   400.0
```

This works accordingly for the other arithmetic operators as shown in Table 5-4.

Table 5-4. Arithmetic operators

Operator	Method
*	mul
+	add
-	sub
/	div
**	pow

When you have a DataFrame and a Series in your calculation, by default the Series is broadcast along the index:

```
In [59]: # A Series taken from a row
         rainfall.loc[1, :]

Out[59]: City 1     100.2
         City 2     300.4
         City 3    1100.6
         Name: 1, dtype: float64

In [60]: rainfall + rainfall.loc[1, :]

Out[60]:    City 1  City 2  City 3
         0   400.3   700.7  2101.1
         1   200.4   600.8  2201.2
```

Hence, to add a Series column-wise, you need to use the add method with an explicit axis argument:

```
In [61]: # A Series taken from a column
         rainfall.loc[:, "City 2"]

Out[61]: 0    400.3
         1    300.4
         Name: City 2, dtype: float64

In [62]: rainfall.add(rainfall.loc[:, "City 2"], axis=0)

Out[62]:    City 1  City 2  City 3
         0   700.4   800.6  1400.8
         1   400.6   600.8  1401.0
```

While this section is about DataFrames with numbers and how they behave in arithmetic operations, the next section shows your options when it comes to manipulating text in DataFrames.

Working with Text Columns

As we have seen at the beginning of this chapter, columns with text or mixed data types have the data type `object`. To perform operations on columns with text strings, use the `str` attribute that gives you access to Python's string methods. We have already met a few string methods in Chapter 3, but it won't hurt to have a look at the available methods in the Python docs (*https://oreil.ly/-e7SC*). For example, to remove leading and trailing white space, use the `strip` method; to make all first letters capitalized, there is the `capitalize` method. Chaining these together will clean up messy text columns that are often the result of manual data entry:

```
In [63]: # Let's create a new DataFrame
         users = pd.DataFrame(data=[" mArk ", "JOHN  ", "Tim", " jenny"],
                              columns=["name"])
         users

Out[63]:      name
         0    mArk
         1    JOHN
         2     Tim
         3   jenny

In [64]: users_cleaned = users.loc[:, "name"].str.strip().str.capitalize()
         users_cleaned

Out[64]: 0     Mark
         1     John
         2      Tim
         3    Jenny
         Name: name, dtype: object
```

Or, to find all names that start with a "J":

```
In [65]: users_cleaned.str.startswith("J")

Out[65]: 0    False
         1     True
         2    False
         3     True
         Name: name, dtype: bool
```

The string methods are easy to use, but sometimes you may need to manipulate a DataFrame in a way that isn't built-in. In that case, create your own function and apply it to your DataFrame, as the next section shows.

Applying a Function

DataFrames offer the `applymap` method, which will apply a function to every individual element, something that is useful if there are no NumPy ufuncs available. For example, there are no ufuncs for string formatting, so we can format every element of a DataFrame like so:

```
In [66]: rainfall

Out[66]:    City 1  City 2  City 3
         0   300.1   400.3  1000.5
         1   100.2   300.4  1100.6

In [67]: def format_string(x):
             return f"{x:,.2f}"

In [68]: # Note that we pass in the function without calling it,
         # i.e., format_string and not format_string()!
         rainfall.applymap(format_string)

Out[68]:    City 1  City 2   City 3
         0  300.10  400.30  1,000.50
         1  100.20  300.40  1,100.60
```

To break this down: the following f-string returns x as a string: `f"{x}"`. To add formatting, append a colon to the variable followed by the formatting string `,.2f`. The comma is the thousands separator and `.2f` means *fixed-point notation with two digits following the decimal point*. To get more details about how to format strings, please refer to the Format Specification Mini-Language (*https://oreil.ly/NgsG8*), which is part of the Python documentation.

For this sort of use case, *lambda expressions* (see sidebar) are widely used as they allow you to write the same in a single line without having to define a separate function. With lambda expressions, we can rewrite the previous example as the following:

```
In [69]: rainfall.applymap(lambda x: f"{x:,.2f}")

Out[69]:    City 1  City 2   City 3
         0  300.10  400.30  1,000.50
         1  100.20  300.40  1,100.60
```

Lambda Expressions

Python allows you to define a function in a single line via *lambda expressions*. Lambda expressions are anonymous functions, which means that it is a function without a name. Consider this function:

```
def function_name(arg1, arg2, ...):
    return return_value
```

This function can be rewritten as a lambda expression like this:

```
lambda arg1, arg2, ...: return_value
```

In essence, you replace `def` with `lambda`, leave away the `return` keyword and the function name, and put everything on one line. As we saw with the `applymap` method, this can be really convenient in this case as we don't need to define a function for something that's just being used a single time.

I have now mentioned all the important data manipulation methods, but before we move on, it's important to understand when pandas uses a view of a DataFrame and when it uses a copy.

View vs. Copy

You may remember from the previous chapter that slicing NumPy arrays returns a view. With DataFrames, it's unfortunately more complicated: it isn't always easily predictable whether `loc` and `iloc` return views or copies, which makes it one of the more confusing topics. Since it's a big difference whether you are changing the view or a copy of a DataFrame, pandas raises the following warning regularly when it thinks that you are setting the data in an unintended way: `SettingWithCopyWarning`. To circumvent this rather cryptic warning, here is some advice:

- Set values on the original DataFrame, not on a DataFrame that has been sliced off another DataFrame

- If you want to have an independent DataFrame after slicing, make an explicit copy:

    ```
    selection = df.loc[:, ["country", "continent"]].copy()
    ```

While things are complicated with `loc` and `iloc`, it's worth remembering that *all* DataFrame methods such as `df.dropna()` or `df.sort_values("column_name")` *always* return a copy.

So far, we've mostly worked with one DataFrame at a time. The next section shows you various ways to combine multiple DataFrames into one, a very common task for which pandas offers powerful tools.

Combining DataFrames

Combining different datasets in Excel can be a cumbersome task and typically involves a lot of VLOOKUP formulas. Fortunately, combining DataFrames is one of pandas' killer features where its data alignment capabilities will make your life really easy, thereby greatly reducing the possibility of introducing errors. Combining and merging DataFrames can be done in various ways; this section looks at just the most common cases using `concat`, `join`, and `merge`. While they have an overlap, each function makes a specific task very simple. I will start with the `concat` function, then explain the different options with `join`, and conclude by introducing `merge`, the most generic function of the three.

Concatenating

To simply glue multiple DataFrames together, the concat function is your best friend. As you can tell by the name of the function, this process has the technical name *concatenation*. By default, concat glues DataFrames together along the rows and aligns the columns automatically. In the following example, I create another DataFrame, more_users, and attach it to the bottom of our sample DataFrame df:

```
In [70]: data = [[15, "France", 4.1, "Becky"],
                 [44, "Canada", 6.1, "Leanne"]]
         more_users = pd.DataFrame(data=data,
                                   columns=["age", "country", "score", "name"],
                                   index=[1000, 1011])
         more_users

Out[70]:       age country  score     name
         1000   15  France    4.1    Becky
         1011   44  Canada    6.1   Leanne

In [71]: pd.concat([df, more_users], axis=0)

Out[71]:        name  age  country  score  continent
         1001   Mark   55    Italy    4.5     Europe
         1000   John   33      USA    6.7    America
         1002    Tim   41      USA    3.9    America
         1003  Jenny   12  Germany    9.0     Europe
         1000  Becky   15   France    4.1        NaN
         1011 Leanne   44   Canada    6.1        NaN
```

Note that you now have duplicate index elements, as concat glues the data together on the indicated axis (rows) and only aligns the data on the other one (columns), thereby matching the column names automatically—even if they are not in the same order in the two DataFrames! If you want to glue two DataFrames together along the columns, set axis=1:

```
In [72]: data = [[3, 4],
                 [5, 6]]
         more_categories = pd.DataFrame(data=data,
                                        columns=["quizzes", "logins"],
                                        index=[1000, 2000])
         more_categories

Out[72]:       quizzes  logins
         1000        3       4
         2000        5       6

In [73]: pd.concat([df, more_categories], axis=1)

Out[73]:        name   age  country  score continent  quizzes  logins
         1000   John  33.0      USA    6.7   America      3.0     4.0
         1001   Mark  55.0    Italy    4.5    Europe      NaN     NaN
         1002    Tim  41.0      USA    3.9   America      NaN     NaN
```

```
1003  Jenny  12.0  Germany   9.0   Europe   NaN   NaN
2000    NaN   NaN      NaN   NaN      NaN   5.0   6.0
```

The special and very useful feature of concat is that it accepts more than two Data-
Frames. We will use this in the next chapter to make a single DataFrame out of multiple CSV files:

```
pd.concat([df1, df2, df3, ...])
```

On the other hand, join and merge only work with two DataFrames, as we'll see next.

Joining and Merging

When you *join* two DataFrames, you combine the columns of each DataFrame into a
new DataFrame while deciding what happens with the rows by relying on set theory.
If you have worked with relational databases before, it's the same concept as the JOIN
clause in SQL queries. Figure 5-3 shows how the four join types (that is the inner, left,
right, and outer join) work by using two sample DataFrames, df1 and df2.

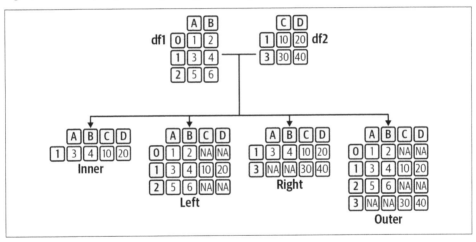

Figure 5-3. Join types

With join, pandas uses the indices of both DataFrames to align the rows. An *inner
join* returns a DataFrame with only those rows where the indices overlap. A *left join*
takes all the rows from the left DataFrame df1 and matches the rows from the right
DataFrame df2 on the index. Where df2 doesn't have a matching row, pandas will fill
in NaN. The left join corresponds to the VLOOKUP case in Excel. The *right join* takes all
rows from the right table df2 and matches them with rows from df1 on the index.
And finally, the *outer join*, which is short for *full outer join*, takes the union of indices
from both DataFrames and matches the values where it can. Table 5-5 is the equivalent of Figure 5-3 in text form.

Table 5-5. Join types

Type	Description
inner	Only rows whose index exists in both DataFrames
left	All rows from the left DataFrame, matching rows from the right DataFrame
right	All rows from the right DataFrame, matching rows from the left DataFrame
outer	The union of row indices from both DataFrames

Let's see how this works in practice, bringing the examples from Figure 5-3 to life:

```
In [74]: df1 = pd.DataFrame(data=[[1, 2], [3, 4], [5, 6]],
                            columns=["A", "B"])
         df1

Out[74]:    A  B
         0  1  2
         1  3  4
         2  5  6

In [75]: df2 = pd.DataFrame(data=[[10, 20], [30, 40]],
                            columns=["C", "D"], index=[1, 3])
         df2

Out[75]:     C   D
         1  10  20
         3  30  40

In [76]: df1.join(df2, how="inner")

Out[76]:    A  B   C   D
         1  3  4  10  20

In [77]: df1.join(df2, how="left")

Out[77]:    A  B    C     D
         0  1  2  NaN   NaN
         1  3  4  10.0  20.0
         2  5  6  NaN   NaN

In [78]: df1.join(df2, how="right")

Out[78]:     A    B   C   D
         1  3.0  4.0  10  20
         3  NaN  NaN  30  40

In [79]: df1.join(df2, how="outer")

Out[79]:     A    B    C     D
         0  1.0  2.0  NaN   NaN
         1  3.0  4.0  10.0  20.0
         2  5.0  6.0  NaN   NaN
         3  NaN  NaN  30.0  40.0
```

If you want to join on one or more DataFrame columns instead of relying on the index, use merge instead of join. merge accepts the on argument to provide one or more columns as the *join condition*: these columns, which have to exist on both Data-Frames, are used to match the rows:

```
In [80]: # Add a column called "category" to both DataFrames
         df1["category"] = ["a", "b", "c"]
         df2["category"] = ["c", "b"]

In [81]: df1

Out[81]:    A  B category
         0  1  2        a
         1  3  4        b
         2  5  6        c

In [82]: df2

Out[82]:     C   D category
         1  10  20        c
         3  30  40        b

In [83]: df1.merge(df2, how="inner", on=["category"])

Out[83]:    A  B category   C   D
         0  3  4        b  30  40
         1  5  6        c  10  20

In [84]: df1.merge(df2, how="left", on=["category"])

Out[84]:    A  B category     C     D
         0  1  2        a   NaN   NaN
         1  3  4        b  30.0  40.0
         2  5  6        c  10.0  20.0
```

Since `join` and `merge` accept quite a few optional arguments to accommodate more complex scenarios, I invite you to have a look at the official documentation (*https://oreil.ly/OZ4WV*) to learn more about them.

You know now how to manipulate one or more DataFrames, which brings us to the next step in our data analysis journey: making sense of data.

Descriptive Statistics and Data Aggregation

One way to make sense of big datasets is to compute a descriptive statistic like the sum or the mean on either the whole dataset or on meaningful subsets. This section starts by looking at how this works with pandas before it introduces two ways to aggregate data into subsets: the `groupby` method and the `pivot_table` function.

Descriptive Statistics

Descriptive statistics allows you to summarize datasets by using quantitative measures. For example, the number of data points is a simple descriptive statistic. Averages like mean, median, or mode are other popular examples. DataFrames and Series allow you to access descriptive statistics conveniently via methods like sum, mean, and count, to name just a few. You will meet many of them throughout this book, and the full list is available via the pandas documentation (*https://oreil.ly/t2q9Q*). By default, they return a Series along axis=0, which means you get the statistic of the columns:

```
In [85]: rainfall

Out[85]:    City 1  City 2  City 3
         0   300.1   400.3  1000.5
         1   100.2   300.4  1100.6

In [86]: rainfall.mean()

Out[86]: City 1     200.15
         City 2     350.35
         City 3    1050.55
         dtype: float64
```

If you want the statistic per row, provide the axis argument:

```
In [87]: rainfall.mean(axis=1)

Out[87]: 0    566.966667
         1    500.400000
         dtype: float64
```

By default, missing values are not included in descriptive statistics like sum or mean. This is in line with how Excel treats empty cells, so using Excel's AVERAGE formula on a range with empty cells will give you the same result as the mean method applied on a Series with the same numbers and NaN values instead of empty cells.

Getting a statistic across all rows of a DataFrame is sometimes not good enough and you need more granular information—the mean per category, for example. Let's see how it's done!

Grouping

Using our sample DataFrame df again, let's find out the average score per continent! To do this, you first group the rows by continent and subsequently apply the mean method, which will calculate the mean *per group*. All nonnumeric columns are automatically excluded:

```
In [88]: df.groupby(["continent"]).mean()

Out[88]: properties   age  score
         continent
         America     37.0   5.30
         Europe      33.5   6.75
```

If you include more than one column, the resulting DataFrame will have a hierarchical index—the MultiIndex we met earlier on:

```
In [89]: df.groupby(["continent", "country"]).mean()
```

```
Out[89]: properties        age  score
         continent country
         America   USA      37.0   5.3
         Europe    Germany  12.0   9.0
                   Italy    55.0   4.5
```

Instead of mean, you can use most of the descriptive statistics that pandas offers and if you want to use your own function, use the agg method. For example, here is how you get the difference between the maximum and minimum value per group:

```
In [90]: selection = df.loc[:, ["age", "score", "continent"]]
         selection.groupby(["continent"]).agg(lambda x: x.max() - x.min())

Out[90]: properties  age  score
         continent
         America       8   2.8
         Europe       43   4.5
```

A popular way to get statistics per group in Excel is to use pivot tables. They introduce a second dimension and are great to look at your data from different perspectives. pandas has a pivot table functionality, too, as we will see next.

Pivoting and Melting

If you are using pivot tables in Excel, you will have no trouble applying pandas' pivot_table function, as it works in largely the same way. The data in the following DataFrame is organized similarly to how records are typically stored in a database; each row shows a sales transaction for a specific fruit in a certain region:

```
In [91]: data = [["Oranges", "North", 12.30],
                 ["Apples", "South", 10.55],
                 ["Oranges", "South", 22.00],
                 ["Bananas", "South", 5.90],
                 ["Bananas", "North", 31.30],
                 ["Oranges", "North", 13.10]]

         sales = pd.DataFrame(data=data,
                              columns=["Fruit", "Region", "Revenue"])
         sales

Out[91]:     Fruit Region  Revenue
         0  Oranges  North    12.30
         1   Apples  South    10.55
         2  Oranges  South    22.00
         3  Bananas  South     5.90
         4  Bananas  North    31.30
         5  Oranges  North    13.10
```

To create a pivot table, you provide the DataFrame as the first argument to the pivot_table function. index and columns define which column of the DataFrame will become the pivot table's row and column labels, respectively. values are going to be aggregated into the data part of the resulting DataFrame by using the `aggfunc`, a function that can be provided as a string or NumPy ufunc. And finally, `margins` correspond to `Grand Total` in Excel, i.e., if you leave `margins` and `margins_name` away, the `Total` column and row won't be shown:

```
In [92]: pivot = pd.pivot_table(sales,
                                index="Fruit", columns="Region",
                                values="Revenue", aggfunc="sum",
                                margins=True, margins_name="Total")
         pivot

Out[92]: Region   North  South  Total
         Fruit
         Apples     NaN  10.55  10.55
         Bananas   31.3   5.90  37.20
         Oranges   25.4  22.00  47.40
         Total     56.7  38.45  95.15
```

In summary, pivoting your data means to take the unique values of a column (`Region` in our case) and turn them into the column headers of the pivot table, thereby aggregating the values from another column. This makes it easy to read off summary information across the dimensions of interest. In our pivot table, you instantly see that there were no apples sold in the north region and that in the south region, most revenues come from oranges. If you want to go the other way around and turn the column headers into the values of a single column, use `melt`. In that sense, `melt` is the opposite of the `pivot_table` function:

```
In [93]: pd.melt(pivot.iloc[:-1,:-1].reset_index(),
                  id_vars="Fruit",
                  value_vars=["North", "South"], value_name="Revenue")

Out[93]:      Fruit Region  Revenue
         0    Apples  North      NaN
         1   Bananas  North    31.30
         2   Oranges  North    25.40
         3    Apples  South    10.55
         4   Bananas  South     5.90
         5   Oranges  South    22.00
```

Here, I am providing our pivot table as the input, but I am using `iloc` to get rid of the total row and column. I also reset the index so that all information is available as regular columns. I then provide `id_vars` to indicate the identifiers and `value_vars` to define which columns I want to "unpivot." Melting can be useful if you want to prepare the data so it can be stored back to a database that expects it in this format.

Working with aggregated statistics helps you understand your data, but nobody likes to read a page full of numbers. To make information easily understandable, nothing works better than creating visualizations, which is our next topic. While Excel uses the term *charts*, pandas generally refers to them as *plots*. I will use these terms interchangeably in this book.

Plotting

Plotting allows you to visualize the findings of your data analysis and may well be the most important step in the whole process. For plotting, we're going to use two libraries: we start by looking at Matplotlib, pandas' default plotting library, before we focus on Plotly, a modern plotting library that gives us a more interactive experience in Jupyter notebooks.

Matplotlib

Matplotlib is a plotting package that has been around for a long time and is included in the Anaconda distribution. With it, you can generate plots in a variety of formats, including vector graphics for high-quality printing. When you call the `plot` method of a DataFrame, pandas will produce a Matplotlib plot by default.

To use Matplotlib in a Jupyter notebook, you need to first run one of two magic commands (see the sidebar "Magic Commands" on page 116): `%matplotlib inline` or `%matplotlib notebook`. They configure the notebook so that plots can be displayed in the notebook itself. The latter command adds a bit more interactivity, allowing you to change the size or zoom factor of the chart. Let's get started and create a first plot with pandas and Matplotlib (see Figure 5-4):

```
In [94]: import numpy as np
         %matplotlib inline
         # Or %matplotlib notebook

In [95]: data = pd.DataFrame(data=np.random.rand(4, 4) * 100000,
                             index=["Q1", "Q2", "Q3", "Q4"],
                             columns=["East", "West", "North", "South"])
         data.index.name = "Quarters"
         data.columns.name = "Region"
         data

Out[95]: Region          East         West        North        South
         Quarters
         Q1          23254.220271  96398.309860  16845.951895  41671.684909
         Q2          87316.022433  45183.397951  15460.819455  50951.465770
         Q3          51458.760432   3821.139360  77793.393899  98915.952421
         Q4          64933.848496   7600.277035  55001.831706  86248.512650

In [96]: data.plot()  # Shortcut for data.plot.line()

Out[96]: <AxesSubplot:xlabel='Quarters'>
```

Note that in this example, I have used a NumPy array to construct a pandas Data-Frame. Providing NumPy arrays allows you to leverage NumPy's constructors that we met in the last chapter; here, we use NumPy to generate a pandas DataFrame based on pseudorandom numbers. Therefore, when you run the sample on your end, you will get different values.

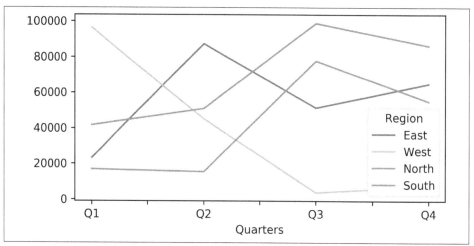

Figure 5-4. Matplotlib plot

Even if you use the magic command `%matplotlib notebook`, you will probably notice that Matplotlib was originally designed for static plots rather than for an interactive experience on a web page. That's why we're going to use Plotly next, a plotting library designed for the web.

Plotly

Plotly is a JavaScript-based library and can—since version 4.8.0—be used as a pandas plotting backend with great interactivity: you can easily zoom in, click on the legend to select or deselect a category, and get tooltips with more info about the data point you're hovering over. Plotly is not included in the Anaconda installation, so if you haven't installed it yet, do so now by running the following command:

```
(base)> conda install plotly
```

Once you run the following cell, the plotting backend of the whole notebook will be set to Plotly and if you would rerun the previous cell, it would also be rendered as a Plotly chart. For Plotly, instead of running a magic command, you just need to set it as backend before being able to plot Figures 5-5 and 5-6:

```
In [97]: # Set the plotting backend to Plotly
         pd.options.plotting.backend = "plotly"
```

```
In [98]: data.plot()
```

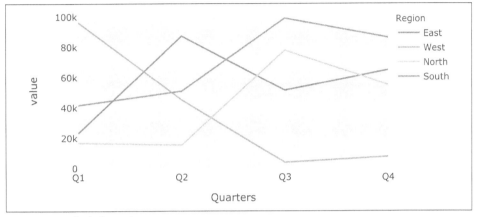

Figure 5-5. Plotly line plot

```
In [99]: # Display the same data as bar plot
         data.plot.bar(barmode="group")
```

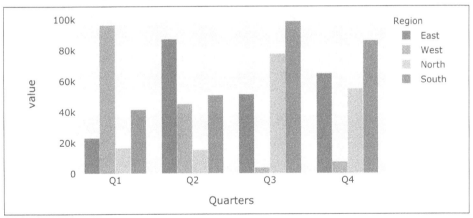

Figure 5-6. Plotly bar plot

> **Differences in Plotting Backends**
>
> If you use Plotly as plotting backend, you'll need to check the accepted arguments of the plot methods directly on the Plotly docs. For example, you can take a look at the `barmode=group` argument in Plotly's bar charts documentation (*https://oreil.ly/Ekurd*).

pandas and the underlying plotting libraries offer a wealth of chart types and options to format the charts in almost any desired way. It's also possible to arrange multiple plots into a series of subplots. As an overview, Table 5-6 shows the available plot types.

Table 5-6. pandas plot types

Type	Description
line	Line Chart, default when running `df.plot()`
bar	Vertical bar chart
barh	Horizontal bar chart
hist	Histogram
box	Box plot
kde	Density plot, can also be used via `density`
area	Area chart
scatter	Scatter plot
hexbin	Hexagonal bin plots
pie	Pie chart

On top of that, pandas offers some higher-level plotting tools and techniques that are made up of multiple individual components. For details, see the pandas visualization documentation (*https://oreil.ly/FxYg9*).

Other Plotting Libraries

The scientific visualization landscape in Python is very active, and besides Matplotlib and Plotly, there are many other high-quality options to choose from that may be the better option for certain use cases:

Seaborn
  Seaborn (*https://oreil.ly/a3U1t*) is built on top of Matplotlib. It improves the default style and adds additional plots like heatmaps, which often simplify your work: you can create advanced statistical plots with only a few lines of code.

Bokeh

> Bokeh (*https://docs.bokeh.org*) is similar to Plotly in technology and functionality: it's based on JavaScript and therefore also works great for interactive charts in Jupyter notebooks. Bokeh is included in Anaconda.

Altair

> Altair (*https://oreil.ly/t06t7*) is a library for statistical visualizations based on the Vega project (*https://oreil.ly/RN6A7*). Altair is also JavaScript-based and offers some interactivity like zooming.

HoloViews

> HoloViews (*https://holoviews.org*) is another JavaScript-based package that focuses on making data analysis and visualization easy. With a few lines of code, you can achieve complex statistical plots.

We will create more plots in the next chapter to analyze time series, but before we get there, let's wrap this chapter up by learning how we can import and export data with pandas!

Importing and Exporting DataFrames

So far, we constructed DataFrames from scratch using nested lists, dictionaries, or NumPy arrays. These techniques are important to know, but typically, the data is already available and you simply need to turn it into a DataFrame. To do this, pandas offers various reader functions. But even if you need to access a proprietary system for which pandas doesn't offer a built-in reader, you often have a Python package to connect to that system, and once you have the data, it's easy enough to turn it into a DataFrame. In Excel, data import is the type of work you would usually handle with Power Query.

After analyzing and changing your dataset, you might want to push the results back into a database or export it to a CSV file or—given the title of the book—present it in an Excel workbook to your manager. To export pandas DataFrames, use one of the exporter methods that DataFrames offer. Table 5-7 shows an overview of the most common import and export methods.

Table 5-7. Importing and exporting DataFrames

Data format/system	Import: pandas (pd) function	Export: DataFrame (df) method
CSV files	pd.read_csv	df.to_csv
JSON	pd.read_json	df.to_json
HTML	pd.read_html	df.to_html
Clipboard	pd.read_clipboard	df.to_clipboard

Data format/system	Import: pandas (pd) function	Export: DataFrame (df) method
Excel files	pd.read_excel	df.to_excel
SQL Databases	pd.read_sql	df.to_sql

We will meet pd.read_sql and pd.to_sql in Chapter 11, where we will use them as part of a case study. And since I am going to dedicate the whole of Chapter 7 to the topic of reading and writing Excel files with pandas, I will focus on importing and exporting CSV files in this section. Let's start with exporting an existing DataFrame!

Exporting CSV Files

If you need to pass a DataFrame to a colleague who might not use Python or pandas, passing it in the form of a CSV file is usually a good idea: pretty much every program knows how to import them. To export our sample DataFrame df to a CSV file, use the to_csv method:

```
In [100]: df.to_csv("course_participants.csv")
```

If you wanted to store the file in a different directory, supply the full path as a raw string, e.g., r"C:\path\to\desired\location\msft.csv".

Use Raw Strings for File Paths on Windows

In strings, the backslash is used to escape certain characters. That's why to work with file paths on Windows, you either need to use double backslashes (C:\\path\\to\\file.csv) or prefix the string with an r to turn it into a *raw string* that interprets the characters literally. This isn't an issue on macOS or Linux, as they use forward slashes in paths.

By providing only the file name as I do, it will produce the file *course_participants.csv* in the same directory as the notebook with the following content:

```
user_id,name,age,country,score,continent
1001,Mark,55,Italy,4.5,Europe
1000,John,33,USA,6.7,America
1002,Tim,41,USA,3.9,America
1003,Jenny,12,Germany,9.0,Europe
```

Now that you know how to use the df.to_csv method, let's see how importing a CSV file works!

Importing CSV Files

Importing a local CSV file is as easy as providing its path to the `read_csv` function. *MSFT.csv* is a CSV file that I downloaded from Yahoo! Finance and it contains the daily historical stock prices for Microsoft—you'll find it in the companion repository, in the *csv* folder:

```
In [101]: msft = pd.read_csv("csv/MSFT.csv")
```

Often, you will need to supply a few more parameters to `read_csv` than just the file name. For example, `sep` allows you to tell pandas what separator or delimiter the CSV file uses in case it isn't the default comma. We will use a few more parameters in the next chapter, but for the full overview, have a look at the pandas documentation (*https://oreil.ly/2GMhW*).

Now that we are dealing with big DataFrames with many thousands of rows, typically the first thing is to run the `info` method to get a summary of the DataFrame. Next, you may want to take a peek at the first and last few rows of the DataFrame using the `head` and `tail` methods. These methods return five rows by default, but this can be changed by providing the desired number of rows as an argument. You can also run the `describe` method to get some basic statistics:

```
In [102]: msft.info()

<class 'pandas.core.frame.DataFrame'>
RangeIndex: 8622 entries, 0 to 8621
Data columns (total 7 columns):
 #   Column     Non-Null Count  Dtype
---  ------     --------------  -----
 0   Date       8622 non-null   object
 1   Open       8622 non-null   float64
 2   High       8622 non-null   float64
 3   Low        8622 non-null   float64
 4   Close      8622 non-null   float64
 5   Adj Close  8622 non-null   float64
 6   Volume     8622 non-null   int64
dtypes: float64(5), int64(1), object(1)
memory usage: 471.6+ KB

In [103]: # I am selecting a few columns because of space issues
          # You can also just run: msft.head()
          msft.loc[:, ["Date", "Adj Close", "Volume"]].head()

Out[103]:          Date  Adj Close      Volume
          0  1986-03-13   0.062205  1031788800
          1  1986-03-14   0.064427   308160000
          2  1986-03-17   0.065537   133171200
          3  1986-03-18   0.063871    67766400
          4  1986-03-19   0.062760    47894400

In [104]: msft.loc[:, ["Date", "Adj Close", "Volume"]].tail(2)
```

```
Out[104]:            Date  Adj Close     Volume
          8620  2020-05-26  181.570007  36073600
          8621  2020-05-27  181.809998  39492600

In [105]: msft.loc[:, ["Adj Close", "Volume"]].describe()

Out[105]:          Adj Close        Volume
          count  8622.000000  8.622000e+03
          mean     24.921952  6.030722e+07
          std      31.838096  3.877805e+07
          min       0.057762  2.304000e+06
          25%       2.247503  3.651632e+07
          50%      18.454313  5.350380e+07
          75%      25.699224  7.397560e+07
          max     187.663330  1.031789e+09
```

Adj Close stands for *adjusted close price* and corrects the stock price for corporate actions such as stock splits. Volume is the number of stocks that were traded. I have summarized the various DataFrame exploration methods we've seen in this chapter in Table 5-8.

Table 5-8. DataFrame exploration methods and attributes

DataFrame (df) Method/Attribute	Description
df.info()	Provides number of data points, index type, dtype, and memory usage.
df.describe()	Provides basic statistics including count, mean, std, min, max, and percentiles.
df.head(n=5)	Returns the first *n* rows of the DataFrame.
df.tail(n=5)	Returns the last *n* rows of the DataFrame.
df.dtypes	Returns the dtype of each column.

The read_csv function also accepts a URL instead of a local CSV file. This is how you read the CSV file directly from the companion repo:

```
In [106]: # The line break in the URL is only to make it fit on the page
          url = ("https://raw.githubusercontent.com/fzumstein/"
                 "python-for-excel/1st-edition/csv/MSFT.csv")
          msft = pd.read_csv(url)

In [107]: msft.loc[:, ["Date", "Adj Close", "Volume"]].head(2)

Out[107]:          Date  Adj Close      Volume
          0  1986-03-13   0.062205  1031788800
          1  1986-03-14   0.064427   308160000
```

We'll continue with this dataset and the read_csv function in the next chapter about time series, where we will turn the Date column into a DatetimeIndex.

Conclusion

This chapter was packed with new concepts and tools to analyze datasets in pandas. We learned how to load CSV files, how to deal with missing or duplicate data, and how to make use of descriptive statistics. We also saw how easy it is to turn your DataFrames into interactive plots. While it may take a while to digest everything, it probably won't take long before you will understand the immense power you are gaining by adding pandas to your tool belt. Along the way, we compared pandas to the following Excel functionality:

AutoFilter functionality
> See "Selecting by boolean indexing" on page 95.

VLOOKUP formula
> See "Joining and Merging" on page 109.

Pivot Table
> See "Pivoting and Melting" on page 113.

Power Query
> This is a combination of "Importing and Exporting DataFrames" on page 119, "Data Manipulation" on page 92, and "Combining DataFrames" on page 107.

The next chapter is about time series analysis, the functionality that led to broad adoption of pandas by the financial industry. Let's see why this part of pandas has such an edge over Excel!

## CHAPTER 6

Time Series Analysis with pandas

A *time series* is a series of data points along a time-based axis that plays a central role in many different scenarios: while traders use historical stock prices to calculate risk measures, the weather forecast is based on time series generated by sensors measuring temperature, humidity, and air pressure. And the digital marketing department relies on time series generated by web pages, e.g., the source and number of page views per hour, and will use them to draw conclusions with regard to their marketing campaigns.

Time series analysis is one of the main driving forces why data scientists and analysts have started to look for a better alternative to Excel. The following points summarize some of the reasons behind this move:

Big datasets

> Time series can quickly grow beyond Excel's limit of roughly one million rows per sheet. For example, if you work with intraday stock prices on a tick data level, you're often dealing with hundreds of thousands of records—per stock and day!

Date and time

> As we have seen in Chapter 3, Excel has various limitations when it comes to handling date and time, the backbone of time series. Missing support for time zones and a number format that is limited to milliseconds are some of them. pandas supports time zones and uses NumPy's `datetime64[ns]` data type, which offers a resolution in up to nanoseconds.

Missing functionality

> Excel misses even basic tools to be able to work with time series data in a decent way. For example, if you want to turn a daily time series into a monthly time series, there is no easy way of doing this despite it being a very common task.

DataFrames allow you to work with various time-based indices: `DatetimeIndex` is the most common one and represents an index with timestamps. Other index types, like `PeriodIndex`, are based on time intervals such as hours or months. In this chapter, however, we are only looking at `DatetimeIndex`, which I will introduce now in more detail.

DatetimeIndex

In this section, we'll learn how to construct a `DatetimeIndex`, how to filter such an index to a specific time range, and how to work with time zones.

Creating a DatetimeIndex

To construct a `DatetimeIndex`, pandas offers the `date_range` function. It accepts a start date, a frequency, and either the number of periods or the end date:

```
In [1]: # Let's start by importing the packages we use in this chapter
        # and by setting the plotting backend to Plotly
        import pandas as pd
        import numpy as np
        pd.options.plotting.backend = "plotly"
```

```
In [2]: # This creates a DatetimeIndex based on a start timestamp,
        # number of periods and frequency ("D" = daily).
        daily_index = pd.date_range("2020-02-28", periods=4, freq="D")
        daily_index
```

```
Out[2]: DatetimeIndex(['2020-02-28', '2020-02-29', '2020-03-01', '2020-03-02'],
              dtype='datetime64[ns]', freq='D')
```

```
In [3]: # This creates a DatetimeIndex based on start/end timestamp.
        # The frequency is set to "weekly on Sundays" ("W-SUN").
        weekly_index = pd.date_range("2020-01-01", "2020-01-31", freq="W-SUN")
        weekly_index
```

```
Out[3]: DatetimeIndex(['2020-01-05', '2020-01-12', '2020-01-19', '2020-01-26'],
              dtype='datetime64[ns]', freq='W-SUN')
```

```
In [4]: # Construct a DataFrame based on the weekly_index. This could be
        # the visitor count of a museum that only opens on Sundays.
        pd.DataFrame(data=[21, 15, 33, 34],
                     columns=["visitors"], index=weekly_index)
```

```
Out[4]:            visitors
        2020-01-05       21
        2020-01-12       15
        2020-01-19       33
        2020-01-26       34
```

Let's now return to the Microsoft stock time series from the last chapter. When you take a closer look at the data types of the columns, you will notice that the Date column has the type `object`, which means that pandas has interpreted the time-stamps as strings:

```
In [5]: msft = pd.read_csv("csv/MSFT.csv")

In [6]: msft.info()

<class 'pandas.core.frame.DataFrame'>
RangeIndex: 8622 entries, 0 to 8621
Data columns (total 7 columns):
 #   Column     Non-Null Count  Dtype
---  ------     --------------  -----
 0   Date       8622 non-null   object
 1   Open       8622 non-null   float64
 2   High       8622 non-null   float64
 3   Low        8622 non-null   float64
 4   Close      8622 non-null   float64
 5   Adj Close  8622 non-null   float64
 6   Volume     8622 non-null   int64
dtypes: float64(5), int64(1), object(1)
memory usage: 471.6+ KB
```

There are two ways to fix this and turn it into a `datetime` data type. The first one is to run the `to_datetime` function on that column. Make sure to assign the transformed column back to the original DataFrame if you want to change it at the source:

```
In [7]: msft.loc[:, "Date"] = pd.to_datetime(msft["Date"])

In [8]: msft.dtypes

Out[8]: Date         datetime64[ns]
        Open                float64
        High                float64
        Low                 float64
        Close               float64
        Adj Close           float64
        Volume                int64
        dtype: object
```

The other possibility is to tell `read_csv` about the columns that contain timestamps by using the `parse_dates` argument. `parse_dates` expects a list of column names or indices. Also, you almost always want to turn timestamps into the index of the Data-Frame since this will allow you to filter the data easily, as we will see in a moment. To spare yourself an extra `set_index` call, provide the column you would like to use as index via the `index_col` argument, again as column name or index:

```
In [9]: msft = pd.read_csv("csv/MSFT.csv",
                           index_col="Date", parse_dates=["Date"])

In [10]: msft.info()

<class 'pandas.core.frame.DataFrame'>
DatetimeIndex: 8622 entries, 1986-03-13 to 2020-05-27
Data columns (total 6 columns):
```

```
 #   Column     Non-Null Count  Dtype
---  ------     --------------  -----
 0   Open       8622 non-null   float64
 1   High       8622 non-null   float64
 2   Low        8622 non-null   float64
 3   Close      8622 non-null   float64
 4   Adj Close  8622 non-null   float64
 5   Volume     8622 non-null   int64
dtypes: float64(5), int64(1)
memory usage: 471.5 KB
```

As info reveals on its second line of output, you are now dealing with a DataFrame that has a DatetimeIndex with values from 1986-03-13 to 2020-05-27. Compare this again with the output under In [6], where it showed a RangeIndex instead with values from 0 to 8621. If you would need to change another data type (let's say you wanted Volume to be a float instead of an int), you again have two options: either provide dtype={"Volume": float} as argument to the read_csv function, or apply the astype method as follows:

```
In [11]: msft.loc[:, "Volume"] = msft["Volume"].astype("float")
         msft["Volume"].dtype

Out[11]: dtype('float64')
```

With time series, it's always a good idea to make sure the index is sorted properly before starting your analysis:

```
In [12]: msft = msft.sort_index()
```

And finally, if you need to access only parts of a DatetimeIndex, like the date part without the time, access the date attribute like this:

```
In [13]: msft.index.date

Out[13]: array([datetime.date(1986, 3, 13), datetime.date(1986, 3, 14),
                datetime.date(1986, 3, 17), ..., datetime.date(2020, 5, 22),
                datetime.date(2020, 5, 26), datetime.date(2020, 5, 27)],
               dtype=object)
```

Instead of date, you can also use parts of a date like year, month, day, etc. To access the same functionality on a regular column with data type datetime, you will have to use the dt attribute, e.g., df["column_name"].dt.date.

With a sorted DatetimeIndex, let's see how we can filter the DataFrame to certain time periods!

Filtering a DatetimeIndex

If your DataFrame has a `DatetimeIndex`, there is an easy way to select rows from a specific time period by using `loc` with a string in the format `YYYY-MM-DD HH:MM:SS`. pandas will turn this string into a slice so it covers the whole period. For example, to select all rows from 2019, provide the year as a *string*, not a number:

```
In [14]: msft.loc["2019", "Adj Close"]

Out[14]: Date
         2019-01-02     99.099190
         2019-01-03     95.453529
         2019-01-04     99.893005
         2019-01-07    100.020401
         2019-01-08    100.745613
                          ...
         2019-12-24    156.515396
         2019-12-26    157.798309
         2019-12-27    158.086731
         2019-12-30    156.724243
         2019-12-31    156.833633
         Name: Adj Close, Length: 252, dtype: float64
```

Let's take this a step further and plot the data between June 2019 and May 2020 (see Figure 6-1):

```
In [15]: msft.loc["2019-06":"2020-05", "Adj Close"].plot()
```

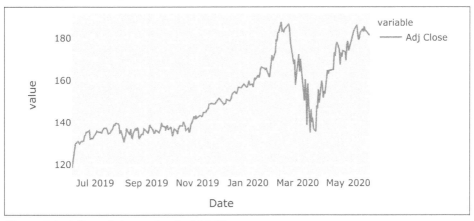

Figure 6-1. Adjusted close price for MSFT

Hover over the Plotly chart to read off the value as a tooltip and zoom in by drawing a rectangle with your mouse. Double-click the chart to get back to the default view.

We'll use the adjusted close price in the next section to learn about time zone handling.

Working with Time Zones

Microsoft is listed on the Nasdaq stock exchange. The Nasdaq is in New York and markets close at 4:00 p.m. To add this additional information to the DataFrame's index, first add the closing hour to the date via `DateOffset`, then attach the correct time zone to the timestamps via `tz_localize`. Since the closing hour is only applicable to the close price, let's create a new DataFrame with it:

```
In [16]: # Add the time information to the date
         msft_close = msft.loc[:, ["Adj Close"]].copy()
         msft_close.index = msft_close.index + pd.DateOffset(hours=16)
         msft_close.head(2)

Out[16]:                      Adj Close
         Date
         1986-03-13 16:00:00   0.062205
         1986-03-14 16:00:00   0.064427

In [17]: # Make the timestamps time-zone-aware
         msft_close = msft_close.tz_localize("America/New_York")
         msft_close.head(2)

Out[17]:                            Adj Close
         Date
         1986-03-13 16:00:00-05:00   0.062205
         1986-03-14 16:00:00-05:00   0.064427
```

If you want to convert the timestamps to UTC time zone, use the DataFrame method `tz_convert`. UTC stands for *Coordinated Universal Time* and is the successor of Greenwich Mean Time (GMT). Note how the closing hours change in UTC depending on whether daylight saving time (DST) is in effect or not in New York:

```
In [18]: msft_close = msft_close.tz_convert("UTC")
         msft_close.loc["2020-01-02", "Adj Close"]  # 21:00 without DST

Out[18]: Date
         2020-01-02 21:00:00+00:00    159.737595
         Name: Adj Close, dtype: float64

In [19]: msft_close.loc["2020-05-01", "Adj Close"]  # 20:00 with DST

Out[19]: Date
         2020-05-01 20:00:00+00:00    174.085175
         Name: Adj Close, dtype: float64
```

Preparing time series like this will allow you to compare close prices from stock exchanges across different time zones even if the time info is missing or stated in the local time zone.

Now that you know what a `DatetimeIndex` is, let's try out a few common time series manipulations in the next section by calculating and comparing stock performance.

Common Time Series Manipulations

In this section, I'll show you how to perform common time series analysis tasks such as calculating stock returns, plotting the performance of various stocks, and visualizing the correlation of their returns in a heatmap. We'll also see how to change the frequency of time series and how to calculate rolling statistics.

Shifting and Percentage Changes

In finance, the *log returns* of stocks are often assumed to be normally distributed. By log returns, I mean the natural logarithm of the ratio of the current and previous price. To get a feeling for the distribution of the daily log returns, let's plot a histogram. First, however, we need to calculate the log returns. In Excel, it's typically done with a formula that involves cells from two rows, as shown in Figure 6-2.

◢	A	B	C
1	Date	Adj Close	
2	3/13/1986	0.062205	
3	3/14/1986	0.064427	=LN(B3/B2)
4	3/17/1986	0.065537	0.017082

Figure 6-2. Calculating log returns in Excel

Logarithms in Excel and Python

Excel uses LN to denote the natural logarithm and LOG for the logarithm with base 10. Python's math module and NumPy, however, use log for the natural logarithm and log10 for the logarithm with base 10.

With pandas, rather than having a formula accessing two different rows, you use the shift method to shift the values down by one row. This allows you to operate on a single row so your calculations can make use of vectorization. shift accepts a positive or negative integer that shifts the time series down or up by the respective number of rows. Let's first see how shift works:

```
In [20]: msft_close.head()

Out[20]:                         Adj Close
        Date
        1986-03-13 21:00:00+00:00   0.062205
        1986-03-14 21:00:00+00:00   0.064427
        1986-03-17 21:00:00+00:00   0.065537
```

```
           1986-03-18 21:00:00+00:00    0.063871
           1986-03-19 21:00:00+00:00    0.062760

In [21]: msft_close.shift(1).head()

Out[21]:                               Adj Close
         Date
         1986-03-13 21:00:00+00:00          NaN
         1986-03-14 21:00:00+00:00     0.062205
         1986-03-17 21:00:00+00:00     0.064427
         1986-03-18 21:00:00+00:00     0.065537
         1986-03-19 21:00:00+00:00     0.063871
```

You are now able to write a single vector-based formula that is easy to read and
understand. To get the natural logarithm, use NumPy's log ufunc, which is applied to
each element. Then we can plot a histogram (see Figure 6-3):

```
In [22]: returns = np.log(msft_close / msft_close.shift(1))
         returns = returns.rename(columns={"Adj Close": "returns"})
         returns.head()

Out[22]:                                returns
         Date
         1986-03-13 21:00:00+00:00          NaN
         1986-03-14 21:00:00+00:00     0.035097
         1986-03-17 21:00:00+00:00     0.017082
         1986-03-18 21:00:00+00:00    -0.025749
         1986-03-19 21:00:00+00:00    -0.017547
```

```
In [23]: # Plot a histogram with the daily log returns
         returns.plot.hist()
```

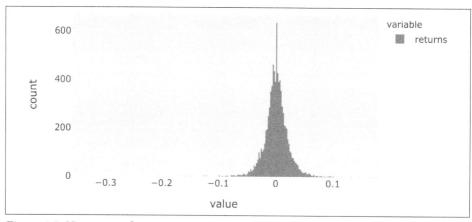

Figure 6-3. Histogram plot

To get *simple returns* instead, use pandas' built-in pct_change method. By default, it
calculates the percentage change from the previous row, which is also the definition
of simple returns:

```
In [24]: simple_rets = msft_close.pct_change()
         simple_rets = simple_rets.rename(columns={"Adj Close": "simple rets"})
         simple_rets.head()

Out[24]:                              simple rets
         Date
         1986-03-13 21:00:00+00:00            NaN
         1986-03-14 21:00:00+00:00       0.035721
         1986-03-17 21:00:00+00:00       0.017229
         1986-03-18 21:00:00+00:00      -0.025421
         1986-03-19 21:00:00+00:00      -0.017394
```

So far, we have looked at just the Microsoft stock. In the next section, we're going to load more time series so we can have a look at other DataFrame methods that require multiple time series.

Rebasing and Correlation

Things get slightly more interesting when we work with more than one time series. Let's load a few additional adjusted close prices for Amazon (AMZN), Google (GOOGL), and Apple (AAPL), also downloaded from Yahoo! Finance:

```
In [25]: parts = []  # List to collect individual DataFrames
         for ticker in ["AAPL", "AMZN", "GOOGL", "MSFT"]:
             # "usecols" allows us to only read in the Date and Adj Close
             # For a refresher about f-strings, see Chapter 3
             adj_close = pd.read_csv(f"csv/{ticker}.csv",
                                     index_col="Date", parse_dates=["Date"],
                                     usecols=["Date", "Adj Close"])
             # Rename the column into the ticker symbol
             # (If you type this example by hand, make sure to keep the
             # following lines correctly indented!)
             adj_close = adj_close.rename(columns={"Adj Close": ticker})
             # Append the stock's DataFrame to the parts list
             parts.append(adj_close)

In [26]: # Combine the 4 DataFrames into a single DataFrame
         adj_close = pd.concat(parts, axis=1)
         adj_close

Out[26]:                   AAPL         AMZN        GOOGL        MSFT
         Date
         1980-12-12    0.405683          NaN          NaN         NaN
         1980-12-15    0.384517          NaN          NaN         NaN
         1980-12-16    0.356296          NaN          NaN         NaN
         1980-12-17    0.365115          NaN          NaN         NaN
         1980-12-18    0.375698          NaN          NaN         NaN
         ...                ...          ...          ...         ...
         2020-05-22  318.890015  2436.879883  1413.239990  183.509995
         2020-05-26  316.730011  2421.860107  1421.369995  181.570007
         2020-05-27  318.109985  2410.389893  1420.280029  181.809998
         2020-05-28  318.250000  2401.100098  1418.239990         NaN
         2020-05-29  317.940002  2442.370117  1433.520020         NaN
```

```
[9950 rows x 4 columns]
```

Did you see the power of `concat`? pandas has automatically aligned the individual time series along the dates. This is why you get NaN values for those stocks that don't go back as far as Apple. And since MSFT has NaN values at the most recent dates, you may have guessed that I downloaded *MSFT.csv* two days before the other ones. Aligning time series by date is a typical operation that is very cumbersome to do with Excel and therefore also very error-prone. Dropping all rows that contain missing values will make sure that all stocks have the same amount of data points:

```
In [27]: adj_close = adj_close.dropna()
         adj_close.info()

<class 'pandas.core.frame.DataFrame'>
DatetimeIndex: 3970 entries, 2004-08-19 to 2020-05-27
Data columns (total 4 columns):
 #   Column  Non-Null Count  Dtype
---  ------  --------------  -----
 0   AAPL    3970 non-null   float64
 1   AMZN    3970 non-null   float64
 2   GOOGL   3970 non-null   float64
 3   MSFT    3970 non-null   float64
dtypes: float64(4)
memory usage: 155.1 KB
```

Let's now rebase the prices so that all time series start at 100. This allows us to compare their relative performance in a chart; see Figure 6-4. To rebase a time series, divide every value by its starting value and multiply by 100, the new base. If you did this in Excel, you would typically write a formula with a combination of absolute and relative cell references, then copy the formula for every row and every time series. In pandas, thanks to vectorization and broadcasting, you are dealing with a single formula:

```
In [28]: # Use a sample from June 2019 - May 2020
         adj_close_sample = adj_close.loc["2019-06":"2020-05", :]
         rebased_prices = adj_close_sample / adj_close_sample.iloc[0, :] * 100
         rebased_prices.head(2)

Out[28]:                  AAPL        AMZN       GOOGL        MSFT
         Date
         2019-06-03  100.000000  100.000000  100.00000  100.000000
         2019-06-04  103.658406  102.178197  101.51626  102.770372

In [29]: rebased_prices.plot()
```

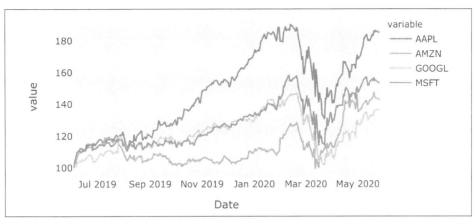

Figure 6-4. Rebased time series

To see how independent the returns of the different stocks are, have a look at their correlations by using the `corr` method. Unfortunately, pandas doesn't provide a built-in plot type to visualize the correlation matrix as a heatmap, so we need to use Plotly directly via its `plotly.express` interface (see Figure 6-5):

```
In [30]: # Correlation of daily log returns
         returns = np.log(adj_close / adj_close.shift(1))
         returns.corr()

Out[30]:              AAPL      AMZN     GOOGL      MSFT
         AAPL    1.000000  0.424910  0.503497  0.486065
         AMZN    0.424910  1.000000  0.486690  0.485725
         GOOGL   0.503497  0.486690  1.000000  0.525645
         MSFT    0.486065  0.485725  0.525645  1.000000

In [31]: import plotly.express as px

In [32]: fig = px.imshow(returns.corr(),
                         x=adj_close.columns,
                         y=adj_close.columns,
                         color_continuous_scale=list(
                             reversed(px.colors.sequential.RdBu)),
                         zmin=-1, zmax=1)
         fig.show()
```

If you want to understand how `imshow` works in detail, have a look at the Plotly Express API docs (*https://oreil.ly/O86li*).

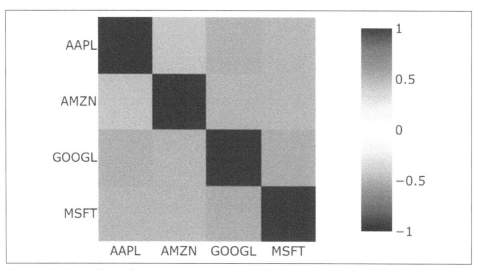

Figure 6-5. Correlation heatmap

At this point, we have already learned quite a few things about time series, including how to combine and clean them and how to calculate returns and correlations. But what if you decide that daily returns are not a good base for your analysis and you want monthly returns? How you change the frequency of time series data is the topic of the next section.

Resampling

A regular task with time series is *up-* and *downsampling*. Upsampling means that the time series is converted into one with a higher frequency, and downsampling means that it is converted into one with a lower frequency. On financial factsheets, you often show monthly or quarterly performance, for example. To turn the daily time series into a monthly one, use the `resample` method that accepts a frequency string like `M` for *end-of-calendar-month* or `BM` for *end-of-business-month*. You can find a list of all frequency strings in the pandas docs (*https://oreil.ly/zStpt*). Similar to how `groupby` works, you then chain a method that defines *how* you are resampling. I am using `last` to always take the last observation of that month:

```
In [33]: end_of_month = adj_close.resample("M").last()
         end_of_month.head()

Out[33]:                 AAPL       AMZN       GOOGL       MSFT
         Date
         2004-08-31  2.132708  38.139999  51.236237  17.673630
         2004-09-30  2.396127  40.860001  64.864868  17.900215
         2004-10-31  3.240182  34.130001  95.415413  18.107374
         2004-11-30  4.146072  39.680000  91.081078  19.344421
         2004-12-31  3.982207  44.290001  96.491493  19.279480
```

Instead of `last`, you can choose any other method that works on `groupby`, like `sum` or `mean`. There is also `ohlc`, which conveniently returns the open, high, low, and close values over that period. This may serve as the source to create the typical candlestick charts that are often used with stock prices.

If that end-of-month time series would be all you have and you need to produce a weekly time series out of it, you have to upsample your time series. By using `asfreq`, you are telling pandas not to apply any transformation and hence you will see most of the values showing NaN. If you wanted to *forward-fill* the last known value instead, use the `ffill` method:

```
In [34]: end_of_month.resample("D").asfreq().head()  # No transformation

Out[34]:             AAPL       AMZN      GOOGL       MSFT
         Date
         2004-08-31  2.132708  38.139999  51.236237  17.67363
         2004-09-01       NaN        NaN        NaN       NaN
         2004-09-02       NaN        NaN        NaN       NaN
         2004-09-03       NaN        NaN        NaN       NaN
         2004-09-04       NaN        NaN        NaN       NaN

In [35]: end_of_month.resample("W-FRI").ffill().head()  # Forward fill

Out[35]:             AAPL       AMZN      GOOGL       MSFT
         Date
         2004-09-03  2.132708  38.139999  51.236237  17.673630
         2004-09-10  2.132708  38.139999  51.236237  17.673630
         2004-09-17  2.132708  38.139999  51.236237  17.673630
         2004-09-24  2.132708  38.139999  51.236237  17.673630
         2004-10-01  2.396127  40.860001  64.864868  17.900215
```

Downsampling data is one way of smoothing a time series. Calculating statistics over a rolling window is another way, as we will see next.

Rolling Windows

When you calculate time series statistics, you often want a rolling statistic such as the *moving average*. The moving average looks at a subset of the time series (let's say 25 days) and takes the mean from this subset before moving the window forward by one day. This will result in a new time series that is smoother and less prone to outliers. If you are into algorithmic trading, you may be looking at the intersection of the moving average with the stock price and take this (or some variation of it) as a trading signal. DataFrames have a `rolling` method, which accepts the number of observations as argument. You then chain it with the statistical method that you want to use —in the case of the moving average, it's the `mean`. By looking at Figure 6-6, you are easily able to compare the original time series with the smoothed moving average:

```
In [36]: # Plot the moving average for MSFT with data from 2019
         msft19 = msft.loc["2019", ["Adj Close"]].copy()
```

```
# Add the 25 day moving average as a new column to the DataFrame
msft19.loc[:, "25day average"] = msft19["Adj Close"].rolling(25).mean()
msft19.plot()
```

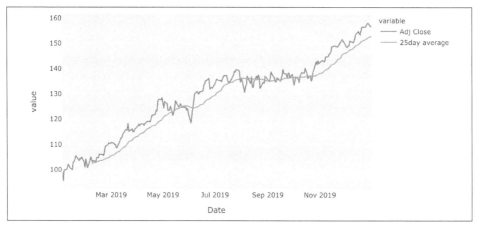

Figure 6-6. Moving average plot

Instead of `mean`, you can use many other statistical measures including `count`, `sum`, `median`, `min`, `max`, `std` (standard deviation), or `var` (variance).

At this point, we have seen the most important functionality of pandas. It's equally important, though, to understand where pandas has its limits, even though they may still be far away right now.

Limitations with pandas

When your DataFrames start to get bigger, it's a good idea to know the upper limit of what a DataFrame can hold. Unlike Excel, where you have a hard limit of roughly one million rows and 12,000 columns per sheet, pandas only has a soft limit: all data must fit into the available memory of your machine. If that's not the case, there might be some easy fixes: only load those columns from your dataset that you need or delete intermediate results to free up some memory. If that doesn't help, there are quite a few projects that will feel familiar to pandas users but work with big data. One of the projects, Dask (*https://dask.org*), works on top of NumPy and pandas and allows you to work with big datasets by splitting it up into multiple pandas DataFrames and distributing the workload across multiple CPU cores or machines. Other big data projects that work with some sort of DataFrame are Modin (*https://oreil.ly/Wd8gi*), Koalas (*https://oreil.ly/V13Be*), Vaex (*https://vaex.io*), PySpark (*https://oreil.ly/E7kmX*), cuDF (*https://oreil.ly/zaeWz*), Ibis (*https://oreil.ly/Gw4wn*), and PyArrow (*https://oreil.ly/DQQGD*). We will briefly touch on Modin in the next chapter but other than that, this is not something we are going to explore further in this book.

Conclusion

Time series analysis is the area where I feel Excel has fallen behind the most, so after reading this chapter, you probably understand why pandas has such a big success in finance, an industry that heavily relies on time series. We've seen how easy it is to work with time zones, resample time series, or produce correlation matrices, functionality that either isn't supported in Excel or requires cumbersome workarounds.

Knowing how to use pandas doesn't mean you have to get rid of Excel, though, as the two worlds can play very nicely together: pandas DataFrames are a great way to transfer data from one world to the other, as we will see in the next part, which is about reading and writing Excel files in ways that bypass the Excel application entirely. This is very helpful as it means you can manipulate Excel files with Python on every operating system that Python supports, including Linux. To start this journey, the next chapter will show you how pandas can be used to automate tedious manual processes like the aggregation of Excel files into summary reports.

## PART III

Reading and Writing Excel Files
Without Excel

## CHAPTER 7

Excel File Manipulation with pandas

After six chapters of intense introductions to tools, Python, and pandas, I will give you a break and start this chapter with a practical case study that allows you to put your newly acquired skills to good use: with just ten lines of pandas code, you will consolidate dozens of Excel files into an Excel report, ready to be sent to your managers. After the case study, I'll give you a more in-depth introduction to the tools that pandas offers to work with Excel files: the `read_excel` function and the `ExcelFile` class for reading, and the `to_excel` method and the `ExcelWriter` class for writing Excel files. pandas does not rely on the Excel application to read and write Excel files, which means that all code samples in this chapter run everywhere Python runs, including Linux.

Case Study: Excel Reporting

This case study is inspired by a few real-world reporting projects I was involved in over the last few years. Even though the projects took place in completely different industries—including telecommunication, digital marketing, and finance—they were still remarkably similar: the starting point is usually a directory with Excel files that need to be processed into an Excel report—often on a monthly, weekly, or daily basis. In the companion repository, in the *sales_data* directory, you will find Excel files with fictitious sales transactions for a telecommunication provider selling different plans (Bronze, Silver, Gold) in a few stores throughout the United States. For every month, there are two files, one in the *new* subfolder for new contracts and one in the *existing* subfolder for existing customers. As the reports come from different systems, they come in different formats: the new customers are delivered as *xlsx* files, while the existing customers arrive in the older *xls* format. Each of the files has up to 10,000 transactions, and our goal is to produce an Excel report that shows the total sales per store and month. To get started, let's have a look at the *January.xlsx* file from the *new* subfolder in Figure 7-1.

⬙	A	B	C	D	E	F	G
1	transaction_id	store	status	transaction_date	plan	contract_type	amount
2	abfbdd6d	Chicago	ACTIVE	1/1/2019	Silver	NEW	14.25
3	136a9997	San Francisco	ACTIVE	1/1/2019	Gold	NEW	19.35
4	c6688f32	San Francisco	ACTIVE	1/1/2019	Bronze	NEW	12.2
5	6ef349c1	Chicago	ACTIVE	1/1/2019	Gold	NEW	19.35
6	22066f29	San Francisco	ACTIVE	1/1/2019	Silver	NEW	14.25

Figure 7-1. The first few rows of January.xlsx

The Excel files in the *existing* subfolder look practically the same, except that they are missing the `status` column and are stored in the legacy *xls* format. As a first step, let's read the new transactions from January with pandas' `read_excel` function:

```
In [1]: import pandas as pd

In [2]: df = pd.read_excel("sales_data/new/January.xlsx")
        df.info()

<class 'pandas.core.frame.DataFrame'>
RangeIndex: 9493 entries, 0 to 9492
Data columns (total 7 columns):
 #   Column            Non-Null Count  Dtype
---  ------            --------------  -----
 0   transaction_id    9493 non-null   object
 1   store             9493 non-null   object
 2   status            9493 non-null   object
 3   transaction_date  9493 non-null   datetime64[ns]
 4   plan              9493 non-null   object
 5   contract_type     9493 non-null   object
 6   amount            9493 non-null   float64
dtypes: datetime64[ns](1), float64(1), object(5)
memory usage: 519.3+ KB
```

The read_excel Function with Python 3.9

This is the same warning as in Chapter 5: if you are running `pd.read_excel` with Python 3.9 or above, make sure to use at least pandas 1.2 or you will get an error when reading *xlsx* files.

As you can see, pandas has properly recognized the data types of all columns, including the date format of `transaction_date`. This allows us to work with the data without further preparation. As this sample is deliberately simple, we can move on with creating a short script called *sales_report_pandas.py* as shown in Example 7-1. This script will read in all Excel files from both directories, aggregate the data, and write the summary table into a new Excel file. Use VS Code to write the script your-self, or open it from the companion repository. For a refresher on how to create or open files in VS Code, have another look at Chapter 2. If you create it yourself, make sure to place it next to the *sales_data* folder—this will allow you to run the script without having to adjust any file paths.

Example 7-1. sales_report_pandas.py

```python
from pathlib import Path

import pandas as pd


# Directory of this file
this_dir = Path(__file__).resolve().parent ❶

# Read in all Excel files from all subfolders of sales_data
parts = []
for path in (this_dir / "sales_data").rglob("*.xls*"): ❷
    print(f'Reading {path.name}')
    part = pd.read_excel(path, index_col="transaction_id")
    parts.append(part)

# Combine the DataFrames from each file into a single DataFrame
# pandas takes care of properly aligning the columns
df = pd.concat(parts)

# Pivot each store into a column and sum up all transactions per date
pivot = pd.pivot_table(df,
                       index="transaction_date", columns="store",
                       values="amount", aggfunc="sum")

# Resample to end of month and assign an index name
summary = pivot.resample("M").sum()
summary.index.name = "Month"

# Write summary report to Excel file
summary.to_excel(this_dir / "sales_report_pandas.xlsx")
```

❶ Up to this chapter, I was using strings to specify file paths. By using the `Path` class from the standard library's `pathlib` module instead, you get access to a powerful set of tools: path objects enable you to easily construct paths by concatenating individual parts via forward slashes, as it's done four lines below with `this_dir /` `"sales_data"`. These paths work across platforms and allow you to apply filters like `rglob` as explained under the next point. `__file__` resolves to the path of the source code file when you run it—using its `parent` will give you therefore the name of the directory of this file. The `resolve` method that we use before calling parent turns the path into an absolute path. If you would run this from a Jupyter notebook instead, you would have to replace this line with `this_dir = Path(".").resolve()`, with the dot representing the current directory. In most cases, functions and classes that accept a path in the form of a string also accept a path object.

❷ The easiest way to read in all Excel files recursively from within a certain directory is to use the `rglob` method of the path object. `glob` is short for *globbing*, which refers to pathname expansion using wildcards. The ? wildcard represents exactly one character, while * stands for any number of characters (including zero). The *r* in `rglob` means *recursive* globbing, i.e., it will look for matching files across all subdirectories—accordingly, `glob` would ignore subdirectories. Using *.xls* as the globbing expression makes sure that the old and new Excel files are found, as it matches both .xls and .xlsx. It's usually a good idea to slightly enhance the expression like this: [!~$]*.xls*. This ignores temporary Excel files (their file name starts with ~$). For more background on how to use globbing in Python, see the Python docs (*https://oreil.ly/fY0qG*).

Run the script, for example, by clicking the Run File button at the top right of VS Code. The script will take a moment to complete and once done, the Excel workbook *sales_report_pandas.xlsx* will show up in the same directory as the script. The content of Sheet1 should look like in Figure 7-2. That's quite an impressive result for only ten lines of code—even if you will need to adjust the width of the first column to be able to see the dates!

	A	B	C	D	E	F	G
1	Month	Boston	Chicago	Las Vegas	New York	an Francisc	ashington DC
2	#########	21784.1	51187.7	23012.75	49872.85	58629.85	14057.6
3	#########	21454.9	52330.85	25493.1	46669.85	55218.65	15235.4
4	#########	20043	48897.25	23451.1	41572.25	52712.95	14177.05
5	#########	18791.05	47396.35	22710.15	41714.3	49324.65	13339.15
6	#########	18036.75	45117.05	21526.55	40610.4	47759.6	13147.1
7	#########	21556.25	49460.45	21985.05	47265.65	53462.4	14284.3
8	#########	19853	47993.8	23444.3	40408.3	50181.6	14161.5
9	#########	22332.9	50838.9	24927.65	45396.85	55336.35	16127.05
10	#########	19924.5	49096.25	24410.7	42830.6	49931.45	14994.4
11	#########	16550.95	42543.8	22827.5	34090.05	44311.65	12846.7
12	#########	21312.9	52011.6	24860.25	46959.85	55056.45	14057.6
13	#########	19722.6	49355.1	24535.75	42364.35	50933.45	14702.15

Figure 7-2. sales_report_pandas.xlsx (as-is, without adjusting any column width)

For simple cases like this one, pandas offers a really easy solution to work with Excel files. However, we can do much better—after all, a title, some formatting (including column width and a consistent number of decimals), and a chart wouldn't hurt. That's exactly what we will take care of in the next chapter by directly using the writer libraries that pandas uses under the hood. Before we get there, however, let's have a more detailed look at how we can read and write Excel files with pandas.

Reading and Writing Excel Files with pandas

The case study was using `read_excel` and `to_excel` with their default arguments to keep things simple. In this section, I will show you the most commonly used arguments and options when reading and writing Excel files with pandas. We'll start with the `read_excel` function and the `ExcelFile` class before looking at the `to_excel` method and the `ExcelWriter` class. Along the way, I'll also introduce Python's `with` statement.

The read_excel Function and ExcelFile Class

The case study used Excel workbooks where the data was conveniently in cell A1 of the first sheet. In reality, your Excel files are probably not so well organized. In this case, pandas offers parameters to fine-tune the reading process. For the next few samples, we're going to use the *stores.xlsx* file that you will find in the *xl* folder of the companion repository. The first sheet is shown in Figure 7-3.

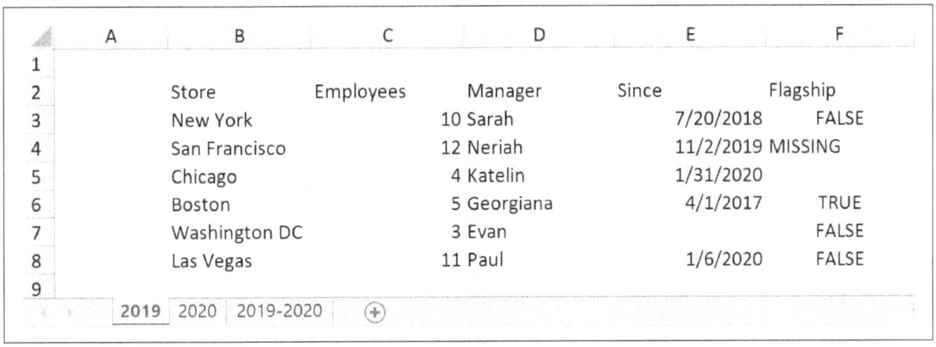

	A	B	C	D	E	F
1						
2		Store	Employees	Manager	Since	Flagship
3		New York		10 Sarah	7/20/2018	FALSE
4		San Francisco		12 Neriah	11/2/2019	MISSING
5		Chicago		4 Katelin	1/31/2020	
6		Boston		5 Georgiana	4/1/2017	TRUE
7		Washington DC		3 Evan		FALSE
8		Las Vegas		11 Paul	1/6/2020	FALSE
9						

2019 | 2020 | 2019-2020 | (+)

Figure 7-3. The first sheet of stores.xlsx

By using the parameters `sheet_name`, `skiprows`, and `usecols`, we can tell pandas about the cell range that we want to read in. As usual, it's a good idea to have a look at the data types of the returned DataFrame by running the `info` method:

```
In [3]: df = pd.read_excel("xl/stores.xlsx",
                           sheet_name="2019", skiprows=1, usecols="B:F")
        df
```

```
Out[3]:           Store  Employees   Manager      Since Flagship
         0     New York         10     Sarah 2018-07-20    False
         1  San Francisco       12    Neriah 2019-11-02  MISSING
         2      Chicago          4   Katelin 2020-01-31      NaN
         3       Boston          5  Georgiana 2017-04-01     True
         4  Washington DC        3      Evan        NaT    False
         5    Las Vegas         11      Paul 2020-01-06    False

In [4]: df.info()

<class 'pandas.core.frame.DataFrame'>
RangeIndex: 6 entries, 0 to 5
Data columns (total 5 columns):
 #   Column     Non-Null Count  Dtype
---  ------     --------------  -----
 0   Store      6 non-null      object
 1   Employees  6 non-null      int64
 2   Manager    6 non-null      object
 3   Since      5 non-null      datetime64[ns]
 4   Flagship   5 non-null      object
dtypes: datetime64[ns](1), int64(1), object(3)
memory usage: 368.0+ bytes
```

Everything looks good except for the Flagship column—its data type should be bool
rather than object. To fix this, we can provide a converter function that deals with
the offensive cells in that column (instead of writing the fix_missing function, we
could have also provided a lambda expression instead):

```
In [5]: def fix_missing(x):
            return False if x in ["", "MISSING"] else x

In [6]: df = pd.read_excel("xl/stores.xlsx",
                           sheet_name="2019", skiprows=1, usecols="B:F",
                           converters={"Flagship": fix_missing})
        df

Out[6]:           Store  Employees   Manager      Since Flagship
         0     New York         10     Sarah 2018-07-20    False
         1  San Francisco       12    Neriah 2019-11-02    False
         2      Chicago          4   Katelin 2020-01-31    False
         3       Boston          5  Georgiana 2017-04-01     True
         4  Washington DC        3      Evan        NaT    False
         5    Las Vegas         11      Paul 2020-01-06    False

In [7]: # The Flagship column now has Dtype "bool"
        df.info()

<class 'pandas.core.frame.DataFrame'>
RangeIndex: 6 entries, 0 to 5
Data columns (total 5 columns):
 #   Column     Non-Null Count  Dtype
---  ------     --------------  -----
 0   Store      6 non-null      object
 1   Employees  6 non-null      int64
 2   Manager    6 non-null      object
```

```
3   Since     5 non-null     datetime64[ns]
4   Flagship  6 non-null     bool
dtypes: bool(1), datetime64[ns](1), int64(1), object(2)
memory usage: 326.0+ bytes
```

The read_excel function also accepts a list of sheet names. In this case, it returns a dictionary with the DataFrame as value and the name of the sheet as key. To read in all sheets, you would need to provide sheet_name=None. Also, note the slight variation of how I am using usecols by providing the column names of the table:

```
In [8]: sheets = pd.read_excel("xl/stores.xlsx", sheet_name=["2019", "2020"],
                               skiprows=1, usecols=["Store", "Employees"])
        sheets["2019"].head(2)

Out[8]:          Store  Employees
        0     New York         10
        1  San Francisco       12
```

If the source file doesn't have column headers, set header=None and provide them via names. Note that sheet_name also accepts sheet indices:

```
In [9]: df = pd.read_excel("xl/stores.xlsx", sheet_name=0,
                           skiprows=2, skipfooter=3,
                           usecols="B:C,F", header=None,
                           names=["Branch", "Employee_Count", "Is_Flagship"])
        df

Out[9]:          Branch  Employee_Count Is_Flagship
        0      New York              10       False
        1  San Francisco             12     MISSING
        2        Chicago              4         NaN
```

To handle NaN values, use a combination of na_values and keep_default_na. The next sample tells pandas to only interpret cells with the word MISSING as NaN and nothing else:

```
In [10]: df = pd.read_excel("xl/stores.xlsx", sheet_name="2019",
                            skiprows=1, usecols="B,C,F", skipfooter=2,
                            na_values="MISSING", keep_default_na=False)
         df

Out[10]:          Store  Employees Flagship
         0      New York         10    False
         1  San Francisco        12      NaN
         2        Chicago         4
         3         Boston         5     True
```

pandas offers an alternative way to read Excel files by using the ExcelFile class. This mostly makes a difference if you want to read in multiple sheets from a file in the legacy *xls* format: in this case, using ExcelFile will be faster as it prevents pandas from reading in the whole file multiple times. ExcelFile can be used as a context manager (see sidebar) so the file is properly closed again.

Context Managers and the with Statement

First of all, the `with` statement in Python doesn't have anything to do with the `With` statement in VBA: in VBA, it is used to run a series of statements on the same object, while in Python, it is used to manage resources like files or database connections. If you want to load the latest sales data to be able to analyze it, you may have to open a file or establish a connection to a database. After you're done reading the data, it's best practice to close the file or connection as soon as possible again. Otherwise, you may run into situations where you can't open another file or can't establish another connection to the database—file handlers and database connections are limited resources. Opening and closing a text file manually works like this (w stands for opening the file in `write` mode, which replaces the file if it already exists):

```
In [11]: f = open("output.txt", "w")
         f.write("Some text")
         f.close()
```

Running this code will create a file called *output.txt* in the same directory as the notebook you are running it from and write "some text" to it. To *read* a file, you would use r instead of w, and to *append* to the end of the file, use a. Since files can also be manipulated from outside of your program, such an operation could fail. You could handle this by using the try/except mechanism that I will introduce in Chapter 11. However, since this is such a common operation, Python is providing the `with` statement to make things easier:

```
In [12]: with open("output.txt", "w") as f:
             f.write("Some text")
```

When code execution leaves the body of the `with` statement, the file is automatically closed, whether or not there is an exception happening. This guarantees that the resources are properly cleaned up. Objects that support the `with` statement are called *context managers*; this includes the `ExcelFile` and `ExcelWriter` objects in this chapter, as well as database connection objects that we will look at in Chapter 11.

Let's see the `ExcelFile` class in action:

```
In [13]: with pd.ExcelFile("xl/stores.xls") as f:
             df1 = pd.read_excel(f, "2019", skiprows=1, usecols="B:F", nrows=2)
             df2 = pd.read_excel(f, "2020", skiprows=1, usecols="B:F", nrows=2)

         df1

Out[13]:          Store  Employees Manager      Since Flagship
         0      New York         10   Sarah 2018-07-20    False
         1  San Francisco         12  Neriah 2019-11-02  MISSING
```

ExcelFile also gives you access to the names of all sheets:

```
In [14]: stores = pd.ExcelFile("xl/stores.xlsx")
         stores.sheet_names

Out[14]: ['2019', '2020', '2019-2020']
```

Finally, pandas allows you to read Excel files from a URL, similar to how we did it with CSV files in Chapter 5. Let's read it directly from the companion repo:

```
In [15]: url = ("https://raw.githubusercontent.com/fzumstein/"
                "python-for-excel/1st-edition/xl/stores.xlsx")
         pd.read_excel(url, skiprows=1, usecols="B:E", nrows=2)

Out[15]:             Store  Employees Manager       Since
         0        New York         10   Sarah  2018-07-20
         1   San Francisco         12  Neriah  2019-11-02
```

Reading xlsb Files via pandas

If you use pandas with a version below 1.3, reading *xlsb* files requires you to explicitly specify the engine in the `read_excel` function or `ExcelFile` class:

```
pd.read_excel("xl/stores.xlsb", engine="pyxlsb")
```

This requires the pyxlsb package to be installed, as it isn't part of Anaconda—we'll get to that as well as to the other engines in the next chapter.

To summarize, Table 7-1 shows you the most commonly used `read_excel` parameters. You will find the complete list in the official docs (*https://oreil.ly/v8Yes*).

Table 7-1. Selected parameters for read_excel

Parameter	Description
`sheet_name`	Instead of providing a sheet name, you could also provide the index of the sheet (zero-based), e.g., `sheet_name=0`. If you set `sheet_name=None`, pandas will read the whole workbook and return a dictionary in the form of `{"sheetname": df}`. To read a selection of sheets, provide a list with sheet names or indices.
`skiprows`	This allows you to skip over the indicated number of rows.
`usecols`	If the Excel file includes the names of the column headers, provide them in a list to select the columns, e.g., `["Store", "Employees"]`. Alternatively, it can also be a list of column indices, e.g., `[1, 2]`, or a string (not a list!) of Excel column names, including ranges, e.g., `"B:D,G"`. You can also provide a function: as an example, to only include the columns that start with `Manager`, use: `usecols=lambda x: x.startswith("Manager")`.
`nrows`	Number of rows you want to read.
`index_col`	Indicates which column should be the index, accepts a column name or an index, e.g., `index_col=0`. If you provide a list with multiple columns, a hierarchical index will be created.

Parameter	Description
header	If you set header=None, the default integer headers are assigned except if you provide the desired names via the names parameter. If you provide a list of indices, hierarchical column headers will be created.
names	Provide the desired names of your columns as list.
na_values	Pandas interprets the following cell values as NaN by default (I introduced NaN in Chapter 5): empty cells, #NA, NA, null, #N/A, N/A, NaN, n/a, -NaN, 1.#IND, nan, #N/A N/A, -1.#QNAN, -nan, NULL, -1.#IND, <NA>, 1.#QNAN. If you'd like to add one or more values to that list, provide them via na_values.
keep_default_na	If you'd like to ignore the default values that pandas interprets as NaN, set keep_default_na=False.
convert_float	Excel stores all numbers internally as floats and by default, pandas transforms numbers without meaningful decimals to integers. If you want to change that behavior, set convert_float=False (this may be a bit faster).
converters	Allows you to provide a function per column to convert its values. For example, to make the text in a certain column uppercase, use the following: converters={"column_name": lambda x: x.upper()}

So much for reading Excel files with pandas—let's now switch sides and learn about writing Excel files in the next section!

The to_excel Method and ExcelWriter Class

The easiest way to write an Excel file with pandas is to use a DataFrame's to_excel method. It allows you to specify to which cell of which sheet you want to write the DataFrame to. You can also decide whether or not to include the column headers and the index of the DataFrame and how to treat data types like np.nan and np.inf that don't have an equivalent representation in Excel. Let's start by creating a DataFrame with different data types and use its to_excel method:

```
In [16]: import numpy as np
         import datetime as dt

In [17]: data = [[dt.datetime(2020,1,1, 10, 13), 2.222, 1, True],
                 [dt.datetime(2020,1,2), np.nan, 2, False],
                 [dt.datetime(2020,1,2), np.inf, 3, True]]
         df = pd.DataFrame(data=data,
                           columns=["Dates", "Floats", "Integers", "Booleans"])
         df.index.name="index"
         df

Out[17]:                      Dates  Floats  Integers  Booleans
         index
         0     2020-01-01 10:13:00   2.222         1      True
         1     2020-01-02 00:00:00     NaN         2     False
         2     2020-01-02 00:00:00     inf         3      True
```

```
In [18]: df.to_excel("written_with_pandas.xlsx", sheet_name="Output",
                      startrow=1, startcol=1, index=True, header=True,
                      na_rep="<NA>", inf_rep="<INF>")
```

Running the `to_excel` command will create the Excel file as shown in Figure 7-4 (you will need to make column C wider to see the dates properly):

	A	B	C	D	E	F
1						
2		index	Dates	Floats	Integers	Booleans
3		0	2020-01-01 10:13:00	2.222	1	TRUE
4		1	2020-01-02 00:00:00	<NA>	2	FALSE
5		2	2020-01-02 00:00:00	<INF>	3	TRUE

Figure 7-4. written_with_pandas.xlsx

If you want to write multiple DataFrames to the same or different sheets, you will need to use the `ExcelWriter` class. The following sample writes the same DataFrame to two different locations on Sheet1 and one more time to Sheet2:

```
In [19]: with pd.ExcelWriter("written_with_pandas2.xlsx") as writer:
             df.to_excel(writer, sheet_name="Sheet1", startrow=1, startcol=1)
             df.to_excel(writer, sheet_name="Sheet1", startrow=10, startcol=1)
             df.to_excel(writer, sheet_name="Sheet2")
```

Since we're using the `ExcelWriter` class as a context manager, the file is automatically written to disk when it exits the context manager, i.e., when the indentation stops. Otherwise, you will have to call `writer.save()` explicitly. For a summary of the most commonly used parameters that `to_excel` accepts, have a look at Table 7-2. You will find the full list of parameters in the official docs (*https://oreil.ly/ESKAG*).

Table 7-2. Selected parameters for to_excel

Parameter	Description
`sheet_name`	Name of the sheet to write to.
`startrow` and `startcol`	`startrow` is the first row where the DataFrame will be written to and `startcol` is the first column. This uses zero-based indexing, so if you want to write your DataFrame into cell B3, use `startrow=2` and `startcol=1`.
`index` and `header`	If you want to hide the index and/or header, set them to `index=False` and `header=False`, respectively.
`na_rep` and `inf_rep`	By default, `np.nan` will be converted to an empty cell, while `np.inf`, NumPy's representation of infinity, will be converted to the string `inf`. Providing values allows you to change this behavior.
`freeze_panes`	Freeze the first couple of rows and columns by supplying a tuple: for example `(2, 1)` will freeze the first two rows and the first column.

As you can see, reading and writing simple Excel files with pandas works well. There are limitations, though—let's see which ones!

Limitations When Using pandas with Excel Files

Using the pandas interface to read and write Excel files works great for simple cases, but there are limits:

- When writing DataFrames to files, you can't include a title or a chart.
- There is no way to change the default format of the header and index in Excel.
- When reading files, pandas automatically transforms cells with errors like #REF! or #NUM! into NaN, making it impossible to search for specific errors in your spreadsheets.
- Working with big Excel files may require extra settings that are easier to control by using the reader and writer packages directly, as we will see in the next chapter.

Conclusion

The nice thing about pandas is that it offers a consistent interface to work with all supported Excel file formats, whether that's *xls*, *xlsx*, *xlsm*, or *xlsb*. This made it easy for us to read a directory of Excel files, aggregate the data, and dump the summary into an Excel report—in only ten lines of code.

pandas, however, doesn't do the heavy lifting itself: under the hood, it selects a reader or writer package to do the job. In the next chapter, I will show you which reader and writer packages pandas uses and how you use them directly or in combination with pandas. This will allow us to work around the limitations we saw in the previous section.

## CHAPTER 8

Excel File Manipulation with Reader and Writer Packages

This chapter introduces you to OpenPyXL, XlsxWriter, pyxlsb, xlrd, and xlwt: these are the packages that can read and write Excel files and are used by pandas under the hood when you call the `read_excel` or `to_excel` functions. Using the reader and writer packages directly allows you to create more complex Excel reports as well as fine-tune the reading process. Also, should you ever work on a project where you only need to read and write Excel files without the need for the rest of the pandas functionality, installing the full NumPy/pandas stack would probably be overkill. We'll start this chapter by learning when to use which package and how their syntax works before looking at a few advanced topics, including how to work with big Excel files and how to combine pandas with the reader and writer packages to improve the styling of DataFrames. To conclude, we will pick up the case study from the beginning of the last chapter again and enhance the Excel report by formatting the table and adding a chart. Like the last chapter, this chapter does not require an installation of Excel, which means that all code samples run on Windows, macOS, and Linux.

The Reader and Writer Packages

The reader and writer landscape can be a bit overwhelming: we are going to look at no less than six packages in this section as almost every Excel file type requires a different package. The fact that each package uses a different syntax that often deviates substantially from the original Excel object model doesn't make it easier—I'll say more about the Excel object model in the next chapter. This means that you will likely have to look up a lot of commands, even if you are a seasoned VBA developer. This section starts with an overview of when you need which package before it introduces a helper module that makes working with these packages a little easier. After that, it presents each of the packages in a cookbook style, where you can look up how the most commonly used commands work.

When to Use Which Package

This section introduces the following six packages to read, write, and edit Excel files:

- OpenPyXL (*https://oreil.ly/3jHQM*)
- XlsxWriter (*https://oreil.ly/7jI3T*)
- pyxlsb (*https://oreil.ly/sEHXS*)
- xlrd (*https://oreil.ly/tSam7*)
- xlwt (*https://oreil.ly/wPSLe*)
- xlutils (*https://oreil.ly/MTFOL*)

To understand which package can do what, have a look at Table 8-1. For example, to read the *xlsx* file format, you will have to use the OpenPyXL package:

Table 8-1. When to use which package

Excel File Format	Read	Write	Edit
xlsx	OpenPyXL	OpenPyXL, XlsxWriter	OpenPyXL
xlsm	OpenPyXL	OpenPyXL, XlsxWriter	OpenPyXL
xltx, xltm	OpenPyXL	OpenPyXL	OpenPyXL
xlsb	pyxlsb	-	-
xls, xlt	xlrd	xlwt	xlutils

If you want to write *xlsx* or *xlsm* files, you need to decide between OpenPyXL and XlsxWriter. Both packages cover similar functionality, but each package may have a few unique features that the other one doesn't have. As both libraries are actively being developed, this is changing over time. Here is a high-level overview of where they differ:

- OpenPyXL can read, write, and edit while XlsxWriter can only write.
- OpenPyXL makes it easier to produce Excel files with VBA macros.
- XlsxWriter is better documented.
- XlsxWriter tends to be faster than OpenPyXL, but depending on the size of the workbook you're writing, the differences may not be significant.

pandas uses the writer package it can find and if you have both OpenPyXL and XlsxWriter installed, XlsxWriter is the default. If you want to choose which package pandas should use, specify the `engine` parameter in the `read_excel` or `to_excel` functions or the `ExcelFile` and `ExcelWriter` classes, respectively. The engine is the package name in lower case, so to write a file with OpenPyXL instead of XlsxWriter, run the following:

```
df.to_excel("filename.xlsx", engine="openpyxl")
```

Once you know which package you need, there is a second challenge waiting for you: most of these packages require you to write quite a bit of code to read or write a range of cells, and each package uses a different syntax. To make your life easier, I created a helper module that I'll introduce next.

The excel.py Module

I have created the `excel.py` module to make your life easier when using the reader and writer packages, as it takes care of the following issues:

Package switching

Having to switch the reader or writer package is a relatively common scenario. For example, Excel files tend to grow in size over time, which many users fight by switching the file format from *xlsx* to *xlsb* as this can substantially reduce the file size. In that case, you will have to switch away from OpenPyXL to pyxlsb. This forces you to rewrite your OpenPyXL code to reflect pyxlsb's syntax.

Data type conversion

This is connected to the previous point: when switching packages, you don't just have to adjust the syntax of your code, but you also need to watch out for different data types that these packages return for the same cell content. For example, OpenPyXL returns None for empty cells, while xlrd returns an empty string.

Cell looping

The reader and writer packages are *low-level* packages: this means that they lack convenience functions that would allow you to tackle common tasks easily. For example, most of the packages require you to loop through every single cell that you are going to read or write.

You will find the `excel.py` module in the companion repository and we will use it in the upcoming sections, but as a preview, here is the syntax to read and write values:

```
import excel
values = excel.read(sheet_object, first_cell="A1", last_cell=None)
excel.write(sheet_object, values, first_cell="A1")
```

The `read` function accepts a `sheet` object from one of the following packages: xlrd, OpenPyXL, or pyxlsb. It also accepts the optional arguments `first_cell` and `last_cell`. They can be provided in either the A1 notation or as row-column-tuple with Excel's one-based indices: `(1, 1)`. The default value for the `first_cell` is A1 whereas the default value for `last_cell` is the bottom right corner of the used range. Hence, if you only provide the `sheet` object, it will read the whole sheet. The `write` function works similarly: it expects a `sheet` object from xlwt, OpenPyXL, or XlsxWriter along with the values as nested list and an optional `first_cell`, which marks the upper left corner of where the nested list will be written to. The `excel.py` module also harmonizes the data type conversion as shown in Table 8-2.

Table 8-2. Data type conversion

Excel representation	Python data type
Empty cell	None
Cell with a date format	`datetime.datetime` (except for pyxlsb)
Cell with a boolean	`bool`
Cell with an error	`str` (the error message)
String	`str`
Float	`float` or `int`

Equipped with the `excel.py` module, we're now ready to dive into the packages: the next four sections are about OpenPyXL, XlsxWriter, pyxlsb, and xlrd/xlwt/xlutils. They follow a cookbook style that allows you to get started quickly with each package. Instead of reading through it sequentially, I would recommend you to pick the package you need based on Table 8-1, then jump directly to the corresponding section.

The with Statement

We'll be using the with statement on various occasions in this chapter. If you need a refresher, have a look at the sidebar "Context Managers and the with Statement" on page 150 in Chapter 7.

OpenPyXL

OpenPyXL is the only package in this section that can both read and write Excel files. You can even use it to edit Excel files—albeit only simple ones. Let's start by looking at how reading works!

Reading with OpenPyXL

The following sample code shows you how to perform common tasks when you use OpenPyXL for reading Excel files. To get the cell values, you need to open the workbook with `data_only=True`. The default is on `False`, which would return the formulas of the cells instead:

```
In [1]: import pandas as pd
        import openpyxl
        import excel
        import datetime as dt

In [2]: # Open the workbook to read cell values.
        # The file is automatically closed again after loading the data.
        book = openpyxl.load_workbook("xl/stores.xlsx", data_only=True)

In [3]: # Get a worksheet object by name or index (0-based)
        sheet = book["2019"]
        sheet = book.worksheets[0]

In [4]: # Get a list with all sheet names
        book.sheetnames

Out[4]: ['2019', '2020', '2019-2020']

In [5]: # Loop through the sheet objects.
        # Instead of "name", openpyxl uses "title".
        for i in book.worksheets:
            print(i.title)

2019
2020
2019-2020

In [6]: # Getting the dimensions,
        # i.e., the used range of the sheet
        sheet.max_row, sheet.max_column

Out[6]: (8, 6)

In [7]: # Read the value of a single cell
        # using "A1" notation and using cell indices (1-based)
```

```
         sheet["B6"].value
         sheet.cell(row=6, column=2).value

Out[7]: 'Boston'

In [8]: # Read in a range of cell values by using our excel module
         data = excel.read(book["2019"], (2, 2), (8, 6))
         data[:2]  # Print the first two rows

Out[8]: [['Store', 'Employees', 'Manager', 'Since', 'Flagship'],
          ['New York', 10, 'Sarah', datetime.datetime(2018, 7, 20, 0, 0), False]]
```

Writing with OpenPyXL

OpenPyXL builds the Excel file in memory and writes out the file once you call the save method. The following code produces the file as shown in Figure 8-1:

```
In [9]: import openpyxl
         from openpyxl.drawing.image import Image
         from openpyxl.chart import BarChart, Reference
         from openpyxl.styles import Font, colors
         from openpyxl.styles.borders import Border, Side
         from openpyxl.styles.alignment import Alignment
         from openpyxl.styles.fills import PatternFill
         import excel

In [10]: # Instantiate a workbook
         book = openpyxl.Workbook()

         # Get the first sheet and give it a name
         sheet = book.active
         sheet.title = "Sheet1"

         # Writing individual cells using A1 notation
         # and cell indices (1-based)
         sheet["A1"].value = "Hello 1"
         sheet.cell(row=2, column=1, value="Hello 2")

         # Formatting: fill color, alignment, border and font
         font_format = Font(color="FF0000", bold=True)
         thin = Side(border_style="thin", color="FF0000")
         sheet["A3"].value = "Hello 3"
         sheet["A3"].font = font_format
         sheet["A3"].border = Border(top=thin, left=thin,
                                     right=thin, bottom=thin)
         sheet["A3"].alignment = Alignment(horizontal="center")
         sheet["A3"].fill = PatternFill(fgColor="FFFF00", fill_type="solid")

         # Number formatting (using Excel's formatting strings)
         sheet["A4"].value = 3.3333
         sheet["A4"].number_format = "0.00"

         # Date formatting (using Excel's formatting strings)
         sheet["A5"].value = dt.date(2016, 10, 13)
```

```
sheet["A5"].number_format = "mm/dd/yy"

# Formula: you must use the English name of the formula
# with commas as delimiters
sheet["A6"].value = "=SUM(A4, 2)"

# Image
sheet.add_image(Image("images/python.png"), "C1")

# Two-dimensional list (we're using our excel module)
data = [[None, "North", "South"],
        ["Last Year", 2, 5],
        ["This Year", 3, 6]]
excel.write(sheet, data, "A10")

# Chart
chart = BarChart()
chart.type = "col"
chart.title = "Sales Per Region"
chart.x_axis.title = "Regions"
chart.y_axis.title = "Sales"
chart_data = Reference(sheet, min_row=11, min_col=1,
                       max_row=12, max_col=3)
chart_categories = Reference(sheet, min_row=10, min_col=2,
                             max_row=10, max_col=3)
# from_rows interprets the data in the same way
# as if you would add a chart manually in Excel
chart.add_data(chart_data, titles_from_data=True, from_rows=True)
chart.set_categories(chart_categories)
sheet.add_chart(chart, "A15")

# Saving the workbook creates the file on disk
book.save("openpyxl.xlsx")
```

If you want to write an Excel template file, you'll need to set the `template` attribute to `True` before saving it:

```
In [11]: book = openpyxl.Workbook()
         sheet = book.active
         sheet["A1"].value = "This is a template"
         book.template = True
         book.save("template.xltx")
```

As you can see in the code, OpenPyXL is setting colors by providing a string like `FF0000`. This value is made up of three hex values (`FF`, `00`, and `00`) that correspond to the red/green/blue values of the desired color. Hex stands for *hexadecimal* and represents numbers using a base of sixteen instead of a base of ten that is used by our standard decimal system.

Finding the Hex Value of a Color

To find the desired hex value of a color in Excel, click on the paint dropdown that you would use to change the fill color of a cell, then select More Colors. Now select your color and read off its hex value from the menu.

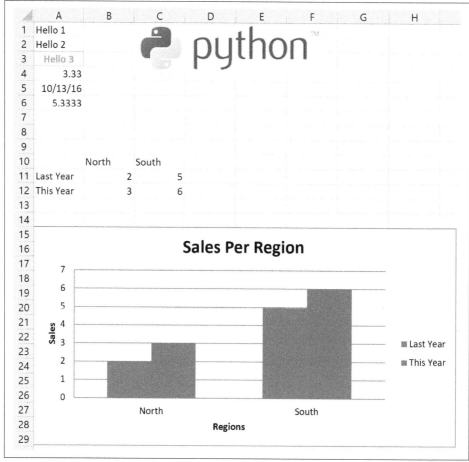

Figure 8-1. The file written by OpenPyXL (openpyxl.xlsx)

Editing with OpenPyXL

There is no reader/writer package that can truly edit Excel files: in reality, OpenPyXL reads the file with everything it understands, then writes the file again from scratch—including any changes you make in between. This can be very powerful for simple Excel files that contain mainly formatted cells with data and formulas, but it's limited when you have charts and other more advanced content in your spreadsheet as

OpenPyXL will either change them or drop them altogether. For example, as of v3.0.5, OpenPyXL will rename charts and drop their title. Here is a simple editing example:

```
In [12]: # Read the stores.xlsx file, change a cell
         # and store it under a new location/name.
         book = openpyxl.load_workbook("xl/stores.xlsx")
         book["2019"]["A1"].value = "modified"
         book.save("stores_edited.xlsx")
```

If you want to write an *xlsm* file, OpenPyXL has to work off an existing file that you need to load with the keep_vba parameter set to True:

```
In [13]: book = openpyxl.load_workbook("xl/macro.xlsm", keep_vba=True)
         book["Sheet1"]["A1"].value = "Click the button!"
         book.save("macro_openpyxl.xlsm")
```

The button in the example file is calling a macro that shows a message box. Open-PyXL covers a lot more functionality than I am able to cover in this section; it is therefore a good idea to have a look at the official docs (*https://oreil.ly/7qfYL*). We will also see more functionality at the end of this chapter when we pick up the case study from the previous chapter again.

XlsxWriter

As the name suggests, XlsxWriter can only write Excel files. The following code produces the same workbook as we previously produced with OpenPyXL, which is shown in Figure 8-1. Note that XlsxWriter uses zero-based cell indices, while Open-PyXL uses one-based cell indices—make sure to take this into account if you switch between packages:

```
In [14]: import datetime as dt
         import xlsxwriter
         import excel

In [15]: # Instantiate a workbook
         book = xlsxwriter.Workbook("xlsxwriter.xlsx")

         # Add a sheet and give it a name
         sheet = book.add_worksheet("Sheet1")

         # Writing individual cells using A1 notation
         # and cell indices (0-based)
         sheet.write("A1", "Hello 1")
         sheet.write(1, 0, "Hello 2")

         # Formatting: fill color, alignment, border and font
         formatting = book.add_format({"font_color": "#FF0000",
                                       "bg_color": "#FFFF00",
                                       "bold": True, "align": "center",
                                       "border": 1, "border_color": "#FF0000"})
```

```
sheet.write("A3", "Hello 3", formatting)

# Number formatting (using Excel's formatting strings)
number_format = book.add_format({"num_format": "0.00"})
sheet.write("A4", 3.3333, number_format)

# Date formatting (using Excel's formatting strings)
date_format = book.add_format({"num_format": "mm/dd/yy"})
sheet.write("A5", dt.date(2016, 10, 13), date_format)

# Formula: you must use the English name of the formula
# with commas as delimiters
sheet.write("A6", "=SUM(A4, 2)")

# Image
sheet.insert_image(0, 2, "images/python.png")

# Two-dimensional list (we're using our excel module)
data = [[None, "North", "South"],
        ["Last Year", 2, 5],
        ["This Year", 3, 6]]
excel.write(sheet, data, "A10")

# Chart: see the file "sales_report_xlsxwriter.py" in the
# companion repo to see how you can work with indices
# instead of cell addresses
chart = book.add_chart({"type": "column"})
chart.set_title({"name": "Sales per Region"})
chart.add_series({"name": "=Sheet1!A11",
                  "categories": "=Sheet1!B10:C10",
                  "values": "=Sheet1!B11:C11"})
chart.add_series({"name": "=Sheet1!A12",
                  "categories": "=Sheet1!B10:C10",
                  "values": "=Sheet1!B12:C12"})
chart.set_x_axis({"name": "Regions"})
chart.set_y_axis({"name": "Sales"})
sheet.insert_chart("A15", chart)

# Closing the workbook creates the file on disk
book.close()
```

In comparison to OpenPyXL, XlsxWriter has to take a more complicated approach to write *xlsm* files as it is a pure writer package. First, you need to extract the macro code from an existing Excel file on the Anaconda Prompt (the example uses the *macro.xlsm* file, which you'll find in the *xl* folder of the companion repo):

Windows

Start by changing into the *xl* directory, then find the path to *vba_extract.py*, a script that comes with XlsxWriter:

```
(base)> cd C:\Users\username\python-for-excel\xl
(base)> where vba_extract.py
C:\Users\username\Anaconda3\Scripts\vba_extract.py
```

Then use this path in the following command:

```
(base)> python C:\...\Anaconda3\Scripts\vba_extract.py macro.xlsm
```

macOS

On macOS, the command is available as executable script and can be run like this:

```
(base)> cd /Users/username/python-for-excel/xl
(base)> vba_extract.py macro.xlsm
```

This will save the file *vbaProject.bin* in the directory where you are running the command. I have also included the extracted file in the *xl* folder of the companion repo. We will use it in the following sample to write a workbook with a macro button:

```
In [16]: book = xlsxwriter.Workbook("macro_xlsxwriter.xlsm")
         sheet = book.add_worksheet("Sheet1")
         sheet.write("A1", "Click the button!")
         book.add_vba_project("xl/vbaProject.bin")
         sheet.insert_button("A3", {"macro": "Hello", "caption": "Button 1",
                                     "width": 130, "height": 35})
         book.close()
```

pyxlsb

Compared to the other reader libraries, pyxlsb offers less functionality but it's your only option when it comes to reading Excel files in the binary *xlsb* format. pyxlsb is not part of Anaconda, so you will need to install it if you haven't already done this. It is currently not available via Conda either, so use pip to install it:

```
(base)> pip install pyxlsb
```

You read sheets and cell values as follows:

```
In [17]: import pyxlsb
         import excel
```

```
In [18]: # Loop through sheets. With pyxlsb, the workbook
         # and sheet objects can be used as context managers.
         # book.sheets returns a list of sheet names, not objects!
         # To get a sheet object, use get_sheet() instead.
         with pyxlsb.open_workbook("xl/stores.xlsb") as book:
             for sheet_name in book.sheets:
                 with book.get_sheet(sheet_name) as sheet:
                     dim = sheet.dimension
                     print(f"Sheet '{sheet_name}' has "
                           f"{dim.h} rows and {dim.w} cols")
```

```
Sheet '2019' has 7 rows and 5 cols
Sheet '2020' has 7 rows and 5 cols
Sheet '2019-2020' has 20 rows and 5 cols

In [19]: # Read in the values of a range of cells by using our excel module.
         # Instead of "2019", you could also use its index (1-based).
         with pyxlsb.open_workbook("xl/stores.xlsb") as book:
             with book.get_sheet("2019") as sheet:
                 data = excel.read(sheet, "B2")
         data[:2]  # Print the first two rows

Out[19]: [['Store', 'Employees', 'Manager', 'Since', 'Flagship'],
          ['New York', 10.0, 'Sarah', 43301.0, False]]
```

pyxlsb currently offers no way of recognizing cells with dates, so you will have to manually convert values from date-formatted cells into datetime objects like so:

```
In [20]: from pyxlsb import convert_date
         convert_date(data[1][3])

Out[20]: datetime.datetime(2018, 7, 20, 0, 0)
```

Remember, when you read the *xlsb* file format with a pandas version below 1.3, you need to specify the engine explicitly:

```
In [21]: df = pd.read_excel("xl/stores.xlsb", engine="pyxlsb")
```

xlrd, xlwt, and xlutils

The combination of xlrd, xlwt, and xlutils offers roughly the same functionality for the legacy *xls* format that OpenPyXL offers for the *xlsx* format: xlrd reads, xlwt writes, and xlutils edits *xls* files. These packages aren't actively developed anymore, but they are likely going to be relevant as long as there are still *xls* files around. xlutils is not part of Anaconda, so install it if you haven't already:

```
(base)> conda install xlutils
```

Let's get started with the reading part!

Reading with xlrd

The following sample code shows you how to read the values from an Excel workbook with xlrd:

```
In [22]: import xlrd
         import xlwt
         from xlwt.Utils import cell_to_rowcol2
         import xlutils
         import excel

In [23]: # Open the workbook to read cell values. The file is
         # automatically closed again after loading the data.
         book = xlrd.open_workbook("xl/stores.xls")
```

```
In [24]: # Get a list with all sheet names
         book.sheet_names()

Out[24]: ['2019', '2020', '2019-2020']

In [25]: # Loop through the sheet objects
         for sheet in book.sheets():
             print(sheet.name)

2019
2020
2019-2020

In [26]: # Get a sheet object by name or index (0-based)
         sheet = book.sheet_by_index(0)
         sheet = book.sheet_by_name("2019")

In [27]: # Dimensions
         sheet.nrows, sheet.ncols

Out[27]: (8, 6)

In [28]: # Read the value of a single cell
         # using "A1" notation and using cell indices (0-based).
         # The "*" unpacks the tuple that cell_to_rowcol2 returns
         # into individual arguments.
         sheet.cell(*cell_to_rowcol2("B3")).value
         sheet.cell(2, 1).value

Out[28]: 'New York'

In [29]: # Read in a range of cell values by using our excel module
         data = excel.read(sheet, "B2")
         data[:2]  # Print the first two rows

Out[29]: [['Store', 'Employees', 'Manager', 'Since', 'Flagship'],
          ['New York', 10.0, 'Sarah', datetime.datetime(2018, 7, 20, 0, 0),
          False]]
```

Used Range

Unlike OpenPyXL and pyxlsb, xlrd returns the dimensions of cells with a value, instead of the *used range* of a sheet when using sheet.nrows and sheet.ncols. What Excel returns as used range often contains empty rows and columns at the bottom and at the right border of the range. This can, for example, happen when you delete the content of rows (by hitting the Delete key), rather than deleting the rows themselves (by right-clicking and selecting Delete).

Writing with xlwt

The following code reproduces what we have done previously with OpenPyXL and XlsxWriter as shown in Figure 8-1. xlwt, however, cannot produce charts and only supports the bmp format for pictures:

```
In [30]: import xlwt
         from xlwt.Utils import cell_to_rowcol2
         import datetime as dt
         import excel

In [31]: # Instantiate a workbook
         book = xlwt.Workbook()

         # Add a sheet and give it a name
         sheet = book.add_sheet("Sheet1")

         # Writing individual cells using A1 notation
         # and cell indices (0-based)
         sheet.write(*cell_to_rowcol2("A1"), "Hello 1")
         sheet.write(r=1, c=0, label="Hello 2")

         # Formatting: fill color, alignment, border and font
         formatting = xlwt.easyxf("font: bold on, color red;"
                                  "align: horiz center;"
                                  "borders: top_color red, bottom_color red,"
                                        "right_color red, left_color red,"
                                        "left thin, right thin,"
                                        "top thin, bottom thin;"
                                  "pattern: pattern solid, fore_color yellow;")
         sheet.write(r=2, c=0, label="Hello 3", style=formatting)

         # Number formatting (using Excel's formatting strings)
         number_format = xlwt.easyxf(num_format_str="0.00")
         sheet.write(3, 0, 3.3333, number_format)

         # Date formatting (using Excel's formatting strings)
         date_format = xlwt.easyxf(num_format_str="mm/dd/yyyy")
         sheet.write(4, 0, dt.datetime(2012, 2, 3), date_format)

         # Formula: you must use the English name of the formula
         # with commas as delimiters
         sheet.write(5, 0, xlwt.Formula("SUM(A4, 2)"))

         # Two-dimensional list (we're using our excel module)
         data = [[None, "North", "South"],
                 ["Last Year", 2, 5],
                 ["This Year", 3, 6]]
         excel.write(sheet, data, "A10")

         # Picture (only allows to add bmp format)
         sheet.insert_bitmap("images/python.bmp", 0, 2)
```

```
# This writes the file to disk
book.save("xlwt.xls")
```

Editing with xlutils

xlutils acts as a bridge between xlrd and xlwt. This makes it explicit that this is not a true editing operation: the spreadsheet is read including the formatting via xlrd (by setting `formatting_info=True`) and then written out again by xlwt, including the changes that were made in between:

```
In [32]: import xlutils.copy

In [33]: book = xlrd.open_workbook("xl/stores.xls", formatting_info=True)
         book = xlutils.copy.copy(book)
         book.get_sheet(0).write(0, 0, "changed!")
         book.save("stores_edited.xls")
```

At this point, you know how to read and write an Excel workbook in a specific format. The next section moves on with a few advanced topics that include working with big Excel files and using pandas and the reader and writer packages together.

Advanced Reader and Writer Topics

If your files are bigger and more complex than the simple Excel files we used in the examples so far, relying on the default options may not be good enough anymore. Therefore, we start this section by looking at how to work with bigger files. Then, we'll learn how to use pandas together with the reader and writer packages: this will open up the ability to style your pandas DataFrames the way you want. To conclude this section, we will use everything we learned in this chapter to make the Excel report from last chapter's case study look much more professional.

Working with Big Excel Files

Working with big files can cause two issues: the reading and writing process may be slow or your computer may run out of memory. Usually, the memory issue is of bigger concern as it will cause your program to crash. When exactly a file is considered *big* always depends on the available resources on your system and your definition of *slow*. This section shows optimization techniques offered by the individual packages, allowing you to work with Excel files that push the limits. I'll start by looking at the options for the writer libraries, followed by the options for the reader libraries. At the end of this section, I'll show you how to read the sheets of a workbook in parallel to reduce processing time.

Writing with OpenPyXL

When writing large files with OpenPyXL, make sure to have the lxml package installed, as this makes the writing process faster. It is included in Anaconda, so there's nothing you need to do about that. The critical option, though, is the `write_only=True` flag, which makes sure that the memory consumption remains low. It, however, forces you to write row by row by using the `append` method and won't allow you to write single cells anymore:

```
In [34]: book = openpyxl.Workbook(write_only=True)
         # With write_only=True, book.active doesn't work
         sheet = book.create_sheet()
         # This will produce a sheet with 1000 x 200 cells
         for row in range(1000):
             sheet.append(list(range(200)))
         book.save("openpyxl_optimized.xlsx")
```

Writing with XlsxWriter

XlsxWriter has a similar option like OpenPyXL called `constant_memory`. It forces you to write sequential rows, too. You enable the option by providing an `options` dictionary like this:

```
In [35]: book = xlsxwriter.Workbook("xlsxwriter_optimized.xlsx",
                                     options={"constant_memory": True})
         sheet = book.add_worksheet()
         # This will produce a sheet with 1000 x 200 cells
         for row in range(1000):
             sheet.write_row(row , 0, list(range(200)))
         book.close()
```

Reading with xlrd

When reading big files in the legacy *xls* format, xlrd allows you to load sheets on demand, like this:

```
In [36]: with xlrd.open_workbook("xl/stores.xls", on_demand=True) as book:
             sheet = book.sheet_by_index(0)  # Only loads the first sheet
```

If you wouldn't use the workbook as a context manager as we do here, you would need to call `book.release_resources()` manually to properly close the workbook again. To use xlrd in this mode with pandas, use it like this:

```
In [37]: with xlrd.open_workbook("xl/stores.xls", on_demand=True) as book:
             with pd.ExcelFile(book, engine="xlrd") as f:
                 df = pd.read_excel(f, sheet_name=0)
```

Reading with OpenPyXL

To keep memory under control when reading big Excel files with OpenPyXL, you should load the workbook with `read_only=True`. However, when using `read_only=True`, OpenPyXL doesn't close the file automatically anymore, so you need to make sure to call the `close` method when you're done (OpenPyXL doesn't support the `with` statement). If your file contains links to external workbooks, you may additionally want to use `keep_links=False` to make it faster. `keep_links` makes sure that the references to external workbooks are kept, which may unnecessarily slow down the process if you are only interested in reading the values of a workbook:

```
In [38]: book = openpyxl.load_workbook("xl/big.xlsx",
                                       data_only=True, read_only=True,
                                       keep_links=False)
         # Perform the desired read operations here
         book.close()  # Required with read_only=True
```

Reading sheets in parallel

When you use pandas' `read_excel` function to read in multiple sheets of a big workbook, you will find that this takes a long time (we'll get to a concrete example in a moment). The reason is that pandas reads sheets sequentially, i.e., one after another. To speed things up, you could read the sheets in parallel. While there is no easy way to parallelize the writing of workbooks due to how the files are structured internally, reading multiple sheets in parallel is simple enough. However, since parallelization is an advanced topic, I left it out of the Python introduction and won't go into details here either.

In Python, if you want to take advantage of the multiple CPU cores that every modern computer has, you use the multiprocessing package that is part of the standard library. This will spawn multiple Python interpreters (usually one per CPU core), which work on a task in parallel. Instead of processing one sheet after another, you have one Python interpreter process the first sheet, while at the same time a second Python interpreter is processing the second sheet, etc. However, every additional Python interpreter takes some time to start up and uses additional memory, so if you have small files, they will most likely run slower when you parallelize the reading process instead of faster. In the case of a big file with multiple big sheets, multiprocessing can speed up the process substantially, though—always assuming that your system has the required memory to handle the workload. If you run the Jupyter notebook on Binder as shown in Chapter 2, you won't have enough memory and hence, the parallelized version will run slower. In the companion repo, you will find *parallel_pandas.py*, which is a simple implementation for reading the sheets in parallel, using OpenPyXL as the engine. It's simple to use, so you won't need to know anything about multiprocessing:

```
import parallel_pandas
parallel_pandas.read_excel(filename, sheet_name=None)
```

By default, it will read in all sheets but you can provide a list of sheet names that you want to process. Like pandas, the function returns a dictionary in the following form: {"sheetname": df}, i.e., keys are the sheet names and the values are the DataFrames.

The %%time Magic Command

In the following samples, I am going to make use of the %%time cell magic. I introduced magic commands in Chapter 5 in connection with Matplotlib. %%time is a cell magic that can be very useful for simple performance tuning as it makes it easy to compare the execution time of two cells with different code snippets. *Wall time* is the elapsed time from the start to the end of the program, i.e., the cell. If you are on macOS or Linux, you will not just get the wall time but an additional line for *CPU times* along these lines:

```
CPU times: user 49.4 s, sys: 108 ms, total: 49.5 s
```

CPU times measures the time spent on the CPU, which can be lower than the wall time (if the program has to wait for the CPU to become available) or higher (if the program is running on multiple CPU cores in parallel). To measure the time more accurately, use %%timeit instead of %%time, which runs the cell multiple times and takes the average of all runs. %%time and %%timeit are cell magics, i.e., they need to be on the first line of the cell and will measure the execution time of the whole cell. If, instead, you want to measure just a single line, start that line with %time or %timeit.

Let's see how much faster the parallelized version reads the *big.xlsx* file that you will find in the companion repo's *xl* folder:

```
In [39]: %%time
         data = pd.read_excel("xl/big.xlsx",
                              sheet_name=None, engine="openpyxl")

Wall time: 49.5 s

In [40]: %%time
         import parallel_pandas
         data = parallel_pandas.read_excel("xl/big.xlsx", sheet_name=None)

Wall time: 12.1 s
```

To get the DataFrame that represents Sheet1, you would write data["Sheet1"] in both cases. Looking at the wall time of both samples, you'll see that the parallelized version was multiple times faster than pd.read_excel with this particular workbook and on my laptop with 6 CPU cores. If you want it even faster, parallelize OpenPyXL directly: you will also find an implementation for that in the companion repository (*parallel_openpyxl.py*), together with an implementation for xlrd to read the legacy *xls* format in parallel (*parallel_xlrd.py*). Going through the underlying packages instead of pandas will allow you to skip the transformation into a DataFrame or only apply the cleaning steps that you need, which will most likely help you make things faster—if that is your biggest concern.

Reading a Sheet in Parallel with Modin

If you are only reading in one huge sheet, it is worth looking at Modin (*https://oreil.ly/wQszH*), a project that acts as a drop-in replacement for pandas. It parallelizes the reading process of a single sheet and provides impressive speed improvements. Since Modin requires a specific version of pandas, it could downgrade the version that comes with Anaconda when you install it. If you want to test it, I would recommend that you create a separate Conda environment for this to ensure you are not messing up your base environment. See Appendix A for more detailed instructions on how to create a Conda environment:

```
(base)> conda create --name modin python=3.8 -y
(base)> conda activate modin
(modin)> conda install -c conda-forge modin -y
```

On my machine and using the *big.xlsx* file, running the following code took roughly five seconds while it took pandas about twelve seconds:

```
import modin.pandas
data = modin.pandas.read_excel("xl/big.xlsx",
                               sheet_name=0, engine="openpyxl")
```

Now that you know how to deal with big files, let's move on and see how we can use pandas and the low-level packages together to improve the default formatting when writing DataFrames to Excel files!

Formatting DataFrames in Excel

To format DataFrames in Excel the way we want, we can write code that uses pandas together with OpenPyXL or XlsxWriter. We'll first use this combination to add a title to the exported DataFrame. We'll then format a DataFrame's header and index before wrapping this section up by formatting the data part of a DataFrame. Combining pandas with OpenPyXL for reading can also be occasionally useful, so let's start with this:

```
In [41]: with pd.ExcelFile("xl/stores.xlsx", engine="openpyxl") as xlfile:
             # Read a DataFrame
             df = pd.read_excel(xlfile, sheet_name="2020")

             # Get the OpenPyXL workbook object
             book = xlfile.book
```

```
# From here on, it's OpenPyXL code
sheet = book["2019"]
value = sheet["B3"].value  # Read a single value
```

When writing workbooks, it works analogously, allowing us to easily add a title to our DataFrame report:

```
In [42]: with pd.ExcelWriter("pandas_and_openpyxl.xlsx",
                             engine="openpyxl") as writer:
             df = pd.DataFrame({"col1": [1, 2, 3, 4], "col2": [5, 6, 7, 8]})
             # Write a DataFrame
             df.to_excel(writer, "Sheet1", startrow=4, startcol=2)

             # Get the OpenPyXL workbook and sheet objects
             book = writer.book
             sheet = writer.sheets["Sheet1"]

             # From here on, it's OpenPyXL code
             sheet["A1"].value = "This is a Title"  # Write a single cell value
```

These samples use OpenPyXL, but it works conceptually the same with the other packages. Let's now continue with finding out how we can format the index and header of a DataFrame.

Formatting a DataFrame's index and headers

The easiest way to get complete control over the formatting of the index and column headers is to simply write them yourself. The following sample shows you how to do this with OpenPyXL and XlsxWriter, respectively. You can see the output in Figure 8-2. Let's start by creating a DataFrame:

```
In [43]: df = pd.DataFrame({"col1": [1, -2], "col2": [-3, 4]},
                           index=["row1", "row2"])
         df.index.name = "ix"
         df

Out[43]:       col1  col2
         ix
         row1     1    -3
         row2    -2     4
```

To format the index and headers with OpenPyXL, do as follows:

```
In [44]: from openpyxl.styles import PatternFill

In [45]: with pd.ExcelWriter("formatting_openpyxl.xlsx",
                             engine="openpyxl") as writer:
             # Write out the df with the default formatting to A1
             df.to_excel(writer, startrow=0, startcol=0)

             # Write out the df with custom index/header formatting to A6
             startrow, startcol = 0, 5
             # 1. Write out the data part of the DataFrame
```

```
df.to_excel(writer, header=False, index=False,
            startrow=startrow + 1, startcol=startcol + 1)
# Get the sheet object and create a style object
sheet = writer.sheets["Sheet1"]
style = PatternFill(fgColor="D9D9D9", fill_type="solid")

# 2. Write out the styled column headers
for i, col in enumerate(df.columns):
    sheet.cell(row=startrow + 1, column=i + startcol + 2,
               value=col).fill = style

# 3. Write out the styled index
index = [df.index.name if df.index.name else None] + list(df.index)
for i, row in enumerate(index):
    sheet.cell(row=i + startrow + 1, column=startcol + 1,
               value=row).fill = style
```

To format the index and headers with XlsxWriter instead, you'll need to adjust the code slightly:

```
In [46]: # Formatting index/headers with XlsxWriter
         with pd.ExcelWriter("formatting_xlsxwriter.xlsx",
                             engine="xlsxwriter") as writer:
             # Write out the df with the default formatting to A1
             df.to_excel(writer, startrow=0, startcol=0)

             # Write out the df with custom index/header formatting to A6
             startrow, startcol = 0, 5
             # 1. Write out the data part of the DataFrame
             df.to_excel(writer, header=False, index=False,
                         startrow=startrow + 1, startcol=startcol + 1)
             # Get the book and sheet object and create a style object
             book = writer.book
             sheet = writer.sheets["Sheet1"]
             style = book.add_format({"bg_color": "#D9D9D9"})

             # 2. Write out the styled column headers
             for i, col in enumerate(df.columns):
                 sheet.write(startrow, startcol + i + 1, col, style)

             # 3. Write out the styled index
             index = [df.index.name if df.index.name else None] + list(df.index)
             for i, row in enumerate(index):
                 sheet.write(startrow + i, startcol, row, style)
```

With the index and header formatted, let's see how we can style the data part!

▲	A	B	C	D	E	F	G	H
1	ix	col1	col2			ix	col1	col2
2	row1	1	3			row1	1	3
3	row2	2	4			row2	2	4

Figure 8-2. A DataFrame with the default format (left) and with a custom format (right)

Formatting a DataFrame's data part

The possibilities you have to format the data part of a DataFrame depend on the package you're using: if you use pandas' `to_excel` method, OpenPyXL can apply a format to each cell, while XlsxWriter can only apply formats on a row or column basis. For example, to set the number format of the cells to three decimals and center-align the content as shown in Figure 8-3, do the following with OpenPyXL:

```
In [47]: from openpyxl.styles import Alignment

In [48]: with pd.ExcelWriter("data_format_openpyxl.xlsx",
                             engine="openpyxl") as writer:
             # Write out the DataFrame
             df.to_excel(writer)

             # Get the book and sheet objects
             book = writer.book
             sheet = writer.sheets["Sheet1"]

             # Formatting individual cells
             nrows, ncols = df.shape
             for row in range(nrows):
                 for col in range(ncols):
                     # +1 to account for the header/index
                     # +1 since OpenPyXL is 1-based
                     cell = sheet.cell(row=row + 2,
                                       column=col + 2)
                     cell.number_format = "0.000"
                     cell.alignment = Alignment(horizontal="center")
```

For XlsxWriter, adjust the code as follows:

```
In [49]: with pd.ExcelWriter("data_format_xlsxwriter.xlsx",
                             engine="xlsxwriter") as writer:
             # Write out the DataFrame
             df.to_excel(writer)

             # Get the book and sheet objects
             book = writer.book
             sheet = writer.sheets["Sheet1"]

             # Formatting the columns (individual cells can't be formatted)
             number_format = book.add_format({"num_format": "0.000",
                                              "align": "center"})
```

```
sheet.set_column(first_col=1, last_col=2,
                 cell_format=number_format)
```

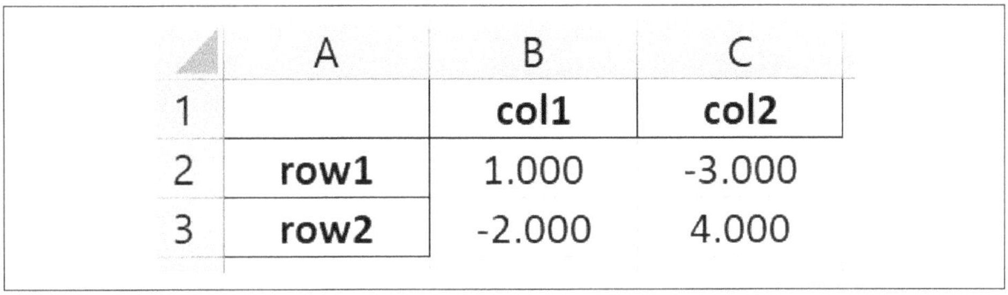

◢	A	B	C
1		col1	col2
2	row1	1.000	-3.000
3	row2	-2.000	4.000

Figure 8-3. A DataFrame with a formatted data part

As an alternative, pandas offers *experimental* support for the `style` property of Data-Frames. Experimental means that the syntax can change at any point in time. Since styles were introduced to format the DataFrames in HTML format, they use CSS syntax. CSS stands for *cascading style sheets* and is used to define the style of HTML elements. To apply the same format as in the previous example (three decimals and center align), you'll need to apply a function to every element of a `Styler` object via `applymap`. You get a `Styler` object via the `df.style` attribute:

```
In [50]: df.style.applymap(lambda x: "number-format: 0.000;"
                                     "text-align: center")\
         .to_excel("styled.xlsx")
```

The outcome of this code is the same as shown in Figure 8-3. For more details on the DataFrame style approach, please refer directly to the styling docs (*https://oreil.ly/_JzfP*).

Without having to rely on the style attribute, pandas offers support to format the date and datetime objects as shown in Figure 8-4:

```
In [51]: df = pd.DataFrame({"Date": [dt.date(2020, 1, 1)],
                            "Datetime": [dt.datetime(2020, 1, 1, 10)]})
         with pd.ExcelWriter("date.xlsx",
                             date_format="yyyy-mm-dd",
                             datetime_format="yyyy-mm-dd hh:mm:ss") as writer:
             df.to_excel(writer)
```

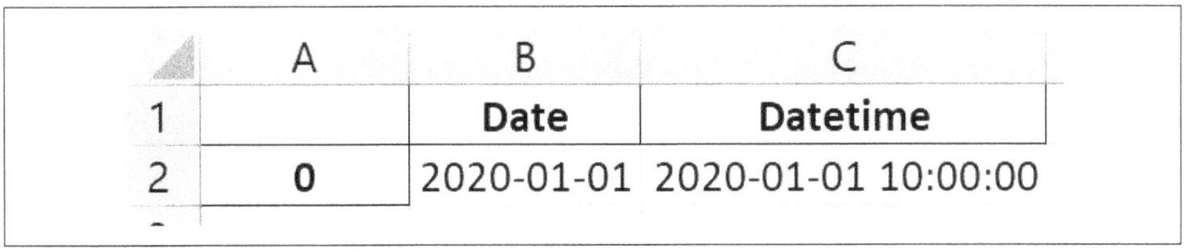

◢	A	B	C
1		Date	Datetime
2	0	2020-01-01	2020-01-01 10:00:00

Figure 8-4. A DataFrame with formatted dates

Other Reader and Writer Packages

Apart from the packages that we have looked at in this chapter, there are a few others that may be interesting for specific use cases:

pyexcel
> pyexcel (*http://pyexcel.org*) offers a harmonized syntax across different Excel packages and other file formats including CSV files and OpenOffice files.

PyExcelerate
> The goal of PyExcelerate (*https://oreil.ly/yJax7*) is to write Excel files in the fastest possible way.

pylightxl
> pylightxl (*https://oreil.ly/efjt4*) can read *xlsx* and *xlsm* files and write *xlsx* files.

styleframe
> styleframe (*https://oreil.ly/nQUg9*) wraps pandas and OpenPyXL to produce Excel files with nicely formatted DataFrames.

oletools
> oletools (*https://oreil.ly/SG-Jy*) is not a classic reader or writer package but can be used to analyze Microsoft Office documents, e.g., for malware analysis. It offers a convenient way to extract VBA code from Excel workbooks.

Now that you know how to format DataFrames in Excel, it's time to take another stab at the case study from the previous chapter and see if we can improve the Excel report with the knowledge of this chapter!

Case Study (Revisited): Excel Reporting

Having made it to the end of this chapter, you know enough to be able to go back to the Excel report from last chapter's case study and make it visually more appealing. If you like, go back to *sales_report_pandas.py* in the companion repository and try to turn it into the report as shown in Figure 8-5.

The red numbers are sales figures that are below 20,000. I haven't touched every aspect of formatting in this chapter (like how to apply conditional formatting), so you will have to use the documentation of the package you choose to work with. To compare your solution, I have included two versions of the script that produce this report in the companion repo. The first version is based on OpenPyXL (*sales_report_openpyxl.py*) and the other one is based on XlsxWriter (*sales_report_xlsxwriter.py*). Seeing the scripts side-by-side may also allow you to make a more educated decision about which package you want to pick for your next writer task. We will get back to this case study one more time in the next chapter: there, we'll rely on an installation of Microsoft Excel to work with report templates.

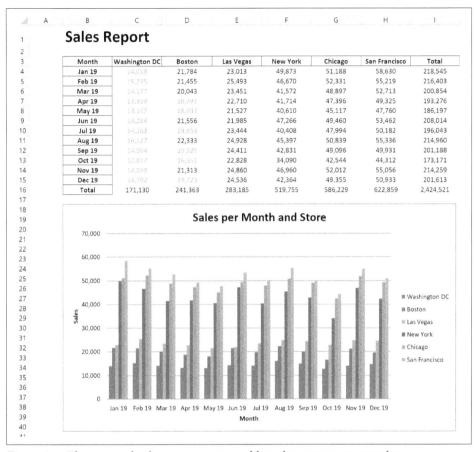

Figure 8-5. The revisited sales report as created by sales_report_openpyxl.py

Conclusion

In this chapter, I introduced you to the reader and writer packages that pandas uses under the hood. Using them directly allows us to read and write Excel workbooks without needing to have pandas installed. However, using them in combination with pandas enables us to enhance the Excel DataFrame reports by adding titles, charts, and formatting. While the current reader and writer packages are incredibly power-ful, I still hope that we'll see a "NumPy moment" one day that unites the efforts of all the developers into a single project. It would be great to know which package to use without having to look at a table first and without having to use a different syntax for each type of Excel file. In that sense, it makes sense to start with pandas and only fall back to the reader and writer packages when you need additional functionality that pandas doesn't cover.

Excel, however, is so much more than just a data file or a report: the Excel application is one of the most intuitive user interfaces where users can type in a few numbers and get it to display the information they are looking for. Automating the Excel application instead of reading and writing Excel files opens up a whole new range of functionality that we are going to explore in Part IV. The next chapter starts this journey by showing you how to control Excel from Python remotely.

## PART IV

Programming the Excel Application with xlwings

## CHAPTER 9

Excel Automation

So far, we've learned how to replace typical Excel tasks with pandas (Part II) and how to use Excel files both as a data source as well as a file format for your reports (Part III). This chapter kicks off Part IV, where we switch away from manipulating Excel *files* with the reader and writer packages and begin automating the Excel *application* with xlwings.

The main use case of xlwings is to build interactive applications where Excel spreadsheets act as the user interface, allowing you to call Python by clicking a button or calling a user-defined function—that's the type of functionality that isn't covered by the reader and writer packages. But that doesn't mean that xlwings can't be used to read and write files, as long as you are on either macOS or Windows and have Excel installed. One advantage that xlwings has in this area is the ability to truly edit Excel files, in all formats, without changing or losing any of the existing content or formatting. Another advantage is that you can read the cell values from an Excel workbook without the need to save it first. It can, however, also make perfect sense to use an Excel reader/writer package and xlwings together, as we will see when we pick up the reporting case study from Chapter 7 one more time.

I'll start this chapter by introducing you to the Excel object model as well as xlwings: we'll first learn the basics like connecting to a workbook or reading and writing cell values before digging a bit deeper to understand how converters and options allow us to work with pandas DataFrames and NumPy arrays. We also look at how to interact with charts, pictures, and defined names before moving on to the last section, which explains how xlwings works under the hood: this will give you the required knowledge to make your scripts performant as well as work around missing functionality.

From this chapter on, you will need to run the code samples on either Windows or macOS, as they depend on a local installation of Microsoft Excel.[1]

Getting Started with xlwings

One goal of xlwings is to serve as a drop-in replacement for VBA, allowing you to interact with Excel from Python on Windows and macOS. Since Excel's grid is the perfect layout to display Python's data structures like nested lists, NumPy arrays, and pandas DataFrames, one of xlwings' core features is to make reading and writing them from and to Excel as easy as possible. I'll start this section by introducing you to Excel as a data viewer—this is useful when you are interacting with DataFrames in a Jupyter notebook. I'll then explain the Excel object model before exploring it interactively with xlwings. To wrap this section up, I'll show you how to call VBA code that you may still have in legacy workbooks. Since xlwings is part of Anaconda, we don't need to install it manually.

Using Excel as Data Viewer

You probably noticed in the previous chapters that by default, Jupyter notebooks hide the majority of data for bigger DataFrames and only show the top and bottom rows as well as the first and last few columns. One way to get a better feeling for your data is to plot it—this allows you to spot outliers or other irregularities. Sometimes, however, it's just really helpful to be able to scroll through a data table. After reading Chapter 7, you know how to use the to_excel method on your DataFrame. While this works, it can be a bit cumbersome: you need to give the Excel file a name, find it on the file system, open it, and, after making changes to your DataFrame, you need to close the Excel file and run the whole process again. A better idea may be to run df.to_clipboard(), which copies the DataFrame df to the clipboard, allowing you to paste it into Excel, but there is an even simpler way—use the view function that comes with xlwings:

```
In [1]: # First, let's import the packages that we'll use in this chapter
        import datetime as dt
        import xlwings as xw
        import pandas as pd
        import numpy as np
```

---

1 On Windows, you need at least Excel 2007, and on macOS, you need at least Excel 2016. Alternatively, you can install the desktop version of Excel, which is part of your Microsoft 365 subscription. Check your subscription for details on how to do this.

```
In [2]: # Let's create a DataFrame based on pseudorandom numbers and
        # with enough rows that only the head and tail are shown
        df = pd.DataFrame(data=np.random.randn(100, 5),
                          columns=[f"Trial {i}" for i in range(1, 6)])
        df

Out[2]:     Trial 1   Trial 2   Trial 3   Trial 4   Trial 5
        0  -1.313877  1.164258 -1.306419 -0.529533 -0.524978
        1  -0.854415  0.022859 -0.246443 -0.229146 -0.005493
        2  -0.327510 -0.492201 -1.353566 -1.229236  0.024385
        3  -0.728083 -0.080525  0.628288 -0.382586 -0.590157
        4  -1.227684  0.498541 -0.266466  0.297261 -1.297985
        ..       ...       ...       ...       ...       ...
        95 -0.903446  1.103650  0.033915  0.336871  0.345999
        96 -1.354898 -1.290954 -0.738396 -1.102659  0.115076
        97 -0.070092 -0.416991 -0.203445 -0.686915 -1.163205
        98 -1.201963  0.471854 -0.458501 -0.357171  1.954585
        99  1.863610  0.214047 -1.426806  0.751906 -2.338352

        [100 rows x 5 columns]

In [3]: # View the DataFrame in Excel
        xw.view(df)
```

The view function accepts all common Python objects, including numbers, strings, lists, dictionaries, tuples, NumPy arrays, and pandas DataFrames. By default, it opens a new workbook and pastes the object into cell A1 of the first sheet—it even adjusts the column widths by using Excel's AutoFit functionality. Instead of opening a new workbook every time, you can also reuse the same one by providing the view function an xlwings sheet object as the second argument: xw.view(df, mysheet). How you get access to such a sheet object and how it fits into the Excel object model is what I will explain next.[2]

---

2 Note that xlwings 0.22.0 introduced the xw.load function, which is similar to xw.view, but works in the opposite direction: it allows you to load an Excel range easily into a Jupyter notebook as a pandas DataFrame, see the docs (*https://oreil.ly/x7sTR*).

The Excel Object Model

When you work with Excel programmatically, you interact with its components like a workbook or a sheet. These components are organized in the *Excel object model*, a hierarchical structure that represents Excel's graphical user interface (see Figure 9-1). Microsoft largely uses the same object model with all programming languages they officially support, whether that's VBA, Office Scripts (the JavaScript interface for Excel on the web), or C#. In contrast to the reader and writer packages from Chapter 8, xlwings follows the Excel object model very closely, only with a breath of fresh air: for example, xlwings uses the names `app` instead of `application` and `book` instead of `workbook`:

- An `app` contains the `books` collection
- A `book` contains the `sheets` collection
- A `sheet` gives access to `range` objects and collections such as `charts`
- A `range` contains one or more contiguous cells as its items

The dashed boxes are *collections* and contain one or more objects of the same type. An `app` corresponds to an Excel instance, i.e., an Excel application that runs as a separate process. Power users sometimes use multiple Excel instances in parallel to open the same workbook twice, for example, to calculate a workbook with different inputs in parallel. With the more recent versions of Excel, Microsoft made it slightly more complicated to open multiple instances of Excel manually: start Excel, then right-click on its icon in the Windows taskbar. In the appearing menu, left-click on the Excel entry while holding down the Alt key at the same time (make sure to keep the Alt key pressed until after you release your mouse button)—a pop-up will ask if you want to start a new instance of Excel. On macOS, there is no manual way of launching more than one instance of the same program but you can launch multiple Excel instances programmatically via xlwings, as we will see later. To summarize, an Excel instance is a *sandboxed* environment, which means that one instance can't communicate with the other one.[3] The `sheet` object gives you access to collections like charts, pictures, and defined names—topics that we will look into in the second section of this chapter.

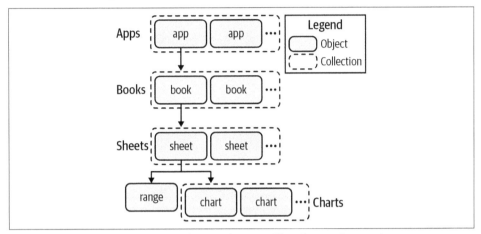

Figure 9-1. The Excel object model as implemented by xlwings (excerpt)

Language and Regional Settings

This book is based on the US-English version of Excel. I will occasionally refer to default names like "Book1" or "Sheet1," which will be different if you use Excel in another language. For example, "Sheet1" is called "Feuil1" in French and "Hoja1" in Spanish. Also, the *list separator*, which is the separator that Excel uses in cell formulas, depends on your settings: I will be using the comma, but your version may require a semicolon or another character. For example, instead of writing =SUM(A1, A2), you will need to write =SUMME(A1; A2) on a computer with German regional settings. Further traps to look out for are TRUE or FALSE and the decimal point: for example, with German regional settings, TRUE is called WAHR while the decimal point is a comma instead of a point.

On Windows, if you wanted to change the list separator from a semicolon to a comma, you need to change it outside of Excel via your Windows settings: click on the Windows start button, search for Settings (or click the cog icon), then go to "Time

---

3 See "What are Excel instances, and why is this important?" (*https://oreil.ly/L2FDT*) for more information about separate Excel instances.

& Language" > "Region & language" > "Additional date, time & regional settings" where you finally click on "Region" > "Change location." Under "List separator," you will be able to change it from a semicolon to a comma. Bear in mind that this only works if your "Decimal symbol" (in the same menu) is not also a comma. To override the system-wide decimal and thousands separators (but not the list separator), in Excel go to "Options" > "Advanced," where you will find the settings under "Editing Options."

On macOS, it works similarly, except that you can't change the list separator directly: under System Preferences of your macOS (not Excel), select Language & Region. There, set a specific region either globally (under the General tab) or specifically for Excel (under the Apps tab).

To get a feeling for the Excel object model, as usual, it's best to play around with it interactively. Let's start with the Book class: it allows you to create new workbooks and connect to existing ones; see Table 9-1 for an overview.

Table 9-1. Working with Excel workbooks

Command	Description
xw.Book()	Returns a book object representing a new Excel workbook in the active Excel instance. If there is no active instance, Excel will be started.
xw.Book("Book1")	Returns a book object representing an unsaved workbook with the name Book1 (name without file extension).
xw.Book("Book1.xlsx")	Returns a book object representing a previously saved workbook with the name *Book1.xlsx* (name with file extension). The file has to be either open or in the current working directory.
xw.Book(r"C:\path\Book1.xlsx")	Returns a book object of a previously saved workbook (full file path). The file can be open or closed. The leading r turns the string into a raw string so the backslashes (\) of the path are interpreted literally on Windows (I introduced raw strings in Chapter 5). On macOS, the r isn't required as file paths use forward slashes instead of backslashes.
xw.books.active	Returns a book object representing the active workbook in the active Excel instance.

Let's see how we can walk through the object model hierarchy from the book object down to the range object:

```
In [4]: # Create a new empty workbook and print its name. This is the
        # book we will use to run most of the code samples in this chapter.
        book = xw.Book()
        book.name

Out[4]: 'Book2'

In [5]: # Accessing the sheets collection
        book.sheets
```

```
Out[5]: Sheets([<Sheet [Book2]Sheet1>])

In [6]: # Get a sheet object by index or name. You will need to adjust
        # "Sheet1" if your sheet is called differently.
        sheet1 = book.sheets[0]
        sheet1 = book.sheets["Sheet1"]

In [7]: sheet1.range("A1")

Out[7]: <Range [Book2]Sheet1!$A$1>
```

With the `range` object, we have arrived at the bottom of the hierarchy. The string that gets printed in between angle brackets gives you useful information about that object, but to do something, you usually use the object with an attribute, as the next sample shows:

```
In [8]: # Most common tasks: write values...
        sheet1.range("A1").value = [[1, 2],
                                    [3, 4]]
        sheet1.range("A4").value = "Hello!"

In [9]: # ...and read values
        sheet1.range("A1:B2").value

Out[9]: [[1.0, 2.0], [3.0, 4.0]]

In [10]: sheet1.range("A4").value

Out[10]: 'Hello!'
```

As you can see, by default, the `value` attribute of an xlwings `range` object accepts and returns a nested list for two-dimensional ranges and a scalar for a single cell. Everything we've used so far is almost identical to VBA: assuming that `book` is a VBA or xlwings workbook object, respectively, this is how you access the `value` attribute from cells A1 to B2 in VBA and with xlwings:

```
book.Sheets(1).Range("A1:B2").Value  # VBA
book.sheets[0].range("A1:B2").value  # xlwings
```

The differences are:

Attributes

Python uses lowercase letters, potentially with underscores as suggested by PEP 8, Python's style guide that I introduced in Chapter 3.

Indexing

Python uses square brackets and zero-based indices to access an element in the `sheets` collection.

Table 9-2 gives you an overview of the strings that an xlwings `range` accepts.

Table 9-2. Strings to define a range in A1 notation

Reference	Description
"A1"	A Single Cell
"A1:B2"	Cells from A1 to B2
"A:A"	Column A
"A:B"	Columns A to B
"1:1"	Row 1
"1:2"	Rows 1 to 2

Indexing and slicing work with xlwings range objects—watch the address in between angle brackets (the printed object representation) to see what cell range you end up with:

```
In [11]: # Indexing
         sheet1.range("A1:B2")[0, 0]

Out[11]: <Range [Book2]Sheet1!$A$1>

In [12]: # Slicing
         sheet1.range("A1:B2")[:, 1]

Out[12]: <Range [Book2]Sheet1!$B$1:$B$2>
```

Indexing corresponds to using the Cells property in VBA:

```
book.Sheets(1).Range("A1:B2").Cells(1, 1)  # VBA
book.sheets[0].range("A1:B2")[0, 0]  # xlwings
```

Instead of using range explicitly as an attribute of the sheet object, you can also get a range object by indexing and slicing the sheet object. Using this with A1 notation will allow you to type less, and using this with integer indices makes the Excel sheet feel like a NumPy array:

```
In [13]: # Single cell: A1 notation
         sheet1["A1"]

Out[13]: <Range [Book2]Sheet1!$A$1>

In [14]: # Multiple cells: A1 notation
         sheet1["A1:B2"]

Out[14]: <Range [Book2]Sheet1!$A$1:$B$2>

In [15]: # Single cell: indexing
         sheet1[0, 0]

Out[15]: <Range [Book2]Sheet1!$A$1>

In [16]: # Multiple cells: slicing
         sheet1[:2, :2]
```

```
Out[16]: <Range [Book2]Sheet1!$A$1:$B$2>
```

Sometimes, however, it may be more intuitive to define a range by referring to the top-left and bottom-right cell of a range. The following samples refer to the cell ranges D10 and D10:F11, respectively, allowing you to understand the difference between indexing/slicing a sheet object and working with a range object:

```
In [17]: # D10 via sheet indexing
         sheet1[9, 3]

Out[17]: <Range [Book2]Sheet1!$D$10>

In [18]: # D10 via range object
         sheet1.range((10, 4))

Out[18]: <Range [Book2]Sheet1!$D$10>

In [19]: # D10:F11 via sheet slicing
         sheet1[9:11, 3:6]

Out[19]: <Range [Book2]Sheet1!$D$10:$F$11>

In [20]: # D10:F11 via range object
         sheet1.range((10, 4), (11, 6))

Out[20]: <Range [Book2]Sheet1!$D$10:$F$11>
```

Defining range objects with tuples is very similar to how the Cells property works in VBA, as the following comparison shows—this assumes again that book is either a VBA workbook object or an xlwings book object. Let's first look at the VBA version:

```
With book.Sheets(1)
    myrange = .Range(.Cells(10, 4), .Cells(11, 6))
End With
```

This is equivalent to the following xlwings expression:

```
myrange = book.sheets[0].range((10, 4), (11, 6))
```

Zero vs. One-Based Indices

As a Python package, xlwings consistently uses zero-based indexing whenever you access elements via Python's index or slice syntax, i.e., via square brackets. xlwings range objects, however, use Excel's one-based row and column indices. Having the same row/column indices as Excel's user interface may sometimes be beneficial. If you prefer to only ever use Python's zero-based indexing, simply use the sheet[row_selection, column_selection] syntax.

The following sample shows you how to get from a range object (sheet1["A1"]) all the way up again to the app object. Remember that the app object represents an Excel instance (the output in between angle brackets represents Excel's process ID and will therefore be different on your machine):

```
In [21]: sheet1["A1"].sheet.book.app

Out[21]: <Excel App 9092>
```

Having arrived at the very top of the Excel object model, it's a good moment to see how you can work with multiple Excel instances. You will need to use the app object explicitly if you want to open the same workbook in multiple Excel instances or if you specifically want to distribute your workbooks across different instances for perfor-mance reasons. Another common use case for working with an app object is to open your workbook in a hidden Excel instance: this allows you to run an xlwings script in the background without blocking you from doing other work in Excel in the mean-time:

```
In [22]: # Get one app object from the open workbook
         # and create an additional invisible app instance
         visible_app = sheet1.book.app
         invisible_app = xw.App(visible=False)

In [23]: # List the book names that are open in each instance
         # by using a list comprehension
         [book.name for book in visible_app.books]

Out[23]: ['Book1', 'Book2']

In [24]: [book.name for book in invisible_app.books]

Out[24]: ['Book3']

In [25]: # An app key represents the process ID (PID)
         xw.apps.keys()

Out[25]: [5996, 9092]

In [26]: # It can also be accessed via the pid attribute
         xw.apps.active.pid

Out[26]: 5996

In [27]: # Work with the book in the invisible Excel instance
         invisible_book = invisible_app.books[0]
         invisible_book.sheets[0]["A1"].value = "Created by an invisible app."

In [28]: # Save the Excel workbook in the xl directory
         invisible_book.save("xl/invisible.xlsx")

In [29]: # Quit the invisible Excel instance
         invisible_app.quit()
```

macOS: Accessing the File System Programmatically

If you run the save command on macOS, you will get a Grant File Access pop-up in Excel that you will need to confirm by clicking the Select button before clicking on Grant Access. On macOS, Excel is *sandboxed*, which means that your program can only access files and folders outside of the Excel app by confirming this prompt. Once confirmed, Excel will remember the locations and won't bug you again when you run the script the next time.

If you have the same workbook open in two instances of Excel or if you want to specify in which Excel instance you want to open a workbook, you can't use xw.Book anymore. Instead, you need to use the books collection as laid out in Table 9-3. Note that myapp stands for an xlwings app object. If you would replace myapp.books with xw.books instead, xlwings will use the active app.

Table 9-3. Working with the books collection

Command	Description
myapp.books.add()	Creates a new Excel workbook in the Excel instance that myapp refers to and returns the corresponding book object.
myapp.books.open(r"C:\path\Book.xlsx")	Returns the book if it's already open, otherwise opens it first in the Excel instance that myapp refers to. Remember that the leading r turns the file path into a raw string to interpret the backslashes literally.
myapp.books["Book1.xlsx"]	Returns the book object if it's open. This will raise a KeyError if it isn't open yet. Make sure to use the name and not the full path. Use this if you need to know if a workbook is already open in Excel.

Before we dive deeper into how xlwings can *replace* your VBA macros, let's see how xlwings can *interact* with your existing VBA code: this can be useful if you have a lot of legacy code and don't have the time to migrate everything to Python.

Running VBA Code

If you have legacy Excel projects with lots of VBA code, it may be a lot of work to migrate everything to Python. In that case, you can use Python to run your VBA macros. The following sample uses the *vba.xlsm* file that you will find in the *xl* folder of the companion repo. It contains the following code in Module1:

```
Function MySum(x As Double, y As Double) As Double
    MySum = x + y
End Function
```

```
Sub ShowMsgBox(msg As String)
    MsgBox msg
End Sub
```

To call these functions via Python, you first need to instantiate an xlwings `macro` object that you subsequently call, making it feel as if it was a native Python function:

```
In [30]: vba_book = xw.Book("xl/vba.xlsm")
```

```
In [31]: # Instantiate a macro object with the VBA function
         mysum = vba_book.macro("Module1.MySum")
         # Call a VBA function
         mysum(5, 4)
```

```
Out[31]: 9.0
```

```
In [32]: # It works the same with a VBA Sub procedure
         show_msgbox = vba_book.macro("Module1.ShowMsgBox")
         show_msgbox("Hello xlwings!")
```

```
In [33]: # Close the book again (make sure to close the MessageBox first)
         vba_book.close()
```

Don't Store VBA Functions in Sheet and ThisWorkbook Modules

If you store the VBA function MySum in the workbook module This Workbook or a sheet module (e.g., Sheet1), you have to refer to it as ThisWorkbook.MySum or Sheet1.MySum. However, you won't be able to access the function's return value from Python, so make sure to store VBA functions in a standard VBA code module that you insert by right-clicking on the Modules folder in the VBA editor.

Now that you know how to interact with existing VBA code, we can continue our exploration of xlwings by looking at how to use it with DataFrames, NumPy arrays, and collections like charts, pictures, and defined names.

Converters, Options, and Collections

In the introductory code samples of this chapter, we were already reading and writing a string and a nested list from and to Excel by using the `value` attribute of an xlwings `range` object. I'll start this section by showing you how this works with pandas Data-Frames before having a closer look at the `options` method that allows us to influence how xlwings reads and writes values. We move on with charts, pictures, and defined names, the collections that you usually access from a `sheet` object. Armed with these xlwings basics, we'll have another look at the reporting case study from Chapter 7.

Working with DataFrames

Writing a DataFrame to Excel is no different from writing a scalar or a nested list to Excel: simply assign the DataFrame to the top-left cell of an Excel range:

```
In [34]: data = [["Mark", 55, "Italy", 4.5, "Europe"],
                  ["John", 33, "USA", 6.7, "America"]]
         df = pd.DataFrame(data=data,
                           columns=["name", "age", "country",
                                    "score", "continent"],
                           index=[1001, 1000])
         df.index.name = "user_id"
         df

Out[34]:          name  age country  score continent
         user_id
         1001     Mark   55   Italy    4.5    Europe
         1000     John   33     USA    6.7   America

In [35]: sheet1["A6"].value = df
```

If, however, you would like to suppress the column headers and/or the index, use the options method like this:

```
In [36]: sheet1["B10"].options(header=False, index=False).value = df
```

Reading Excel ranges as DataFrames requires you to provide the DataFrame class as the convert parameter in the options method. By default, it expects that your data has both a header and index, but you can again use the index and header parameters to change this. Instead of using the converter, you could also read in the values first as a nested list and then manually construct your DataFrame, but using the converter makes it quite a bit easier to handle the index and header.

The expand Method

In the following code sample, I am introducing the expand method that makes it easy to read a contiguous block of cells, delivering the same range as if you were doing Shift+Ctrl+Down-Arrow+Right-Arrow in Excel, except that expand jumps over an empty cell in the top-left corner.

```
In [37]: df2 = sheet1["A6"].expand().options(pd.DataFrame).value
         df2

Out[37]:          name   age country  score continent
         user_id
         1001.0   Mark  55.0   Italy    4.5    Europe
         1000.0   John  33.0     USA    6.7   America

In [38]: # If you want the index to be an integer index,
         # you can change its data type
```

```
         df2.index = df2.index.astype(int)
         df2

Out[38]:       name  age country  score continent
         1001  Mark 55.0   Italy    4.5    Europe
         1000  John 33.0     USA    6.7   America

In [39]: # By setting index=False, it will put all the values from Excel into
         # the data part of the DataFrame and will use the default index
         sheet1["A6"].expand().options(pd.DataFrame, index=False).value

Out[39]:    user_id name   age country  score continent
         0   1001.0 Mark  55.0   Italy    4.5    Europe
         1   1000.0 John  33.0     USA    6.7   America
```

Reading and writing DataFrames was a first example of how converters and options work. How they are formally defined and how you use them with other data structures is what we will look into next.

Converters and Options

As we have just seen, the `options` method of the xlwings `range` object allows you to influence the way that values are read and written from and to Excel. That is, `options` are only evaluated when you call the `value` attribute on a `range` object. The syntax is as follows (`myrange` is an xlwings `range` object):

```
myrange.options(convert=None, option1=value1, option2=value2, ...).value
```

Table 9-4 shows the built-in converters, i.e., the values that the `convert` argument accepts. They are called *built-in* as xlwings offers a way to write your own converters, which could be useful if you have to repeatedly apply additional transformations before writing or after reading values—to see how it works, have a look at the xlwings docs (*https://oreil.ly/Ruw8v*).

Table 9-4. Built-in converters

Converter	Description
dict	Simple dictionaries without nesting, i.e., in the form {key1: value1, key2: value2, ...}
np.array	NumPy arrays, requires import numpy as np
pd.Series	pandas Series, requires import pandas as pd
pd.DataFrame	pandas DataFrame, requires import pandas as pd

We have already used the `index` and `header` options with the DataFrame example, but there are more options available, as shown in Table 9-5.

Table 9-5. Built-in options

Option	Description
empty	By default, empty cells are read as None. Change this by providing a value for empty.
date	Accepts a function that is applied to values from date-formatted cells.
numbers	Accepts a function that is applied to numbers.
ndim	*Number of dimensions*: when reading, use ndim to force the values of a range to arrive in a certain dimensionality. Must be either None, 1, or 2. Can be used when reading values as lists or NumPy arrays.
transpose	Transposes the values, i.e., turns the columns into rows or vice versa.
index	To be used with pandas DataFrames and Series: when reading, use it to define whether the Excel range contains the index. Can be True/False or an integer. The integer defines how many columns should be turned into a MultiIndex. For example, 2 will use the two left-most columns as index. When writing, you can decide if you want to write out the index by setting index to True or False.
header	Works the same as index, but applied to the column headers.

Let's have a closer look at ndim: by default, when you read in a single cell from Excel, you will get a scalar (e.g., a float or a string); when you read in a column or row, you will get a simple list; and finally, when you read in a two-dimensional range, you will get a nested (i.e., two-dimensional) list. This is not only consistent in itself, but it is also equivalent to how slicing works with NumPy arrays, as seen in Chapter 4. The one-dimensional case is a special one: sometimes, a column may just be an edge case of what is otherwise a two-dimensional range. In this case, it makes sense to force a range to always arrive as a two-dimensional list by using ndim=2:

```
In [40]: # Horizontal range (one-dimensional)
         sheet1["A1:B1"].value

Out[40]: [1.0, 2.0]

In [41]: # Vertical range (one-dimensional)
         sheet1["A1:A2"].value

Out[41]: [1.0, 3.0]

In [42]: # Horizontal range (two-dimensional)
         sheet1["A1:B1"].options(ndim=2).value

Out[42]: [[1.0, 2.0]]

In [43]: # Vertical range (two-dimensional)
         sheet1["A1:A2"].options(ndim=2).value

Out[43]: [[1.0], [3.0]]

In [44]: # Using the NumPy array converter behaves the same:
         # vertical range leads to a one-dimensional array
         sheet1["A1:A2"].options(np.array).value

Out[44]: array([1., 3.])

In [45]: # Preserving the column orientation
         sheet1["A1:A2"].options(np.array, ndim=2).value
```

```
Out[45]: array([[1.],
               [3.]])

In [46]: # If you need to write out a list vertically,
         # the "transpose" option comes in handy
         sheet1["D1"].options(transpose=True).value = [100, 200]
```

Use ndim=1 to force the value of a single cell to be read as a list instead of a scalar. You won't need ndim with pandas, as a DataFrame is always two-dimensional and a Series is always one-dimensional. Here is one more example showing how the empty, date, and number options work:

```
In [47]: # Write out some sample data
         sheet1["A13"].value = [dt.datetime(2020, 1, 1), None, 1.0]

In [48]: # Read it back using the default options
         sheet1["A13:C13"].value

Out[48]: [datetime.datetime(2020, 1, 1, 0, 0), None, 1.0]

In [49]: # Read it back using non-default options
         sheet1["A13:C13"].options(empty="NA",
                                   dates=dt.date,
                                   numbers=int).value

Out[49]: [datetime.date(2020, 1, 1), 'NA', 1]
```

So far, we have worked with the book, sheet, and range objects. Let's now move on to learn how to deal with collections such as charts that you access from the sheet object!

Charts, Pictures, and Defined Names

In this section, I'll show you how to work with three collections that you access via the sheet or book object: charts, pictures, and defined names.[4] xlwings only supports the most basic chart functionality, but since you can work with templates, you may not even be missing much. And to compensate, xlwings allows you to embed Matplotlib plots as pictures—you may remember from Chapter 5 that Matplotlib is pandas' default plotting backend. Let's start by creating a first Excel chart!

Excel charts

To add a new chart, use the add method of the charts collection, and then set the chart type and source data:

---

4 Another popular collection is tables. To use them, you need at least xlwings 0.21.0; see the docs (*https:// oreil.ly/H2Imd*).

```
In [50]: sheet1["A15"].value = [[None, "North", "South"],
                                ["Last Year", 2, 5],
                                ["This Year", 3, 6]]

In [51]: chart = sheet1.charts.add(top=sheet1["A19"].top,
                                   left=sheet1["A19"].left)
         chart.chart_type = "column_clustered"
         chart.set_source_data(sheet1["A15"].expand())
```

This will produce the chart shown on the lefthand side of Figure 9-2. To look up the available chart types, have a look at the xlwings docs (*https://oreil.ly/2B58q*). If you enjoy working with pandas plots more than with Excel charts, or if you want to use a chart type that is not available in Excel, xlwings has you covered—let's see how!

Pictures: Matplotlib plots

When you use pandas' default plotting backend, you are creating a Matplotlib plot. To bring such a plot over to Excel, you first need to get ahold of its `figure` object, which you provide as an argument to `pictures.add`—this will convert the plot into a picture and send it over to Excel:

```
In [52]: # Read in the chart data as DataFrame
         df = sheet1["A15"].expand().options(pd.DataFrame).value
         df

Out[52]:            North  South
         Last Year    2.0    5.0
         This Year    3.0    6.0

In [53]: # Enable Matplotlib by using the notebook magic command
         # and switch to the "seaborn" style
         %matplotlib inline
         import matplotlib.pyplot as plt
         plt.style.use("seaborn")

In [54]: # The pandas plot method returns an "axis" object from
         # where you can get the figure. "T" transposes the
         # DataFrame to bring the plot into the desired orientation
         ax = df.T.plot.bar()
         fig = ax.get_figure()

In [55]: # Send the plot to Excel
         plot = sheet1.pictures.add(fig, name="SalesPlot",
                                    top=sheet1["H19"].top,
                                    left=sheet1["H19"].left)
         # Let's scale the plot to 70%
         plot.width, plot.height = plot.width * 0.7, plot.height * 0.7
```

To update the picture with a new plot, simply use the `update` method with another `figure` object—technically, this will replace the picture in Excel but will preserve all properties like the location, size, and name:

```
In [56]: ax = (df + 1).T.plot.bar()
         plot = plot.update(ax.get_figure())
```

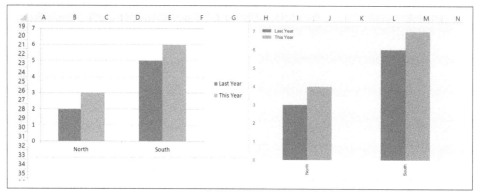

Figure 9-2. An Excel chart (left) and Matplotlib plot (right)

Figure 9-2 shows how the Excel chart and the Matplotlib plot compare after the update call.

Make Sure That Pillow Is Installed

When working with pictures, make sure that Pillow (*https://oreil.ly/ 3HYkf*), Python's go-to library for pictures, is installed: this will make sure that the pictures arrive in the correct size and proportion in Excel. Pillow is part of Anaconda, so if you use a different distribution, you'll need to install it by either running `conda install pillow` or `pip install pillow`. Note that `pictures.add` also accepts a path to a picture on disk instead of a Matplotlib figure.

Charts and pictures are collections that are accessed via a `sheet` object. Defined names, the collection we are going to look at next, can be accessed from the `sheet` or the `book` object. Let's see what difference this makes!

Defined names

In Excel, you create a *defined name* by assigning a name to a range, a formula, or a constant.[5] Assigning a name to a range is probably the most common case and called a *named range*. With a named range, you can refer to the Excel range in formulas and code by using a descriptive name rather than an abstract address in the form of

---

5 Defined names with formulas are also used for *lambda functions*, a new way of defining user-defined functions without VBA or JavaScript, that Microsoft announced as a new feature for Microsoft 365 subscribers in December 2020.

A1:B2. Using them with xlwings makes your code more flexible and solid: reading and writing values from and to named ranges gives you the flexibility to restructure your workbook without having to adjust your Python code: a name sticks to the cell, even if you move it around by inserting a new row, for example. Defined names can be set on either the global book scope or the local sheet scope. The advantage of a name with sheet scope is that you could copy the sheet without running into conflicts with duplicate named ranges. In Excel, you add defined names manually by going to Formulas > Define Name or by selecting a range, then writing the desired name into the Name Box—this is the text box to the left of the formula bar, where you see the cell address by default. Here is how you manage defined names with xlwings:

```
In [57]: # The book scope is the default scope
         sheet1["A1:B2"].name = "matrix1"

In [58]: # For the sheet scope, prepend the sheet name with
         # an exclamation point
         sheet1["B10:E11"].name = "Sheet1!matrix2"

In [59]: # Now you can access the range by name
         sheet1["matrix1"]

Out[59]: <Range [Book2]Sheet1!$A$1:$B$2>

In [60]: # If you access the names collection via the "sheet1" object,
         # it contains only names with that sheet's scope
         sheet1.names

Out[60]: [<Name 'Sheet1!matrix2': =Sheet1!$B$10:$E$11>]

In [61]: # If you access the names collection via the "book" object,
         # it contains all names, including book and sheet scope
         book.names

Out[61]: [<Name 'matrix1': =Sheet1!$A$1:$B$2>, <Name 'Sheet1!matrix2':
         =Sheet1!$B$10:$E$11>]

In [62]: # Names have various methods and attributes.
         # You can, for example, get the respective range object.
         book.names["matrix1"].refers_to_range

Out[62]: <Range [Book2]Sheet1!$A$1:$B$2>

In [63]: # If you want to assign a name to a constant
         # or a formula, use the "add" method.
         # You may need to replace the decimal point with a comma
         # if your are using an international version of Excel.
         book.names.add("EURUSD", "=1.1151")

Out[63]: <Name 'EURUSD': =1.1151>
```

Have a look at the generated defined names in Excel by opening the Name Manager via Formulas > Name Manager (see Figure 9-3). Note that Excel on macOS doesn't have a Name Manager—instead, go to Formulas > Define Name, from where you will see the existing names.

Figure 9-3. Excel's Name Manager after adding a few defined names via xlwings

At this point, you know how to work with the most commonly used components of an Excel workbook. This means that we can look at the reporting case study from Chapter 7 one more time: let's see what changes when we bring xlwings into the picture!

Case Study (Re-Revisited): Excel Reporting

Being able to truly edit Excel files via xlwings enables us to work with template files that will be 100% preserved, no matter how complex they are or in which format they are stored—for example, you can easily edit an *xlsb* file, a case that is currently not supported by any of the writer packages we met in the previous chapter. When you look at *sales_report_openpxyl.py* in the companion repo, you will see that after preparing the summary DataFrame, we had to write almost forty lines of code to create one chart and style one DataFrame with OpenPyXL. With xlwings, you achieve the same in just six lines of code, as shown in Example 9-1. Being able to handle the formatting in the Excel template will save you a lot of work. This, however, comes at a price: xlwings requires an installation of Excel to run—that's usually fine if you have to create these reports infrequently on your own machine, but it may be less ideal if you try to create reports on a server as part of a web application.

First, you need to make sure that your Microsoft Office license covers the installation on a server and second, Excel wasn't made for unattended automation, which means that you may run into stability issues, especially if you need to generate many reports in a short amount of time. That being said, I have seen more than one client doing this successfully, so if you can't use a writer package for whatever reason, running xlwings on a server may very well be an option worth exploring. Just make sure to run each script in a new Excel instance via `app = xw.App()` to ship around the typical stability issues.

You will find the full xlwings script under *sales_report_xlwings.py* in the companion repository (the first half is the same as we used with OpenPyXL and XlsxWriter). It is also a perfect example for combining a reader package with xlwings: while pandas (via OpenPyXL and xlrd) is faster with reading many files from disk, xlwings makes it easier to fill in a preformatted template.

Example 9-1. sales_report_xlwings.py (second part only)

```
# Open the template, paste the data, autofit the columns
# and adjust the chart source. Then save it under a different name.
template = xw.Book(this_dir / "xl" / "sales_report_template.xlsx")
sheet = template.sheets["Sheet1"]
sheet["B3"].value = summary
sheet["B3"].expand().columns.autofit()
sheet.charts["Chart 1"].set_source_data(sheet["B3"].expand()[:-1, :-1])
template.save(this_dir / "sales_report_xlwings.xlsx")
```

When you run this script for the very first time on macOS (for example by opening it in VS Code and clicking the Run File button), you will have to again confirm a pop-up to grant access to the file system, something we've already come across earlier in this chapter.

With formatted Excel templates, you can build beautiful Excel reports very quickly. You also get access to methods like `autofit`, something that's not available with the writer packages as it relies on calculations done by the Excel application: this allows you to properly set the width and height of your cells according to their content. Figure 9-4 shows you the upper part of the sales report as generated by xlwings with a customized table header as well as columns where the `autofit` method has been applied.

When you start using xlwings for more than just filling in a couple of cells in a template, it's good to know a little bit about its internals: the next section looks at how xlwings works under the hood.

Month	Washington DC	Boston	Las Vegas	New York	Chicago	San Francisco	Total
Jan 19	14,058	21,784	23,013	49,873	51,188	58,630	218,545
Feb 19	15,235	21,455	25,493	46,670	52,331	55,219	216,403
Mar 19	14,177	20,043	23,451	41,572	48,897	52,713	200,854
Apr 19	13,339	18,791	22,710	41,714	47,396	49,325	193,276
May 19	13,147	18,037	21,527	40,610	45,117	47,760	186,197
Jun 19	14,284	21,556	21,985	47,266	49,460	53,462	208,014
Jul 19	14,162	19,853	23,444	40,408	47,994	50,182	196,043
Aug 19	16,127	22,333	24,928	45,397	50,839	55,336	214,960
Sep 19	14,994	19,925	24,411	42,831	49,096	49,931	201,188
Oct 19	12,847	16,551	22,828	34,090	42,544	44,312	173,171
Nov 19	14,058	21,313	24,860	46,960	52,012	55,056	214,259
Dec 19	14,702	19,723	24,536	42,364	49,355	50,933	201,613
Total	171,130	241,363	283,185	519,755	586,229	622,859	2,424,521

Figure 9-4. The table of the sales report based on a preformatted template

Advanced xlwings Topics

This section shows you how to make your xlwings code performant and how to work around missing functionality. To understand these topics, though, we first need to say a few words about the way xlwings communicates with Excel.

xlwings Foundations

xlwings depends on other Python packages to communicate with the automation mechanism of the respective operating system:

Windows

On Windows, xlwings relies on the COM technology, short for *Component Object Model*. COM is a standard that allows two processes to communicate with each other—in our case Excel and Python. xlwings uses the Python package pywin32 (*https://oreil.ly/tm7sK*) to handle the COM calls.

macOS

On macOS, xlwings relies on *AppleScript*. AppleScript is Apple's scripting language to automate scriptable applications—fortunately, Excel is such a scriptable application. To run AppleScript commands, xlwings uses the Python package appscript (*https://oreil.ly/tIsDd*).

Windows: How to Prevent Zombie Processes

When you play around with xlwings on Windows, you will sometimes notice that Excel seems to be completely closed, yet when you open the Task Manager (right-click on the Windows taskbar, then select Task Manager), you will see Microsoft Excel under Background processes on the Processes tab. If you don't see any tab, click on "More details" first. Alternatively, go to the Details tab, where you will see Excel listed as "EXCEL.EXE." To terminate a zombie process, right-click the respective row and select "End task" to force Excel to close.

Because these processes are *undead* rather than properly terminated, they are often called *zombie processes*. Leaving them around uses resources and can lead to undesired behavior: for example, files may be blocked or add-ins may not be properly loaded when you open a new instance of Excel. The reason why Excel sometimes doesn't manage to shut down properly is that processes can only be terminated once there are no more COM references, e.g., in the form of an xlwings `app` object. Most commonly, you end up with an Excel zombie process after killing the Python interpreter as this prevents it from properly cleaning up the COM references. Consider this example on an Anaconda Prompt:

```
(base)> python
>>> import xlwings as xw
>>> app = xw.App()
```

Once the new Excel instance is running, quit it again via the Excel user interface: while Excel closes, the Excel process in the Task Manager will keep running. If you shut down the Python session properly by running `quit()` or by using the Ctrl+Z shortcut, the Excel process will eventually be shut down. If, however, you kill the Anaconda Prompt by clicking the "x" at the top right of the window, you will notice that the process sticks around as a zombie process. The same happens if you kill the Anaconda Prompt before closing Excel or if you kill it while it is running a Jupyter server and you hold an xlwings `app` object in one of the Jupyter notebook cells. To minimize the chances of ending up with Excel zombie processes, here are a few suggestions:

- Run `app.quit()` from Python instead of closing Excel manually. This makes sure that the references are cleaned up properly.

- Don't kill interactive Python sessions when you work with xlwings, e.g., if you run a Python REPL on an Anaconda Prompt, shut the Python interpreter down properly by running `quit()` or by using the Ctrl+Z shortcut. When you work with Jupyter notebooks, shut the server down by clicking on Quit on the web interface.

- With interactive Python sessions, it helps to avoid using the `app` object directly, e.g., by using `xw.Book()` instead of `myapp.books.add()`. This should properly terminate Excel even if the Python process is killed.

Now that you have an idea about the underlying technology of xlwings, let's see how we can speed up slow scripts!

Improving Performance

To keep your xlwings scripts performant, there are a few strategies: the most important one is to keep cross-application calls to an absolute minimum. Using raw values can be another option, and finally, setting the right `app` properties may also help. Let's go through these options one after another!

Minimize cross-application calls

It's crucial to know that every cross-application call from Python to Excel is "expensive," i.e., slow. Therefore, such calls should be reduced as much as possible. The easiest way to do this is by reading and writing entire Excel ranges instead of looping through individual cells. In the following example, we read and write 150 cells, first by looping through every cell and then by dealing with the entire range in one call:

```
In [64]: # Add a new sheet and write 150 values
         # to it to have something to work with
         sheet2 = book.sheets.add()
         sheet2["A1"].value = np.arange(150).reshape(30, 5)

In [65]: %%time
         # This makes 150 cross-application calls
         for cell in sheet2["A1:E30"]:
             cell.value += 1

Wall time: 909 ms

In [66]: %%time
         # This makes just two cross-application calls
         values = sheet2["A1:E30"].options(np.array).value
         sheet2["A1:E30"].value = values + 1

Wall time: 97.2 ms
```

These numbers are even more extreme on macOS, where the second option is about 50 times faster than the first one on my machine.

Raw values

xlwings was primarily designed with a focus on convenience rather than speed. However, if you deal with huge cell ranges, you may run into situations where you can save time by skipping xlwings' data cleaning step: xlwings loops through each value when you read and write data, for example, to align data types between Windows and macOS. By using the string `raw` as converter in the `options` method, you skip this step. While this should make all operations faster, the difference may not be significant unless you write large arrays on Windows. Using raw values, however, means that you cannot directly work with DataFrames anymore. Instead, you need to provide your values as nested lists or tuples. Also, you will need to provide the full address of the range you are writing to—providing the top-left cell isn't enough anymore:

```
In [67]: # With raw values, you must provide the full
         # target range, sheet["A35"] doesn't work anymore
         sheet1["A35:B36"].options("raw").value = [[1, 2], [3, 4]]
```

App properties

Depending on the content of your workbook, changing the properties of your app objects can also help to make code run faster. Usually, you want to look at the following properties (myapp is an xlwings app object):

- myapp.screen_updating = False

- myapp.calculation = "manual"

- myapp.display_alerts = False

At the end of the script, make sure to set the attributes back to their original state. If you are on Windows, you may also see a slight performance improvement by running your script in a hidden Excel instance via xw.App(visible=False).

Now that you know how to keep performance under control, let's have a look at how to extend the functionality of xlwings.

How to Work Around Missing Functionality

xlwings provides a Pythonic interface for the most commonly used Excel commands and makes them work across Windows and macOS. There are, however, many methods and attributes of the Excel object model that are not yet covered natively by xlwings—but all is not lost! xlwings gives you access to the underlying pywin32 object on Windows and the appscript object on macOS by using the api attribute on any xlwings object. This way, you have access to the whole Excel object model, but in turn, you lose cross-platform compatibility. For example, assume you wanted to clear the formatting of a cell. Here is how you would go about this:

- Check if the method is available on the xlwings range object, e.g., by using the Tab key after putting a dot at the end of a range object in a Jupyter notebook, by running dir(sheet["A1"]) or by searching the xlwings API reference (*https://oreil.ly/EiXBc*). On VS Code, the available methods should be shown automatically in a tooltip.

- If the desired functionality is missing, use the api attribute to get the underlying object: on Windows, sheet["A1"].api will give you a pywin32 object and on macOS, you will get an appscript object.

- Check Excel's object model in the Excel VBA reference (*https://oreil.ly/UILPo*). To clear the format of a range, you would end up under Range.ClearFormats (*https://oreil.ly/kcEsw*).

- On Windows, in most cases, you can use the VBA method or property directly with your `api` object. If it is a method, make sure to add parentheses in Python: `sheet["A1"].api.ClearFormats()`. If you are doing this on macOS, things are more complicated as appscript uses a syntax that can be difficult to guess. Your best approach is to look at the developer guide that is part of the xlwings source code (*https://oreil.ly/YSS0Y*). Clearing the cell formatting, however, is easy enough: just apply Python's syntax rules on the method name by using lowercase characters with underscores: `sheet["A1"].api.clear_formats()`.

If you need to make sure that `ClearFormats` works across both platforms, you can do it as follows (`darwin` is the core of macOS and used as its name by `sys.platform`):

```
import sys
if sys.platform.startswith("darwin"):
    sheet["A10"].api.clear_formats()
elif sys.platform.startswith("win"):
    sheet["A10"].api.ClearFormats()
```

In any case, it's worth opening an issue on xlwings' GitHub repository (*https://oreil.ly/kFkD0*) to have the functionality included in a future version.

Conclusion

This chapter introduced you to the concept of Excel automation: via xlwings, you can use Python for tasks that you would traditionally do in VBA. We learned about the Excel object model and how xlwings allows you to interact with its components like the `sheet` and `range` objects. Equipped with this knowledge, we went back to the reporting case study from Chapter 7 and used xlwings to fill in a preformatted report template; this showed you that there is a case for using the reader packages and xlwings side by side. We also learned about the libraries that xlwings uses under the hood to understand how we can improve performance and work around missing functionality. My favorite xlwings feature is that it works equally well on macOS as it does on Windows. This is even more exciting as Power Query on macOS doesn't have all the features of the Windows version yet: whatever is missing, you should be able to easily replace it with a combination of pandas and xlwings.

Now that you know the xlwings basics, you are ready for the next chapter: there, we're going to take the next step and call xlwings scripts from Excel itself, allowing you to build Excel tools that are powered by Python.

## CHAPTER 10

Python-Powered Excel Tools

In the last chapter, we learned how to write Python scripts to automate Microsoft Excel. While this is very powerful, the user must feel comfortable using either the Anaconda Prompt or an editor like VS Code to run the scripts. This is most likely not the case if your tools are used by business users. For them, you'll want to hide away the Python part so that the Excel tool feels like a normal macro-enabled workbook again. How you achieve that with xlwings is the topic of this chapter. I'll start by showing you the shortest path to run Python code from Excel before looking at the challenges of deploying xlwings tools—this will also allow us to have a more detailed look at the available settings that xlwings offers. Like the last chapter, this chapter requires you to have an installation of Microsoft Excel on either Windows or macOS.

Using Excel as Frontend with xlwings

The *frontend* is the part of an application that a user sees and interacts with. Other common names for frontend are *graphical user interface* (GUI) or just *user interface* (UI). When I ask xlwings users why they are creating their tool with Excel rather than building a modern web application, what I usually hear is this: "Excel is the interface that our users are familiar with." Relying on spreadsheet cells allows the users to provide inputs quickly and intuitively, making them often more productive than if they have to use a half-baked web interface. I'll start this section by introducing you to the xlwings Excel add-in and the xlwings CLI (command line interface) before creating our first project via the quickstart command. I'll wrap this section up by showing you two ways of calling Python code from Excel: by clicking the Run main button in the add-in and by using the RunPython function in VBA. Let's get started by installing the xlwings Excel add-in!

Excel Add-in

Since xlwings is included in the Anaconda distribution, in the previous chapter, we could run xlwings commands in Python right out of the box. If you, however, want to call Python scripts from Excel, you need to either install the Excel add-in or set the workbook up in the standalone mode. While I will introduce the standalone mode under "Deployment" on page 218, this section shows you how to work with the add-in. To install it, run the following on an Anaconda Prompt:

```
(base)> xlwings addin install
```

You will need to keep the version of the Python package and the version of the add-in in sync whenever you update xlwings. Therefore, you should always run two commands when you update xlwings—one for the Python package and one for the Excel add-in. Depending on whether you use the Conda or pip package manager, this is how you update your xlwings installation:

Conda (use this with the Anaconda Python distribution)
```
(base)> conda update xlwings
(base)> xlwings addin install
```

pip (use this with any other Python distribution)
```
(base)> pip install --upgrade xlwings
(base)> xlwings addin install
```

Antivirus Software

Unfortunately, the xlwings add-in is sometimes flagged as a malicious add-in by antivirus software, especially if you're using a brand-new release. If this happens on your machine, go to the settings of your antivirus software, where you should be able to mark xlwings as safe to run. Usually, it's also possible to report such false positives via the software's home page.

When you type `xlwings` on an Anaconda Prompt, you are using the xlwings CLI. Apart from making the installation of the xlwings add-in easy, it offers a few more commands: I will introduce them whenever we need them, but you can always type `xlwings` on an Anaconda Prompt and hit Enter to print the available options. Let's now have a closer look at what `xlwings addin install` does:

Installation
The actual installation of the add-in is done by copying *xlwings.xlam* from the directory of the Python package into Excel's *XLSTART* folder, which is a special folder: Excel will open all files that are in this folder every time you start Excel. When you run `xlwings addin status` on an Anaconda Prompt, it will print

where the *XLSTART* directory is on your system and whether or not the add-in is installed.

Configuration

When you install the add-in for the very first time, it will also configure it to use the Python interpreter or Conda environment from where you are running the `install` command: as you see in Figure 10-1, the values for `Conda Path` and `Conda Env` are filled in automatically by the xlwings CLI.[1] These values are stored in a file called *xlwings.conf* in the *.xlwings* folder in your home directory. On Windows, this is usually *C:\Users\<username>\.xlwings\xlwings.conf* and on macOS */Users/<username>/.xlwings/xlwings.conf*. On macOS, folders and files with a leading dot are hidden by default. When you are in Finder, type the keyboard shortcut Command-Shift-. to toggle their visibility.

After running the installation command, you'll have to restart Excel to see the xlwings tab in the ribbon as shown in Figure 10-1.

Figure 10-1. The xlwings ribbon add-in after running the install command

The Ribbon Add-in on macOS

On macOS, the ribbon looks a bit different as it's missing the sections about user-defined functions and Conda: while user-defined functions are not supported on macOS, Conda environments don't require special treatment, i.e., are configured as Interpreter under the Python group.

Now that you have the xlwings add-in installed, we'll need a workbook and some Python code to test it out. The fastest way of getting there is by using the `quickstart` command, as I will show you next.

---

1 If you are on macOS or using a Python distribution other than Anaconda, it will configure the Interpreter rather than the Conda settings.

Quickstart Command

To make the creation of your first xlwings tool as easy as possible, the xlwings CLI offers the quickstart command. On an Anaconda Prompt, use the cd command to change into the directory where you want to create your first project (e.g., cd Desk top), then run the following to create a project with the name first_project:

```
(base)> xlwings quickstart first_project
```

The project name has to be a valid Python module name: it can contain characters, numbers, and underscores, but no spaces or dashes, and it must not start with a number. I will show you under "RunPython Function" on page 213 how you can change the name of the Excel file into something that doesn't have to follow these rules. Running the quickstart command will create a folder called *first_project* in your current directory. When you open it in the File Explorer on Windows or the Finder on macOS, you will see two files: *first_project.xlsm* and *first_project.py*. Open both files—the Excel file in Excel and the Python file in VS Code. The easiest way to run the Python code from Excel is by using the Run main button in the add-in—let's see how it works!

Run Main

Before looking at *first_project.py* in more detail, go ahead and click the Run main button on the very left of the xlwings add-in while *first_project.xlsm* is your active file; it will write "Hello xlwings!" into cell A1 of the first sheet. Click the button again and it will change to "Bye xlwings!" Congratulations, you have just run your first Python function from Excel! After all, that wasn't much harder than writing a VBA macro, was it? Let's now have a look at *first_project.py* in Example 10-1.

Example 10-1. first_project.py

```python
import xlwings as xw


def main():
    wb = xw.Book.caller()  ❶
    sheet = wb.sheets[0]
    if sheet["A1"].value == "Hello xlwings!":
        sheet["A1"].value = "Bye xlwings!"
    else:
        sheet["A1"].value = "Hello xlwings!"


@xw.func  ❷
def hello(name):
    return f"Hello {name}!"
```

```
if __name__ == "__main__":  ❸
    xw.Book("first_project.xlsm").set_mock_caller()
    main()
```

❶ xw.Book.caller() is an xlwings book object that refers to the Excel workbook
that is active when you click the Run main button. In our case, it corresponds to
xw.Book("first_project.xlsm"). Using xw.Book.caller() allows you to
rename and move your Excel file around on the file system without breaking the
reference. It also makes sure that you are manipulating the correct workbook if
you have it open in multiple Excel instances.

❷ In this chapter, we will ignore the function hello as this will be the topic of
Chapter 12. If you run the quickstart command on macOS, you won't see the
hello function anyway, as user-defined functions are only supported on Windows.

❸ I will explain the last three lines when we look at debugging in the next chapter.
For the purpose of this chapter, ignore or even delete everything below the first
function.

The Run main button in the Excel add-in is a convenience feature: it allows you to
call a function with the name main in a Python module that has the same name as the
Excel file without having to add a button first to your workbook. It will even work if
you save your workbook in the macro-free *xlsx* format. If, however, you want to call
one or more Python functions that are not called main and are not part of a module
with the same name as the workbook, you have to use the RunPython function from
VBA instead. The next section has the details!

RunPython Function

If you need more control over how you call your Python code, use the VBA function
RunPython. Consequently, RunPython requires your workbook to be saved as a
macro-enabled workbook.

Enable Macros

You need to click on Enable Content (Windows) or Enable Macros
(macOS) when you open a macro-enabled workbook (*xlsm* extension) such as the one that is generated by the quickstart command. On Windows, when you work with *xlsm* files from the
companion repository, you have to additionally click on Enable
Editing or Excel won't open files that are downloaded from the
internet properly.

`RunPython` accepts a string with Python code: most commonly, you import a Python module and run one of its functions. When you open the VBA editor via Alt+F11 (Windows) or Option-F11 (macOS), you will see that the `quickstart` command adds a macro called `SampleCall` in a VBA module with the name "Module1" (see Figure 10-2). If you don't see the `SampleCall`, double-click Module1 in the VBA project tree on the lefthand side.

Figure 10-2. The VBA editor showing Module1

The code looks a bit convoluted, but this is only to make it work dynamically no matter what project name you choose when running the `quickstart` command. As our Python module is called `first_project`, you could replace the code with the following easy-to-understand equivalent:

```
Sub SampleCall()
    RunPython "import first_project; first_project.main()"
End Sub
```

Since it's no fun to write multiline strings in VBA, we use a semicolon that Python accepts instead of a line break. There are a couple of ways you can run this code: for example, while you are in the VBA editor, place your cursor on any line of the `SampleCall` macro and hit F5. Usually, however, you will be running the code from an Excel sheet and not from the VBA editor. Therefore, close the VBA editor and switch back to the workbook. Typing Alt+F8 (Windows) or Option-F8 (macOS) will bring up the macro menu: select `SampleCall` and click on the Run button. Or, to make it more user-friendly, add a button to your Excel workbook and connect it with the `SampleCall`: first, make sure that the Developer tab in the ribbon is shown. If it isn't, go to File > Options > Customize Ribbon and activate the checkbox next to Developer (on macOS, you'll find it under Excel > Preferences > Ribbon & Toolbar instead). To insert a button, go to the Developer tab and in the Controls group, click on Insert > Button (under Form Controls). On macOS, you'll be presented with the button without having to go to Insert first. When you click the button icon, your cursor turns into a small cross: use it to draw a button on your sheet by holding your left mouse button down while drawing a rectangular form. Once you let go of your mouse button, you'll be presented with the Assign Macro menu—select the

SampleCall and click OK. Click the button that you've just created (in my case it's called "Button 1"), and it will run our main function again, as in Figure 10-3.

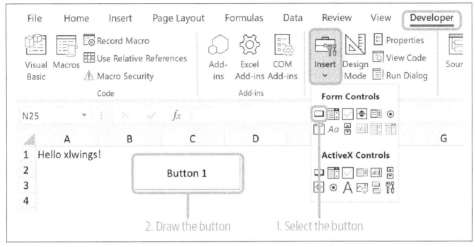

Figure 10-3. Drawing a button on a sheet

 Form Controls vs. ActiveX Controls

On Windows, you have two types of controls: Form Controls and ActiveX Controls. While you could use a button from either group to connect to your SampleCall macro, only the one from the Form Controls will work on macOS too. In the next chapter, we will use Rectangles as buttons to make them look a bit more modern.

Now let's take a look at how we can change the default names that were assigned by the quickstart command: go back to your Python file and rename it from *first_project.py* to *hello.py*. Also, rename your main function into hello_world. Make sure to save the file, then open the VBA editor again via Alt+F11 (Windows) or Option-F11 (macOS) and edit SampleCall as follows to reflect the changes:

```
Sub SampleCall()
    RunPython "import hello; hello.hello_world()"
End Sub
```

Back on the sheet, click the "Button 1" to make sure that everything still works. Finally, you may also want to keep the Python script and the Excel file in two different directories. To understand the implications of this, I'll first need to say a word about Python's *module search path*: if you import a module in your code, Python searches for it in various directories. First, Python checks if there is a built-in module with this name, and if it doesn't find one, moves on to look in the current working directory and in the directories provided by the so-called PYTHONPATH. xlwings automatically adds the directory of the workbook to the PYTHONPATH and allows you to add additional paths via the add-in. To try this out, take the Python script that is now called *hello.py* and move it to a folder called *pyscripts* that you create under your home directory: in my case, this would be *C:\Users\felix\pyscripts* on Windows or */Users/felix/pyscripts* on macOS. When you now click the button again, you will get the following error in a pop-up:

```
Traceback (most recent call last):
  File "<string>", line 1, in <module>
ModuleNotFoundError: No module named 'first_project'
```

To fix this, simply add the path of the *pyscripts* directory to the PYTHONPATH setting in your xlwings ribbon, as in Figure 10-4. When you now click the button one more time, it will work again.

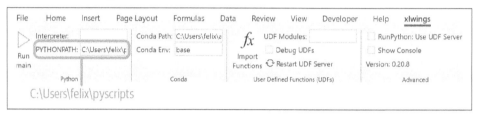

Figure 10-4. The PYTHONPATH setting

What I haven't touched on yet is the name of the Excel workbook: once your RunPython function call uses an explicit module name like first_project instead of the code that was added by quickstart, you are free to rename your Excel workbook anything you want.

Relying on the quickstart command is the easiest way if you start a new xlwings project. If you have an existing workbook, however, you may prefer to set it up manually. Let's see how it's done!

RunPython without quickstart command

If you want to use the RunPython function with an existing workbook that wasn't created by the quickstart command, you need to manually take care of the things that the quickstart command does for you otherwise. Note that the following steps are only required for the RunPython call but not when you want to use the Run main button:

1. First of all, make sure to save your workbook as a macro-enabled workbook with either the *xlsm* or *xlsb* extension.

2. Add a VBA module; to do so, open the VBA editor via Alt+F11 (Windows) or Option-F11 (macOS) and make sure to select the VBAProject of your workbook in the tree view on the lefthand side, then right-click on it and choose Insert > Module, as in Figure 10-5. This will insert an empty VBA module where you can write your VBA macro with the RunPython call.

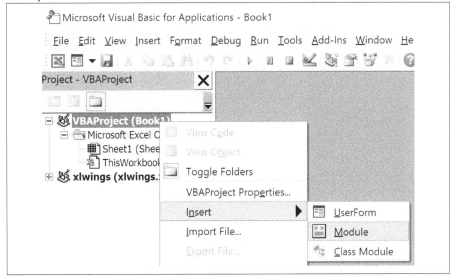

Figure 10-5. Add a VBA module

3. Add a reference to xlwings: RunPython is a function that is part of the xlwings add-in. To use it, you will need to make sure that you have a reference set to xlwings in your VBA Project. Again, start by selecting the correct workbook in the tree view on the lefthand side of the VBA editor, then go to Tools > Reference and activate the checkbox for xlwings, as seen in Figure 10-6.

Your workbook is now ready to be used with the RunPython call again. Once everything works on your machine, the next step is usually to make it work on your colleague's machine—let's go through a couple of options to make this part easier!

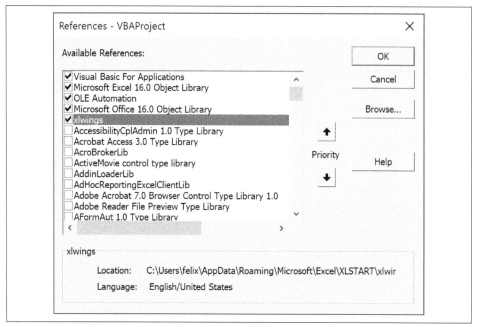

Figure 10-6. RunPython requires a reference to xlwings

Deployment

In software development, the term *deployment* refers to distributing and installing software so that end users are able to use it. In the case of xlwings tools, it helps to know which dependencies are required and which settings can make deployment easier. I'll start with the most important dependency, which is Python, before looking at workbooks that have been set up in the standalone mode to get rid of the xlwings Excel add-in. I'll conclude this section by having a closer look at how configuration works with xlwings.

Python Dependency

To be able to run xlwings tools, your end users must have an installation of Python. But just because they don't have Python yet doesn't mean that there aren't ways to make the installation process easy. Here are a couple of options:

Anaconda or WinPython

Instruct your users to download and install the Anaconda distribution. To be on the safe side, you would have to agree to a specific version of Anaconda to make sure they are using the same versions of the contained packages that you're using. This is a good option if you only use packages that are part of Anaconda. WinPython (*https://oreil.ly/A66KN*) is an interesting alternative to Anaconda, as it is distributed under the MIT open source license and also comes with xlwings pre-installed. As the name suggests, it is only available on Windows.

Shared drive

If you have access to a reasonably fast shared drive, you may be able to install Python directly on there, which will allow everyone to use the tools without a local Python installation.

Frozen executable

On Windows, xlwings allows you to work with *frozen executables*, which are files with the *.exe* extension that contain Python and all the dependencies. A popular package to produce frozen executables is PyInstaller (*https://oreil.ly/AnYlV*). Frozen executables have the advantage that they are only packaging up what your program needs and can produce a single file, which can make distribution easier. For more details on how to work with frozen executables, have a look at the xlwings docs (*https://oreil.ly/QWz7i*). Note that frozen executables will not work when you use xlwings for user-defined functions, the functionality that I will introduce in Chapter 12.

While Python is a hard requirement, the installation of the xlwings add-in is not, as I will explain next.

Standalone Workbooks: Getting Rid of the xlwings Add-in

In this chapter, we have always relied on the xlwings add-in to call Python code either by clicking the Run main button or by using the RunPython function. Even if the xlwings CLI makes it easy to install the add-in, it may still be a hassle for less technical users who don't feel comfortable using the Anaconda Prompt. Also, since the xlwings add-in and the xlwings Python package need to have the same version, you may run into a conflict where your recipients already have the xlwings add-in installed, but with a different version than your tool requires. There is a simple solution, though: xlwings doesn't require the Excel add-in and can be set up as a *standalone workbook* instead. In this case, the VBA code of the add-in is stored directly in your workbook. As usual, the easiest way to get everything set up is by using the quickstart command, this time with the --standalone flag:

```
(base)> xlwings quickstart second_project --standalone
```

When you open the generated *second_project.xlsm* workbook in Excel and press Alt+F11 (Windows) or Option-F11 (macOS), you will see the xlwings module and the Dictionary class module that are required in place of the add-in. Most importantly, a standalone project must not have a reference to xlwings anymore. While this is configured automatically when using the --standalone flag, it is important that you remove the reference in case you want to convert an existing workbook: go to Tools > References in your VBA editor and clear the checkbox for xlwings.

Building a Custom Add-in

While this section shows you how to get rid of the dependency of the xlwings add-in, you may sometimes want to build your own add-in for deployment. This makes sense if you want to use the same macros with many different workbooks. You will find instructions on how to build your own custom add-in in the xlwings docs (*https://oreil.ly/hFvlj*).

Having touched upon Python and the add-in, let's now have a more in-depth look at how the xlwings configuration works.

Configuration Hierarchy

As mentioned at the beginning of this chapter, the ribbon stores its configuration in the user's home directory, under *.xlwings\xlwings.conf*. The *configuration* consists of individual *settings*, like the PYTHONPATH that we already saw at the beginning of this chapter. The settings you set in your add-in can be overridden on the directory and workbook level—xlwings looks for settings in the following locations and order:

Workbook configuration
First, xlwings looks for a sheet called *xlwings.conf*. This is the recommended way to configure your workbook for deployment as you don't have to handle an additional config file. When you run the quickstart command, it will create a sample configuration on a sheet called "_xlwings.conf": remove the leading underscore in the name to activate it. If you don't want to use it, feel free to delete the sheet.

Directory configuration
Next, xlwings looks for a file called *xlwings.conf* in the same directory as your Excel workbook.

User configuration
Finally, xlwings looks for a file called *xlwings.conf* in the *.xlwings* folder in the user's home directory. Normally, you don't edit this file directly—instead, it is created and edited by the add-in whenever you change a setting.

If xlwings doesn't find any settings in these three locations, it falls back to default values.

When you edit the settings via the Excel add-in, it will automatically edit the *xlwings.conf* file. If you want to edit the file directly, look up the exact format and available settings by going to the xlwings docs (*https://oreil.ly/U9JTY*), but I'll point out the most helpful settings in the context of deployment next.

Settings

The most critical setting is certainly the Python interpreter—if your Excel tool can't find the correct Python interpreter, nothing will work. The PYTHONPATH setting allows you to control where you place your Python source files, and the Use UDF Server setting keeps the Python interpreter running in between calls on Windows, which can greatly improve performance.

Python Interpreter

xlwings relies on a locally installed Python installation. This, however, doesn't necessarily mean that the recipient of your xlwings tool needs to mess around with the configuration before they can use the tool. As mentioned previously, you could tell them to install the Anaconda distribution with the default settings, which will install it in the user's home directory. If you use *environment variables* in your configuration, xlwings will find the correct path to the Python interpreter. An environment variable is a variable set on the user's computer that allows programs to query information specific to this environment, like the name of the current user's home folder. As an example, on Windows, set the Conda Path to %USERPROFILE%\anaconda3 and on macOS, set Interpreter_Mac to $HOME/opt/anaconda3/bin/python. These paths will then dynamically resolve to Anaconda's default installation path.

PYTHONPATH

By default, xlwings looks for the Python source file in the same directory as the Excel file. This may not be ideal when you give your tool to users who aren't familiar with Python as they could forget to keep the two files together when moving the Excel file around. Instead, you can put your Python source files in a dedicated folder (this could be on a shared drive) and add this folder to the PYTHONPATH setting. Alternatively, you could also place your source files on a path that is already part of the Python module search path. One way to achieve this would be to distribute your source code as a Python package—installing it will place it in Python's *site-packages* directory, where Python will find your code. For more information on how to build a Python package, see the Python Packaging User Guide (*https://oreil.ly/_kJoj*).

RunPython: Use UDF Server (Windows only)

You may have noticed that a RunPython call can be rather slow. This is because xlwings starts a Python interpreter, runs the Python code, and finally shuts the interpreter down again. This may not be so bad during development, as it makes sure that all modules are loaded from scratch every time you call the RunPython command. Once your code is stable, though, you might want to activate the checkbox "RunPython: Use UDF Server" that is only available on Windows. This will use the same Python server as the user-defined functions use (the topic of Chapter 12) and keep the Python session running in between calls, which will be much faster. Note, however, that you need to click the Restart UDF Server button in the ribbon after code changes.

---

xlwings PRO

While this book makes use of only the free and open source version of xlwings, there is also a commercial PRO package available to fund the continued maintenance and development of the open source package. Some of the additional functionality that xlwings PRO offers are:

- Python code can be embedded in Excel, thereby getting rid of external source files.

- The reports package allows you to turn your workbooks into templates with placeholders. This gives nontechnical users the power to edit the template without having to change the Python code.

- Installers can be built easily to get rid of any deployment headaches: end users can install Python including all dependencies with a single click, giving them the feeling of dealing with normal Excel workbooks without having to manually configure anything.

For further details about xlwings PRO and to request a trial license, see the xlwings home page (*https://oreil.ly/QEuoo*).

Conclusion

This chapter started by showing you how easy it is to run Python code from Excel: with Anaconda installed, you only need to run `xlwings addin install` followed by `xlwings quickstart myproject`, and you are ready to click the Run main button in the xlwings add-in or use the `RunPython` VBA function. The second part introduced a few settings that make it easier to deploy your xlwings tool to your end users. The fact that xlwings comes preinstalled with Anaconda helps a lot in lowering the entry barriers for new users.

In this chapter, we were merely using the Hello World example to learn how everything works. The next chapter takes these foundations to build the Python Package Tracker, a full-fledged business application.

## CHAPTER 11

The Python Package Tracker

In this chapter, we will create a typical business application that downloads data from the internet and stores it in a database before visualizing it in Excel. This will help you understand what role xlwings plays in such an application and allows you to see how easy it is to connect to external systems with Python. In an attempt to build a project that is close to a real-world application yet relatively simple to follow, I have come up with the *Python Package Tracker*, an Excel tool that shows the number of releases per year for a given Python package. Despite being a case study, you might actually find the tool useful to understand if a certain Python package is being actively developed or not.

After getting acquainted with the application, we'll go through a few topics that we need to understand to be able to follow its code: we'll see how we can download data from the internet and how we can interact with databases before we learn about exception handling in Python, an important concept when it comes to application development. Once we're done with these preliminaries, we'll go through the components of the Python Package Tracker to see how everything fits together. To wrap this chapter up, we'll look into how debugging xlwings code works. Like the last two chapters, this chapter requires you to have an installation of Microsoft Excel on either Windows or macOS. Let's get started by taking the Python Package Tracker for a test drive!

What We Will Build

Head over to the companion repository, where you will find the *packagetracker* folder. There are a couple of files in that folder, but for now just open the Excel file *package-tracker.xlsm* and head over to the Database sheet: we first need to get some data into the database to have something to work with. As shown in Figure 11-1, type in a package name, for example "xlwings," then click on Add Package. You can choose any package name that exists on the Python Package Index (*https://pypi.org*) (PyPI).

macOS: Confirm Access to Folder

When you add the very first package on macOS, you will have to confirm a pop-up so that the application can access the *package-tracker* folder. This is the same pop-up we already came across in Chapter 9.

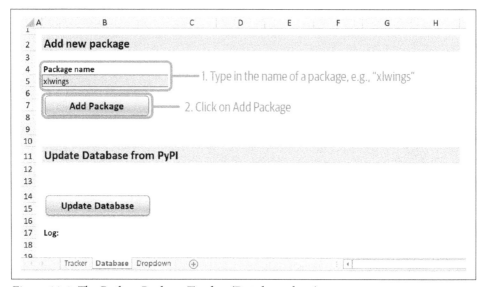

Figure 11-1. The Python Package Tracker (Database sheet)

If everything works according to plan, you will see the message "Added xlwings successfully" to the right of where you typed in the package name. Also, you will see a Last updated timestamp under the Update Database section as well as an updated Log section where it says that it downloaded xlwings successfully and stored it to the database. Let's do this one more time and add the pandas package so we have some more data to play around with. Now, switch to the Tracker sheet and select xlwings from the dropdown in cell B5 before clicking on Show History. Your screen should now look similar to Figure 11-2, showing the latest release of the package as well as a chart with the number of releases over the years.

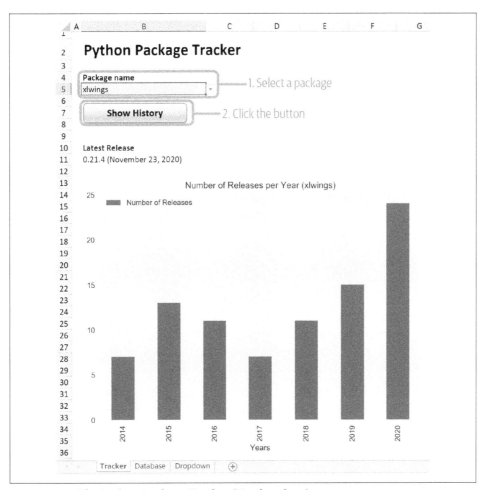

Figure 11-2. The Python Package Tracker (Tracker sheet)

You could now go back to the Database sheet and add additional packages. Whenever you want to update the database with the latest information from PyPI, click on the Update Database button: this will synchronize your database with the latest data from PyPI.

After taking a look at how the Python Package Tracker works from a user's perspective, let's now introduce its core functionality.

Core Functionality

In this section, I will introduce you to the core functionality of the Python Package Tracker: how to fetch data via web APIs and how to query databases. I'll also show you how to handle exceptions, a topic that will inevitably arise when writing application code. Let's get started with web APIs!

Web APIs

Web APIs are one of the most popular ways for an application to fetch data from the internet: API stands for *application programming interface* and defines how you interact with an application programmatically. A web API, therefore, is an API that is accessed over a network, usually the internet. To understand how web APIs work, let's take a step back and see what happens (in simplified terms) when you open a web page in your browser: after entering a URL into the address bar, your browser sends a *GET request* to the server, asking for the web page you want. A GET request is a method of the HTTP protocol that your browser uses to communicate with the server. When the server receives the request, it responds by sending back the requested HTML document, which your browser displays: *voilà*, your web page has loaded. The HTTP protocol has various other methods; the most common one—apart from the GET request—is the *POST request*, which is used to send data to the server (for example, when you fill in a contact form on a web page).

While it makes sense for servers to send back a nicely formatted HTML page to interact with humans, applications don't care about design and are only interested in the data. Therefore, a GET request to a web API works like requesting a web page, but you usually get back the data in *JSON* instead of HTML format. JSON stands for *JavaScript Object Notation* and is a data structure that is understood by pretty much every programming language, which makes it ideal to exchange data between different systems. Although the notation is using JavaScript syntax, it's very close to how you use (nested) dictionaries and lists in Python. The differences are the following:

- JSON only accepts double quotes for strings
- JSON uses `null` where Python uses `None`
- JSON uses lowercase `true` and `false` while they are capitalized in Python
- JSON only accepts strings as keys whereas Python dictionaries accept a wide range of objects as keys

The `json` module from the standard library allows you to convert a Python dictionary to a JSON string and vice versa:

```
In [1]: import json

In [2]: # A Python dictionary...
        user_dict = {"name": "Jane Doe",
                     "age": 23,
                     "married": False,
                     "children": None,
                     "hobbies": ["hiking", "reading"]}

In [3]: # ...converted to a JSON string
        # by json.dumps ("dump string"). The "indent" parameter is
        # optional and prettifies the printing.
        user_json = json.dumps(user_dict, indent=4)
        print(user_json)
{
    "name": "Jane Doe",
    "age": 23,
    "married": false,
    "children": null,
    "hobbies": [
        "hiking",
        "reading"
    ]
}

In [4]: # Convert the JSON string back to a native Python data structure
        json.loads(user_json)

Out[4]: {'name': 'Jane Doe',
         'age': 23,
         'married': False,
         'children': None,
         'hobbies': ['hiking', 'reading']}
```

REST API

Instead of web API, you will often see the term *REST* or *RESTful* API. REST stands for *representational state transfer* and defines a web API that adheres to certain constraints. At its core, the idea of REST is that you access information in the form of *stateless resources*. Stateless means that every request to a REST API is completely independent of any other request and needs to always provide the full set of information that it requests. Note that the term *REST API* is often misused to mean any sort of web API, even if it doesn't adhere to the REST constraints.

Consuming web APIs is usually really simple (we'll see how this works with Python in a moment), and almost every service offers one. If you want to download your favorite Spotify playlist, you would issue the following GET request (see the Spotify Web API Reference (*https://oreil.ly/zcyUh*)):

```
GET https://api.spotify.com/v1/playlists/playlist_id
```

Or, if you want to get information about your latest Uber trips, you would run the following GET request (see the Uber REST API (*https://oreil.ly/FTp-Y*)):

```
GET https://api.uber.com/v1.2/history
```

To use these APIs, though, you need to be authenticated, which usually means that you require an account and a token that you can send along with your requests. For the Python Package Tracker, we'll need to fetch data from PyPI to get information about the releases of a specific package. Fortunately, PyPI's web API doesn't require any authentication, so we have one thing less to worry about. When you have a look at the PyPI JSON API docs (*https://oreil.ly/yTVjL*), you will see that there are only two *endpoints*, i.e., URL fragments that are appended to the common *base URL*, *https://pypi.org/pypi*:

```
GET /project_name/json
GET /project_name/version/json
```

The second endpoint gives you the same information as the first one, but for a specific version only. For the Python Package Tracker, the first endpoint is all we need to get the details about the past releases of a package, so let's see how this works. In Python, a simple way to interact with a web API is by using the Requests package that comes preinstalled with Anaconda. Run the following commands to fetch PyPI data about pandas:

```
In [5]: import requests
```

```
In [6]: response = requests.get("https://pypi.org/pypi/pandas/json")
        response.status_code
```

```
Out[6]: 200
```

Every response comes with an HTTP status code: for example, 200 means *OK* and 404 means *Not Found*. You can look up the full list of HTTP response status codes in the Mozilla web docs (*https://oreil.ly/HySVq*). You may be familiar with the status code 404 as your browser sometimes displays it when you click on a dead link or type in an address that doesn't exist. Similarly, you will also get a 404 status code if you run a GET request with a package name that doesn't exist on PyPI. To look at the content of the response, it's easiest to call the json method of the response object, which will transform the JSON string of the response into a Python dictionary:

```
In [7]: response.json()
```

The response is very long, so I am printing a short subset here to allow you to understand the structure:

```
Out[7]: {
            'info': {
                'bugtrack_url': None,
                'license': 'BSD',
                'maintainer': 'The PyData Development Team',
```

```
                    'maintainer_email': 'pydata@googlegroups.com',
                    'name': 'pandas'
                },
                'releases': {
                    '0.1': [
                        {
                            'filename': 'pandas-0.1.tar.gz',
                            'size': 238458,
                            'upload_time': '2009-12-25T23:58:31'
                        },
                        {
                            'filename': 'pandas-0.1.win32-py2.5.exe',
                            'size': 313639,
                            'upload_time': '2009-12-26T17:14:35'
                        }
                    ]
                }
            }
```

To get a list with all releases and their dates, something we need for the Python Package Tracker, we can run the following code to loop through the `releases` dictionary:

```
In [8]: releases = []
        for version, files in response.json()['releases'].items():
            releases.append(f"{version}: {files[0]['upload_time']}")
        releases[:3]  # show the first 3 elements of the list

Out[8]: ['0.1: 2009-12-25T23:58:31',
         '0.10.0: 2012-12-17T16:52:06',
         '0.10.1: 2013-01-22T05:22:09']
```

Note that we are arbitrarily picking the release timestamp from the package that appears first in the list. A specific release often has multiple packages to account for different versions of Python and operating systems. To wrap this topic up, you may remember from Chapter 5 that pandas has a `read_json` method to return a Data-Frame directly from a JSON string. This, however, wouldn't help us here as the response from PyPI isn't in a structure that can be directly transformed into a DataFrame.

This was a short introduction to web APIs to understand their use in the code base of the Python Package Tracker. Let's now see how we can communicate with databases, the other external system that we make use of in our application!

Databases

To be able to use the data from PyPI even when you're not connected to the internet, you need to store it after downloading. While you could store your JSON responses as text files on disk, a far more comfortable solution is to use a database: this allows you to query your data in an easy way. The Python Package Tracker is using SQLite (*https://sqlite.org*), a *relational database*. Relational database systems get their name from *relation*, which refers to the database table itself (and not to the relation between tables, which is a common misconception): their highest goal is data integrity, which they achieve by splitting the data up into different tables (a process called *normalization*) and by applying constraints to avoid inconsistent and redundant data. Relational databases use SQL (Structured Query Language) to perform database queries and are among the most popular server-based relational database systems are SQL Server (*https://oreil.ly/XZOI9*), Oracle (*https://oreil.ly/VKWE0*), PostgreSQL (*https://oreil.ly/VAEqY*), and MySQL (*https://mysql.com*). As an Excel user, you may also be familiar with the file-based Microsoft Access (*https://oreil.ly/bRh6Q*) database.

NoSQL Databases

These days, relational databases have strong competition from *NoSQL* databases that store redundant data in an attempt to achieve the following advantages:

No table joins

Since relational databases split their data across multiple tables, you often need to combine the information from two or more tables by *joining* them, which sometimes can be slow. This is not required with NoSQL databases, which can result in better performance for certain types of queries.

No database migrations

With relational database systems, every time you make a change to the table structure, e.g., by adding a new column to a table, you must run a database *migration*. A migration is a script that brings the database into the desired new structure. This makes the deployment of new versions of an application more complex, potentially resulting in downtime, something that is easier to avoid with NoSQL databases.

Easier to scale

NoSQL databases are easier to distribute across multiple servers as there are no tables that are dependent on each other. This means that an application that uses a NoSQL database may scale better when your user base skyrockets.

NoSQL databases come in many flavors: some databases are simple key-value stores, i.e., work similarly to a dictionary in Python (e.g., Redis (*https://redis.io*)); others allow the storage of documents, often in JSON format (e.g., MongoDB (*https://mongodb.com*)). Some databases even combine the relational and NoSQL worlds: PostgreSQL, which happens to be one of the most popular databases in the Python community, is traditionally a relational database but also allows you to store data in JSON format—without losing the ability to query it via SQL.

SQLite, the database we're going to use, is a file-based database like Microsoft Access. However, in contrast to Microsoft Access, which only works on Windows, SQLite works on all platforms that Python supports. On the other hand, SQLite doesn't allow you to build a user interface like Microsoft Access, but Excel comes in handy for this part.

Let's now have a look at the structure of the Package Tracker's database before finding out how we can use Python to connect to databases and make SQL queries. Then, to conclude this introduction about databases, we'll have a look at SQL injections, a popular vulnerability of database-driven applications.

The Package Tracker database

The database of the Python Package Tracker couldn't be any simpler as it only has two tables: the table `packages` stores the package name and the table `package_versions` stores the version strings and the date of the upload. The two tables can be joined on the `package_id`: rather than storing the `package_name` with every row in the `package_versions` table, it has been *normalized* into the `packages` table. This gets rid of redundant data—name changes, for example, only have to be done in a single field across the entire database. To get a better idea about how the database looks with the xlwings and pandas packages loaded, have a look at Tables 11-1 and 11-2.

Table 11-1. The packages table

package_id	package_name
1	xlwings
2	pandas

Table 11-2. The package_versions table (first three rows of each package_id)

package_id	version_string	uploaded_at
1	0.1.0	2014-03-19 18:18:49.000000
1	0.1.1	2014-06-27 16:26:36.000000
1	0.2.0	2014-07-29 17:14:22.000000
...	...	...
2	0.1	2009-12-25 23:58:31.000000
2	0.2beta	2010-05-18 15:05:11.000000
2	0.2b1	2010-05-18 15:09:05.000000
...	...	...

Figure 11-3 is a database diagram that shows the two tables again schematically. You can read off the table and column names and get information about the primary and foreign keys:

Primary key

Relational databases require every table to have a *primary key*. A primary key is one or more columns that uniquely identify a row (a row is also called a *record*). In the case of the packages table, the primary key is package_id and in the case of the package_versions table, the primary key is a so-called *composite key*, i.e., a combination of package_id and version_string.

Foreign key

The column package_id in the package_versions table is a *foreign key* to the same column in the packages table, symbolized by the line that connects the tables: a foreign key is a constraint that, in our case, ensures that every package_id in the package_versions table exists in the packages table—this guarantees data integrity. The branches at the right end of the connection line symbolize the nature of the relationship: one package can have many package_versions, which is called a *one-to-many* relationship.

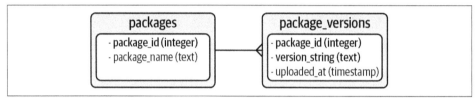

Figure 11-3. Database diagram (primary keys are bold)

To have a look at the content of the database tables and run SQL queries, you could install a VS Code extension called SQLite (please see the SQLite extension docs (*https://oreil.ly/nP4mC*) for more details) or use a dedicated SQLite management software, of which there are plenty. We, however, will be using Python to run SQL queries. Before anything else, let's see how we can connect to a database!

Database connections

To connect to a database from Python, you need a *driver*, i.e., a Python package that knows how to communicate with the database you are using. Each database requires a different driver and each driver uses a different syntax, but luckily, there is a powerful package called SQLAlchemy (*https://sqlalchemy.org*) that abstracts away most of the differences between the various databases and drivers. SQLAlchemy is mostly used as an *object relational mapper* (ORM) that translates your database records into Python objects, a concept that many developers—albeit not all—find more natural to work with. To keep things simple, we're ignoring the ORM functionality and only using SQLAlchemy to make it easier to run raw SQL queries. SQLAlchemy is also used behind the scenes when you use pandas to read and write database tables in the form of DataFrames. Running a database query from pandas involves three levels of packages—pandas, SQLAlchemy, and the database driver—as shown in Figure 11-4. You can run database queries from each of these three levels.

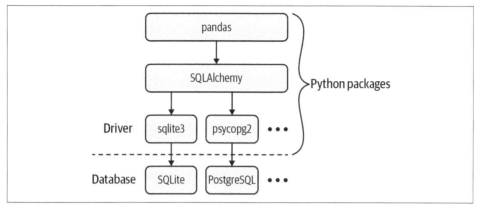

Figure 11-4. Accessing databases from Python

Table 11-3 shows you which driver SQLAlchemy uses by default (some databases can be used with more than one driver). It also gives you the format of the database connection string—we'll use the connection string in a moment when we will run actual SQL queries.

Table 11-3. SQLAlchemy default drivers and connection strings

Database	Default Driver	Connection String
SQLite	sqlite3	sqlite:///filepath
PostgreSQL	psycopg2	postgresql://username:password@host:port/database
MySQL	mysql-python	mysql://username:password@host:port/database
Oracle	cx_oracle	oracle://username:password@host:port/database
SQL Server	pyodbc	mssql+pyodbc://username:password@host:port/database

Except for SQLite, you usually need a password to connect to a database. And since connection strings are URLs, you will have to use the URL encoded version of your passwords if you have any special characters in them. Here is how you can print the URL encoded version of your password:

```
In [9]: import urllib.parse

In [10]: urllib.parse.quote_plus("pa$$word")

Out[10]: 'pa%24%24word'
```

Having introduced pandas, SQLAlchemy, and the database driver as the three levels from which we can connect to databases, let's see how they compare in practice by making a few SQL queries!

SQL queries

Even if you are new to SQL, you should have no trouble understanding the few SQL queries that I will use in the following samples and in the Python Package Tracker. SQL is a *declarative language*, which means that you tell the database *what you want* instead of *what to do*. Some queries almost read like plain English:

```
SELECT * FROM packages
```

This tells the database that you want to *select all columns from the packages table*. In production code, you wouldn't want to use the wildcard * which means *all columns* but rather specify each column explicitly as this makes your query less error-prone:

```
SELECT package_id, package_name FROM packages
```

 Database Queries vs. pandas DataFrames

SQL is a *set-based* language, which means that you operate on a set of rows rather than looping through individual rows. This is very similar to how you work with pandas DataFrames. The SQL query:

```
SELECT package_id, package_name FROM packages
```

corresponds to the following pandas expression (assuming that packages is a DataFrame):

```
packages.loc[:, ["package_id", "package_name"]]
```

The following code samples use the *packagetracker.db* file that you will find in the *packagetracker* folder of the companion repo. The examples expect that you have already added xlwings and pandas to the database via the Python Package Tracker's Excel frontend like we did at the beginning of this chapter—otherwise you would get only empty results. Following Figure 11-4 from bottom to top, we will first make our SQL query from the driver directly, then use SQLAlchemy and finally pandas:

```
In [11]: # Let's start with the imports
         import sqlite3
         from sqlalchemy import create_engine
         import pandas as pd

In [12]: # Our SQL query: "select all columns from the packages table"
         sql = "SELECT * FROM packages"

In [13]: # Option 1: Database driver (sqlite3 is part of the standard library)
         # Using the connection as context manager automatically commits
         # the transaction or rolls it back in case of an error.
         with sqlite3.connect("packagetracker/packagetracker.db") as con:
             cursor = con.cursor()  # We need a cursor to run SQL queries
             result = cursor.execute(sql).fetchall()  # Return all records
         result

Out[13]: [(1, 'xlwings'), (2, 'pandas')]
```

```
In [14]: # Option 2: SQLAlchemy
         # "create_engine" expects the connection string of your database.
         # Here, we can execute a query as a method of the connection object.
         engine = create_engine("sqlite:///packagetracker/packagetracker.db")
         with engine.connect() as con:
             result = con.execute(sql).fetchall()
         result

Out[14]: [(1, 'xlwings'), (2, 'pandas')]

In [15]: # Option 3: pandas
         # Providing a table name to "read_sql" reads the full table.
         # Pandas requires an SQLAlchemy engine that we reuse from
         # the previous example.
         df = pd.read_sql("packages", engine, index_col="package_id")
         df

Out[15]:             package_name
         package_id
         1                xlwings
         2                 pandas

In [16]: # "read_sql" also accepts an SQL query
         pd.read_sql(sql, engine, index_col="package_id")

Out[16]:             package_name
         package_id
         1                xlwings
         2                 pandas

In [17]: # The DataFrame method "to_sql" writes DataFrames to tables
         # "if_exists" has to be either "fail", "append" or "replace"
         # and defines what happens if the table already exists
         df.to_sql("packages2", con=engine, if_exists="append")

In [18]: # The previous command created a new table "packages2" and
         # inserted the records from the DataFrame df as we can
         # verify by reading it back
         pd.read_sql("packages2", engine, index_col="package_id")

Out[18]:             package_name
         package_id
         1                xlwings
         2                 pandas

In [19]: # Let's get rid of the table again by running the
         # "drop table" command via SQLAlchemy
         with engine.connect() as con:
             con.execute("DROP TABLE packages2")
```

Whether you should use the database driver, SQLAlchemy, or pandas to run your queries largely depends on your preferences: I personally like the fine-grained control you get by using SQLAlchemy and enjoy that I can use the same syntax with different databases. On the other hand, pandas' `read_sql` is convenient to get the result of a query in the form of a DataFrame.

Foreign Keys with SQLite

Somewhat surprisingly, SQLite does not respect foreign keys by default when running queries. However, if you use SQLAlchemy, you can easily enforce foreign keys; see the SQLAlchemy docs (*https://oreil.ly/6YPvC*). This will also work if you run the queries from pandas. You will find the respective code at the top of the *database.py* module in the *packagetracker* folder of the companion repository.

Now that you know how to run simple SQL queries, let's wrap this section up by looking at SQL injections, which can pose a security risk to your application.

SQL injection

If you don't protect your SQL queries properly, a malicious user can run arbitrary SQL code by injecting SQL statements into data input fields: for example, instead of selecting a package name like xlwings in the dropdown of the Python Package Tracker, they could send an SQL statement that changes your intended query. This can expose sensitive information or perform destructive actions like deleting a table. How can you prevent this? Let's first have a look at the following database query, which the Package Tracker runs when you select xlwings and click on Show History:[1]

```
SELECT v.uploaded_at, v.version_string
FROM packages p
INNER JOIN package_versions v ON p.package_id = v.package_id
WHERE p.package_id = 1
```

This query joins the two tables together and only returns those rows where the package_id is 1. To help you understand this query based on what we learned in Chapter 5, if packages and package_versions were pandas DataFrames, you could write:

```
df = packages.merge(package_versions, how="inner", on="package_id")
df.loc[df["package_id"] == 1, ["uploaded_at", "version_string"]]
```

It's obvious that the package_id needs to be a variable where we now have a hardcoded 1 to return the correct rows depending on the package that is selected. Knowing about f-strings from Chapter 3, you could be tempted to change the last line of the SQL query like this:

```
f"WHERE p.package_id = {package_id}"
```

While this would technically work, you must never do this as it opens up the door for SQL injection: for example, somebody could send '1 OR TRUE' instead of an integer

---

1 In reality, the tool uses package_name instead of package_id to simplify the code.

representing the `package_id`. The resulting query would return the rows of the whole table instead of just those where the `package_id` is 1. Therefore, always use the syntax that SQLAlchemy offers you for placeholders (they start with a colon):

```
In [20]: # Let's start by importing SQLAlchemy's text function
         from sqlalchemy.sql import text
```

```
In [21]: # ":package_id" is the placeholder
         sql = """
         SELECT v.uploaded_at, v.version_string
         FROM packages p
         INNER JOIN package_versions v ON p.package_id = v.package_id
         WHERE p.package_id = :package_id
         ORDER BY v.uploaded_at
         """
```

```
In [22]: # Via SQLAlchemy
         with engine.connect() as con:
             result = con.execute(text(sql), package_id=1).fetchall()
         result[:3]  # Print the first 3 records
```

```
Out[22]: [('2014-03-19 18:18:49.000000', '0.1.0'),
          ('2014-06-27 16:26:36.000000', '0.1.1'),
          ('2014-07-29 17:14:22.000000', '0.2.0')]
```

```
In [23]: # Via pandas
         pd.read_sql(text(sql), engine, parse_dates=["uploaded_at"],
                     params={"package_id": 1},
                     index_col=["uploaded_at"]).head(3)
```

```
Out[23]:                          version_string
         uploaded_at
         2014-03-19 18:18:49            0.1.0
         2014-06-27 16:26:36            0.1.1
         2014-07-29 17:14:22            0.2.0
```

Wrapping the SQL query with SQLAlchemy's `text` function has the advantage that you can use the same syntax for placeholders across different databases. Otherwise, you'd have to use the placeholder that the database driver uses: `sqlite3` uses `?` and `psycopg2` uses `%s`, for example.

You may argue that SQL injection isn't much of an issue when your users have direct access to Python and could run arbitrary code on the database anyway. But if you take your xlwings prototype and transform it into a web application one day, it will become a huge issue, so it's better to do it properly from the beginning.

Besides web APIs and databases, there is another topic that we have jumped over so far that is indispensable for solid application development: exception handling. Let's see how it works!

Exceptions

I mentioned exception handling in Chapter 1 as an example of where VBA with its *GoTo* mechanism has fallen behind. In this section, I show you how Python uses the *try/except* mechanism to handle errors in your programs. Whenever something is outside of your control, errors can and will happen. For example, the email server may be down when you try to send an email, or a file may be missing that your program expects—in the case of the Python Package Tracker, this could be the database file. Dealing with user input is another area where you have to prepare for inputs that don't make sense. Let's get some practice—if the following function is called with a zero, you will get a ZeroDivisionError:

```
In [24]: def print_reciprocal(number):
             result = 1 / number
             print(f"The reciprocal is: {result}")

In [25]: print_reciprocal(0)  # This will raise an error

---------------------------------------------------------------------------
ZeroDivisionError                         Traceback (most recent call last)
<ipython-input-25-095f19ebb9e9> in <module>
----> 1 print_reciprocal(0)  # This will raise an error

<ipython-input-24-88fdfd8a4711> in print_reciprocal(number)
      1 def print_reciprocal(number):
----> 2     result = 1 / number
      3     print(f"The reciprocal is: {result}")

ZeroDivisionError: division by zero
```

To let your program react gracefully to such errors, use the try/except statements (this is the equivalent of the VBA sample in Chapter 1):

```
In [26]: def print_reciprocal(number):
             try:
                 result = 1 / number
             except Exception as e:
                 # "as e" makes the Exception object available as variable "e"
                 # "repr" stands for "printable representation" of an object
                 # and gives you back a string with the error message
                 print(f"There was an error: {repr(e)}")
                 result = "N/A"
             else:
                 print("There was no error!")
             finally:
                 print(f"The reciprocal is: {result}")
```

Whenever an error occurs in the try block, code execution moves on to the except block where you can handle the error: this allows you to give the user helpful feedback or write the error to a log file. The else clause only runs if there is no error raised during the try block and the finally block runs always, whether or not an error was raised. Often, you will get away with just the try and except blocks. Let's see the output of the function given different inputs:

```
In [27]: print_reciprocal(10)

There was no error!
The reciprocal is: 0.1

In [28]: print_reciprocal("a")

There was an error: TypeError("unsupported operand type(s) for /: 'int'
 and 'str'")
The reciprocal is: N/A

In [29]: print_reciprocal(0)

There was an error: ZeroDivisionError('division by zero')
The reciprocal is: N/A
```

The way that I have used the except statement means that any exception that happens in the try block will cause the code execution to continue in the except block. Usually, that is not what you want. You want to check for an error as specific as possible and handle only those you expect. Your program may otherwise fail for something completely unexpected, which makes it hard to debug. To fix this, rewrite the function as follows, checking explicitly for the two errors that we expect (I am leaving away the else and finally statements):

```
In [30]: def print_reciprocal(number):
             try:
                 result = 1 / number
                 print(f"The reciprocal is: {result}")
             except (TypeError, ZeroDivisionError):
                 print("Please type in any number except 0.")
```

Let's run the code again:

```
In [31]: print_reciprocal("a")

Please type in any number except 0.
```

If you want to handle an error differently depending on the exception, handle them separately:

```
In [32]: def print_reciprocal(number):
             try:
                 result = 1 / number
                 print(f"The reciprocal is: {result}")
             except TypeError:
                 print("Please type in a number.")
             except ZeroDivisionError:
                 print("The reciprocal of 0 is not defined.")

In [33]: print_reciprocal("a")

Please type in a number.
```

```
In [34]: print_reciprocal(0)

The reciprocal of 0 is not defined.
```

Now that you know about error handling, web APIs, and databases, you are ready to move on to the next section, where we'll go through each component of the Python Package Tracker.

Application Structure

In this section, we'll look behind the scenes of the Python Package Tracker to understand how everything works. First, we'll walk through the application's frontend, i.e., the Excel file, before looking at its backend, i.e., the Python code. To wrap this section up, we'll see how debugging an xlwings project works, a useful skill with projects of the size and complexity of the Package Tracker.

In the *packagetracker* directory in the companion repo, you'll find four files. Do you remember when I talked about *separation of concerns* in Chapter 1? We are now able to map these files to the different layers as shown in Table 11-4:

Table 11-4. Separation of concerns

Layer	File	Description
Presentation layer	`packagetracker.xlsm`	This is the frontend and as such the only file the end-user interacts with.
Business layer	`packagetracker.py`	This module handles the data download via web API and does the number crunching with pandas.
Data layer	`database.py`	This module handles all database queries.
Database	`packagetracker.db`	This is an SQLite database file.

In this context, it's worth mentioning that the presentation layer, i.e., the Excel file, doesn't contain a single cell formula, which makes the tool much easier to audit and control.

Model-View-Controller (MVC)

Separation of concerns has many faces and the breakdown as shown in Table 11-4 is just one possibility. Another popular design pattern that you may run into relatively quickly is called *model-view-controller* (MVC). In the MVC world, the core of the application is the *model* where all the data and usually most of the business logic is handled. While the *view* corresponds to the presentation layer, the *controller* is only a thin layer that sits between the model and the view to make sure that they are always in sync. To keep things simple, I am not using the MVC pattern in this book.

Now that you know what each file is responsible for, let's move on and have a closer look at how the Excel frontend has been set up!

Frontend

When you build a web application, you differentiate between the *frontend*, which is the part of the application that runs in your browser, and the *backend*, which is the code that runs on the server. We can apply the same terminology with xlwings tools: the frontend is the Excel file and the backend is the Python code that you call via RunPython. If you want to build the frontend from scratch, begin with running the following command on an Anaconda Prompt (make sure to cd first into the directory of your choice):

```
(base)> xlwings quickstart packagetracker
```

Navigate to the *packagetracker* directory and open *packagetracker.xlsm* in Excel. Start by adding the three tabs, Tracker, Database and Dropdown, as shown in Figure 11-5.

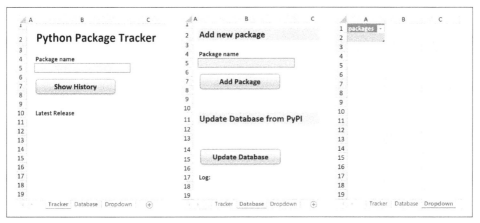

Figure 11-5. Building the user interface

While you should be able to take over the text and formatting from Figure 11-5, I need to give you a few more details about the things that aren't visible:

Buttons
> To make the tool look a bit less like Windows 3.1, I didn't use the standard macro buttons that we used in the previous chapter. Instead, I went to Insert > Shapes and inserted a Rounded Rectangle. If you want to use the standard button, that's fine, too, but at this point, don't assign a macro just yet.

Named ranges

To make the tool a little easier to maintain, we will use named ranges rather than cell addresses in the Python code. Therefore, add the named ranges as shown in Table 11-5.

Table 11-5. Named ranges

Sheet	Cell	Name
Tracker	B5	package_selection
Tracker	B11	latest_release
Database	B5	new_package
Database	B13	updated_at
Database	B18	log

One way to add named ranges is to select the cell, then write the name into the Name Box and finally confirm by hitting Enter, as in Figure 11-6.

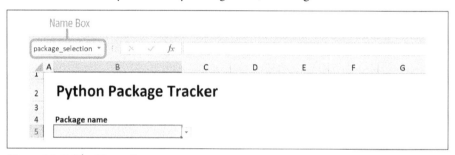

Figure 11-6. The Name Box

Tables

On the Dropdown sheet, after typing "packages" into cell A1, select A1, then go to Insert > Table and make sure to activate the checkbox next to "My table has headers." To finalize, with the table selected, go to the ribbon tab Table Design (Windows) or Table (macOS) and rename the table from `Table1` to `drop down_content`, as shown in Figure 11-7.

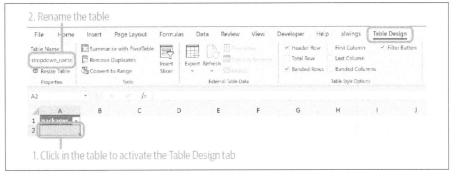

Figure 11-7. Renaming an Excel table

Data Validation

We use data validation to provide the dropdown in cell B5 on the Tracker sheet. To add it, select cell B5, then go to Data > Data Validation and under Allow, select List. Under source set the following formula:

```
=INDIRECT("dropdown_content[packages]")
```

Then, confirm with OK. This is just a reference to the body of the table, but since Excel doesn't accept a table reference directly, we have to wrap it in an INDIRECT formula, which resolves the table to its address. Still, by using a table, it will properly resize the range that is shown in the dropdown when we add more packages.

Conditional Formatting

When you add a package, there can be a few errors that we'd like to show to the user: the field could be empty, the package may already exist on the database, or it may be missing on PyPI. To show the error in red and other messages in black, we'll use a simple trick based on conditional formatting: we want a red font whenever the message contains the word "error." On the Database sheet, select cell C5, which is where we'll write out the message. Then go to Home > Conditional Formatting > Highlight Cells Rules > Text that contains. Enter the value **error** and select Red Text in the dropdown as shown in Figure 11-8, then click on OK. Apply the same conditional format to cell C5 on the Tracker sheet.

Figure 11-8. Conditional Formatting on Windows (left) and macOS (right)

Gridlines

On the Tracker and Database sheets, the gridlines have been hidden by unchecking the View checkbox under Page Layout > Gridlines.

At this point, the user interface is complete and should look like Figure 11-5. We now need to add the `RunPython` calls in the VBA editor and connect them with the buttons. Click Alt+F11 (Windows) or Option-F11 (macOS) to open the VBA editor, then, under the VBAProject of *packagetracker.xlsm*, double-click Module1 on the left-hand side under Modules to open it. Delete the existing `SampleCall` code and replace it with the following macros:

```
Sub AddPackage()
    RunPython "import packagetracker; packagetracker.add_package()"
End Sub

Sub ShowHistory()
    RunPython "import packagetracker; packagetracker.show_history()"
End Sub

Sub UpdateDatabase()
    RunPython "import packagetracker; packagetracker.update_database()"
End Sub
```

Next, right-click on each button, select Assign Macro and select the macro that corresponds to the button. Figure 11-9 shows the Show History button, but it works the same for the Add Package and Update Database buttons.

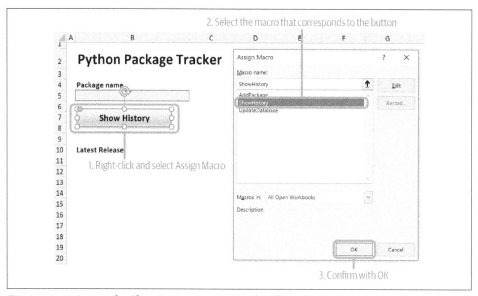

Figure 11-9. Assign the ShowHistory macro to the Show History button

The frontend is now done and we can move on with the Python backend.

Backend

The code of the two Python files *packagetracker.py* and *database.py* is too long to be shown here, so you will need to open them from the companion repository in VS Code. I will, however, refer to a couple of code snippets in this section to explain a few key concepts. Let's see what happens when you click the Add Package button on the Database sheet. The button has the following VBA macro assigned:

```
Sub AddPackage()
    RunPython "import packagetracker; packagetracker.add_package()"
End Sub
```

As you see, the RunPython function calls the add_package Python function in the packagetracker module as shown in Example 11-1.

No Production Code

The application is kept as simple as possible to make it easy to follow—it doesn't check for every possible thing that can go wrong. In a production environment, you'd want to make it more robust: for example, you would show a user-friendly error if it can't find the database file.

Example 11-1. The add_package function in packagetracker.py (without comments)

```
def add_package():
    db_sheet = xw.Book.caller().sheets["Database"]
    package_name = db_sheet["new_package"].value
    feedback_cell = db_sheet["new_package"].offset(column_offset=1)

    feedback_cell.clear_contents()

    if not package_name:
        feedback_cell.value = "Error: Please provide a name!" ❶
        return
    if requests.get(f"{BASE_URL}/{package_name}/json",
                    timeout=6).status_code != 200: ❷
        feedback_cell.value = "Error: Package not found!"
        return

    error = database.store_package(package_name) ❸
    db_sheet["new_package"].clear_contents()

    if error:
        feedback_cell.value = f"Error: {error}"
    else:
        feedback_cell.value = f"Added {package_name} successfully."
```

```
        update_database()  ❹
        refresh_dropdown()  ❺
```

❶ The "error" in the feedback message will trigger the red font in Excel via conditional formatting.

❷ By default, Requests is waiting forever for a response which could lead the application to "hang" in cases where PyPI has an issue and is responding slowly. That's why for production code, you should always include an explicit `timeout` parameter.

❸ The `store_package` function returns `None` if the operation was successful and a string with the error message otherwise.

❹ To keep things simple, the whole database is updated. In a production environment, you would only add the records of the new package.

❺ This will update the table on the Dropdown sheet with the content of the `packages` table. Together with the data validation that we have set up in Excel, this makes sure that all packages appear in the dropdown on the Tracker sheet. You would need to give the users a way to call this function directly if you allow the database to be populated from outside of your Excel file. This is the case as soon as you have multiple users using the same database from different Excel files.

You should be able to follow the other functions in the *packagetracker.py* file with the help of the comments in the code. Let's now turn our attention to the *database.py* file. The first few lines are shown in Example 11-2.

Example 11-2. database.py (excerpt with the relevant imports)

```
from pathlib import Path

import sqlalchemy
import pandas as pd

...

# We want the database file to sit next to this file.
# Here, we are turning the path into an absolute path.
this_dir = Path(__file__).resolve().parent  ❶
db_path = this_dir / "packagetracker.db"

# Database engine
engine = sqlalchemy.create_engine(f"sqlite:///{db_path}")
```

❶ If you need a refresher of what this line does, have a look at the beginning of Chapter 7, where I explain it in the code of the sales report.

While this snippet is concerned with putting together the path of the database file, it also shows you how to get around a common error when you work with any sort of file, whether that's a picture, a CSV file, or, like in this case, a database file. When you put together a quick Python script, you may just use a relative path as I have done in most of the Jupyter notebook samples:

```
engine = sqlalchemy.create_engine("sqlite:///packagetracker.db")
```

This works as long as your file is in your working directory. However, when you run this code from Excel via RunPython, the working directory can be different, which will cause Python to look for the file in the wrong folder—you will get a File not found error. You can solve this issue by providing an absolute path or by creating a path the way we do in Example 11-2. This makes sure that Python is looking for the file in the same directory as the source file even if you execute the code from Excel via RunPython.

If you want to create the Python Package Tracker from scratch, you will need to create the database manually: run the *database.py* file as a script, for example by clicking the Run File button in VS Code. This will create the database file *packagetracker.db* with the two tables. The code that creates the database is found at the very bottom of *database.py*:

```
if __name__ == "__main__":
    create_db()
```

While the last line calls the create_db function, the meaning of the preceding if statement is explained in the following tip.

if __name__ == "__main__"

You will see this if statement at the bottom of many Python files. It makes sure that this code only runs when you run the file *as a script*, for example, from an Anaconda Prompt by running python database.py or by clicking the Run File button in VS Code. It, however, will not be triggered when you run the file *by importing it as a module*, i.e., by doing import database in your code. The reason for this is that Python assigns the name __main__ to the file if you run it directly as script, whereas it will be called by its module name (database) when you run it via the import statement. Since Python tracks the file name in a variable called __name__, the if statement will evaluate to True only when you run it as script; it will not be triggered when you import it from the *packagetracker.py* file.

The rest of the `database` module runs SQL statements both via SQLAlchemy and pandas' `to_sql` and `read_sql` methods so you get a feeling for both approaches.

Moving to PostgreSQL

If you wanted to replace SQLite with PostgreSQL, a server-based database, there are only a few things you need to change. First of all, you need to run `conda install psycopg2` (or `pip install psycopg2-binary` if you are not using the Anaconda distribution) to install the PostgreSQL driver. Then, in *database.py*, change the connection string in the `create_engine` function to the PostgreSQL version as shown in Table 11-3. Finally, to create the tables, you would need to change the `INTEGER` data type of `packages.package_id` to the PostgreSQL specific notation of `SERIAL`. Creating an auto-incrementing primary key is an example of where the SQL dialects differ.

When you create tools of the complexity of the Python Package Tracker, you probably run into a few issues along the way: for example, you might have renamed a named range in Excel and forgot to adjust the Python code accordingly. This is a good moment to look into how debugging works!

Debugging

To easily debug your xlwings scripts, run your functions directly from VS Code, instead of running them by clicking a button in Excel. The following lines at the very bottom of the *packagetracker.py* file will help you with debugging the `add_package` function (this is the same code that you will also find at the bottom of a `quickstart` project):

```
if __name__ == "__main__":  ❶
    xw.Book("packagetracker.xlsm").set_mock_caller()  ❷
    add_package()
```

❶ We have just seen how this if statement works when we were looking at the *database.py* code; see the previous tip.

❷ As this code is only executed when you run the file directly from Python as a script, the `set_mock_caller()` command is only meant for debugging purposes: when you run the file in VS Code or from an Anaconda Prompt, it sets the `xw.Book.caller()` to `xw.Book("packagetracker.xlsm")`. The only purpose of doing this is to be able to run your script from both sides, Python and Excel, without having to switch the book object within the `add_package` function back and forth between `xw.Book("packagetracker.xlsm")` (when you call it from VS Code) and `xw.Book.caller()` (when you call it from Excel).

Open *packagetracker.py* in VS Code and set a breakpoint on any line within the `add_package` function by clicking to the left of the line numbers. Then hit F5 and select "Python File" in the dialog to start the debugger and to make your code stop at the breakpoint. Make sure to hit F5 instead of using the Run File button, as the Run File button ignores breakpoints.

Debugging with VS Code and Anaconda

On Windows, when you run the VS Code debugger for the first time with code that uses pandas, you might be greeted by an error: "Exception has occurred: ImportError, Unable to import required dependencies: numpy." This happens because the debugger is up and running before the Conda environment has been activated properly. As a workaround, stop the debugger by clicking the stop icon and hit F5 again—it will work the second time.

If you are not familiar with how the debugger in VS Code works, have a look at Appendix B where I explain all the relevant functionality and buttons. We will also pick the topic up again in the respective section of the next chapter. If you want to debug a different function, stop the current debug session, then adjust the function name at the bottom of your file. For example, to debug the `show_history` function, change the last line in *packagetracker.py* as follows before hitting F5 again:

```
if __name__ == "__main__":
    xw.Book("packagetracker.xlsm").set_mock_caller()
    show_history()
```

On Windows, you could also activate the Show Console checkbox in the xlwings add-in, which will show a Command Prompt while the `RunPython` call is running.[2] This allows you to print additional information to help you debug the issue. For example, you could print the value of a variable to inspect it on the Command Prompt. After the code has been run, however, the Command Prompt will be closed. If you need to keep it open for a little longer, there is an easy trick: add `input()` as the last line in your function. This causes Python to wait for user input instead of closing the Command Prompt right away. When you're done with inspecting the output, hit Enter in the Command Prompt to close it—just make sure to remove the `input()` line again before unchecking the Show Console option!

---

2 At the time of this writing, this option is not yet available on macOS.

Conclusion

This chapter showed you that it's possible to build reasonably complex applications with a minimum of effort. Being able to leverage powerful Python packages like Requests or SQLAlchemy makes all the difference to me when I compare this with VBA, where talking to external systems is so much harder. If you have similar use cases, I would highly recommend you look more closely into both Requests and SQL-Alchemy—being able to efficiently deal with external data sources will allow you to make copy/paste a thing of the past.

Instead of clicking buttons, some users prefer to create their Excel tools by using cell formulas. The next chapter shows you how xlwings enables you to write user-defined functions in Python, allowing you to reuse most of the xlwings concepts we've learned so far.

## CHAPTER 12

User-Defined Functions (UDFs)

The previous three chapters showed you how to automate Excel with a Python script and how to run such a script from Excel at the click of a button. This chapter introduces user-defined functions (UDFs) as another option to call Python code from Excel with xlwings. UDFs are Python functions that you use in Excel cells in the same way as you use built-in functions like SUM or AVERAGE. As in the previous chapter, we will start with the quickstart command that allows us to try out a first UDF in no time. We then move on to a case study about fetching and processing data from Google Trends as an excuse to work with more complex UDFs: we'll learn how to work with pandas DataFrames and plots as well as how to debug UDFs. To conclude this chapter, we'll dig into a few advanced topics with a focus on performance. Unfortunately, xlwings doesn't support UDFs on macOS, which makes this chapter the only chapter requiring you to run the samples on Windows.[1]

A Note for macOS and Linux Users

Even if you are not on Windows, you may still want to have a look at the Google Trends case study as you could easily adapt it to work with a RunPython call on macOS. You could also produce a report by using one of the writer libraries from Chapter 8, which even works on Linux.

---

1 The Windows implementation uses a COM server (I've introduced the COM technology briefly in Chapter 9). Since COM doesn't exist on macOS, UDFs would have to be reimplemented from scratch, which is a lot of work and simply hasn't been done yet.

Getting Started with UDFs

This section starts with the prerequisites for writing UDFs before we can use the `quickstart` command to run our first UDF. To follow along with the examples in this chapter, you'll need the xlwings add-in installed and have the Excel option "Trust access to the VBA project object mode" enabled:

Add-in
> I assume you have the xlwings add-in installed as explained in Chapter 10. This is not a hard requirement, though: while it makes development easy, especially to click the Import Functions button, it is not required for deployment and can be replaced by setting the workbook up in the standalone mode—for the details, see Chapter 10.

Trust access to the VBA project object model
> To be able to write your first UDFs, you will need to change a setting in Excel: go to File > Options > Trust Center > Trust Center Settings > Macro Settings and activate the checkbox to "Trust access to the VBA project object model," as in Figure 12-1. This enables xlwings to automatically insert a VBA module into your workbook when you click the Import Functions button in the add-in, as we'll see shortly. Since you only rely on this setting during the import process, you should look at it as a developer setting that end users don't need to be concerned about.

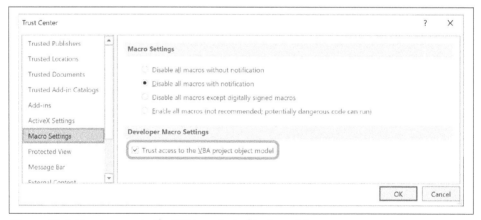

Figure 12-1. Trust access to the VBA project object model

With these two prerequisites in place, you're ready to run your first UDF!

UDF Quickstart

As usual, the easiest way to get off the ground is to use the `quickstart` command. Before you run the following on an Anaconda Prompt, make sure to change into the directory of your choice via the cd command. For example, if you are in your home directory and want to change to the desktop, run cd Desktop first:

```
(base)> xlwings quickstart first_udf
```

Navigate to the *first_udf* folder in the File Explorer and open *first_udf.xlsm* in Excel and *first_udf.py* in VS Code. Then, in the xlwings ribbon add-in, click the Import Functions button. By default, this is a silent action, i.e., you will only see something in case of an error. However, if you activate the checkbox Show Console in the Excel add-in and click the Import Functions button again, a Command Prompt opens and prints the following:

```
xlwings server running [...]
Imported functions from the following modules: first_udf
```

The first line prints a few more details that we can ignore, though—the important part is that once this line is printed, Python is up and running. The second line confirms that it imported the functions from the `first_udf` module correctly. Now type **=hello("xlwings")** into cell A1 of the active sheet in *first_udf.xlsm* and after hitting Enter, you will see the formula evaluated as shown in Figure 12-2.

Figure 12-2. first_udf.xlsm

Let's break this down to see how everything works: start by looking at the `hello` function in *first_udf.py* (Example 12-1), which is the part of the `quickstart` code that we've ignored so far.

Example 12-1. first_udf.py (excerpt)

```
import xlwings as xw


@xw.func
def hello(name):
    return f"Hello {name}!"
```

Every function that you mark with `@xw.func` will get imported into Excel when you click on Import Functions in the xlwings add-in. Importing a function makes it available in Excel so you can use it in your cell formulas—we'll get to the technical details in a moment. `@xw.func` is a *decorator*, which means that you have to place it directly on top of the function definition. If you want to know a bit more about how decorators work, have a look at the sidebar.

Function Decorators

A decorator is a function name that you put on top of a function definition, starting with the @ sign. It's a simple way to change the behavior of a function and is used by xlwings to recognize which functions you want to make available in Excel. To help you understand how a decorator works, the following example shows the definition of a decorator called verbose that will print some text before and after the function print_hello is run. Technically, the decorator takes the function (print_hello) and provides it as argument func to the verbose function. The inner function called wrapper can then do whatever needs to be done; in this case, it prints a value before and after calling the print_hello function. The name of the inner function doesn't matter:

```
In [1]: # This is the definition of the function decorator
        def verbose(func):
            def wrapper():
                print("Before calling the function.")
                func()
                print("After calling the function.")
            return wrapper

In [2]: # Using a function decorator
        @verbose
        def print_hello():
            print("hello!")

In [3]: # Effect of calling the decorated function
        print_hello()

Before calling the function.
hello!
After calling the function.
```

At the end of this chapter, you'll find Table 12-1 with a summary of all decorators that xlwings offers.

By default, if the function arguments are cell ranges, xlwings delivers you the values of these cell ranges instead of the xlwings range object. In the vast majority of cases, this is very convenient and allows you to call the hello function with a cell as argument. For example, you could write "xlwings" into cell A2, then change the formula in A1 into the following:

```
=hello(A2)
```

The result will be the same as in Figure 12-2. I will show you in the last section of this chapter how to change this behavior and make the arguments arrive as xlwings range objects instead—as we will see then, there are occasions where you will need this. In VBA, the equivalent `hello` function would look like this:

```
Function hello(name As String) As String
    hello = "Hello " & name & "!"
End Function
```

When you click the Import Functions button in the add-in, xlwings inserts a VBA module called `xlwings_udfs` into your Excel workbook. It contains a VBA function for each Python function you import: these wrapper VBA functions take care of running the respective function in Python. While nobody stops you from looking at the `xlwings_udfs` VBA module by opening the VBA editor with Alt+F11, you can ignore it as the code is autogenerated and any changes would get lost when you click the Import Functions button again. Let's now play around with our `hello` function in *first_udf.py* and replace `Hello` in the return value with `Bye`:

```
@xw.func
def hello(name):
    return f"Bye {name}!"
```

To recalculate the function in Excel, either double-click the cell A1 to edit the formula (or select the cell and press F2 to activate the edit mode), then hit Enter. Alternatively, type the keyboard shortcut Ctrl+Alt+F9: this will *force* the recalculation of all worksheets in all open workbooks including the `hello` formula. Note that F9 (recalculate all worksheets in all open workbooks) or Shift+F9 (recalculate the active worksheet) will not recalculate the UDF as Excel only triggers a recalculation of UDFs if a dependent cell changed. To change this behavior, you could make the function *volatile* by adding the respective argument to the `func` decorator:

```
@xw.func(volatile=True)
def hello(name):
    return f"Bye {name}!"
```

Volatile functions are evaluated every time Excel performs a recalculation—whether or not the function's dependencies have changed. A few of Excel's built-in functions are volatile like =RAND() or =NOW() and using lots of them will make your workbook slower, so don't overdo it. When you change a function's name or arguments or the `func` decorator as we just did, you will need to reimport your function by clicking the Import Functions button again: this will restart the Python interpreter before importing the updated function. When you now change the function back from `Bye` to `Hello`, it is enough to use the keyboard shortcuts Shift+F9 or F9 to cause the formula to recalculate as the function is now volatile.

Save the Python File After Changing It

A common gotcha is forgetting to save the Python source file after making changes. Therefore, always double-check that the Python file is saved before hitting the Import Functions button or recalculating the UDFs in Excel.

By default, xlwings imports functions from a Python file in the same directory with the same name as the Excel file. Renaming and moving your Python source file requires similar changes as in Chapter 10, when we were doing the same with RunPython calls: go ahead and rename the file from *first_udf.py* to *hello.py*. To let xlwings know about that change, add the name of the module, i.e., hello (without the *.py* extension!) to UDF Modules in the xlwings add-in, as shown in Figure 12-3.

Figure 12-3. The UDF Modules setting

Click the Import Functions button to reimport the function. Then recalculate the formula in Excel to be sure everything still works.

Import Functions from Multiple Python Modules

If you want to import functions from multiple modules, use a semicolon between their names in the UDF Modules setting, e.g., hello;another_module.

Now go ahead and move *hello.py* to your desktop: this requires you to add the path of your desktop to the PYTHONPATH in the xlwings add-in. As seen in Chapter 10, you could use environment variables to achieve this, i.e., you could set the PYTHONPATH setting in the add-in to *%USERPROFILE%\Desktop*. If you still have the path to the *pyscripts* folder in there from Chapter 10, either overwrite it or leave it in there, separating the paths with a semicolon. After these changes, click the Import Functions button again, then recalculate the function in Excel to verify that everything still works.

Configuration and Deployment

In this chapter, I am always referring to changing a setting in the add-in; however, everything from Chapter 10 with regard to configuration and deployment can be applied to this chapter too. This means that a setting could also be changed in the xlwings.conf sheet or a config file sitting in the same directory as the Excel file. And instead of using the xlwings add-in, you could use a workbook that has been set up in the standalone mode. With UDFs, it also makes sense to build your own custom add-in—this allows you to share your UDFs among all workbooks without having to import them into each workbook. For more information about building your own custom add-in, see the xlwings docs (*https://oreil.ly/uNo0g*).

If you change the Python code of your UDF, xlwings automatically picks up the changes whenever you save the Python file. As mentioned, you only need to reimport your UDFs if you change something in the function's name, arguments, or decorators. If, however, your source file imports code from other modules, and you change something in these modules, the easiest way to let Excel pick up all changes is to click on Restart UDF Server.

At this point, you know how to write a simple UDF in Python and how to use it in Excel. The case study in the next section will introduce you to more realistic UDFs that make use of pandas DataFrames.

Case Study: Google Trends

In this case study, we'll use data from Google Trends to learn how to work with pandas DataFrames and dynamic arrays, one of the most exciting new features in Excel that Microsoft officially launched in 2020. We then create a UDF that connects directly to Google Trends as well as one that uses a DataFrame's plot method. To wrap this section up, we'll have a look at how debugging works with UDFs. Let's get started with a short introduction to Google Trends!

Introduction to Google Trends

Google Trends (*https://oreil.ly/G6TpC*) is a Google service that allows you to analyze the popularity of Google search queries over time and across regions. Figure 12-4 shows Google Trends after adding a few popular programming languages, selecting Worldwide as the region and 1/1/16 - 12/26/20 as the time range. Each search term has been selected with the *Programming language* context that appears in a dropdown after typing in the search term. This makes sure that we ignore Python, the snake, and Java, the island. Google indexes the data within the selected timeframe and location with 100 representing the maximum search interest. In our sample, it means that within the given timeframe and location, the highest search interest was in Java in February 2016. For more details about Google Trends, have a look at their official blog post (*https://oreil.ly/_aw8f*).

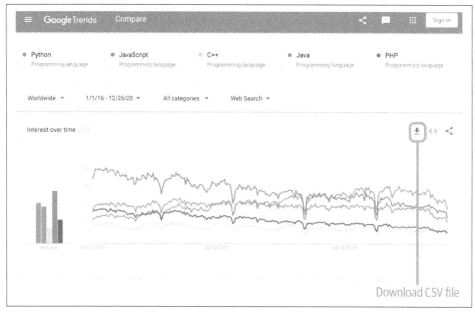

Figure 12-4. Interest over time; data source Google Trends (https://oreil.ly/SR8zD)

Random Samples

Google Trends numbers are based on random samples, which means that you may see a picture that is slightly different from Figure 12-4 even if you use the same location, timeframe, and search terms as on the screenshot.

I hit the download button that you see in Figure 12-4 to get a CSV file from where I copied the data into the Excel workbook of a `quickstart` project. In the next section, I'll show you where to find this workbook—we will use it to analyze the data with a UDF right from within Excel!

Working with DataFrames and Dynamic Arrays

Having it made this far in the book, you shouldn't be surprised that pandas Data-Frames are also a UDF's best friend. To see how DataFrames and UDFs work together and to learn about dynamic arrays, navigate to the *describe* folder in the *udfs* directory of the companion repository and open *describe.xlsm* in Excel and *describe.py* in

VS Code. The Excel file contains the data from Google Trends and in the Python file, you'll find a simple function to start with, as shown in Example 12-2.

Example 12-2. describe.py

```
import xlwings as xw
import pandas as pd


@xw.func
@xw.arg("df", pd.DataFrame, index=True, header=True)
def describe(df):
    return df.describe()
```

Compared to the `hello` function from the `quickstart` project, you'll notice a second decorator:

```
@xw.arg("df", pd.DataFrame, index=True, header=True)
```

`arg` is short for *argument* and allows you to apply the same converters and options as I was using in Chapter 9 when I was introducing the xlwings syntax. In other words, the decorator offers the same functionality for UDFs as the `options` method for xlwings `range` objects. Formally, this is the syntax of the `arg` decorator:

```
@xw.arg("argument_name", convert=None, option1=value1, option2=value2, ...)
```

To help you make the connection back to Chapter 9, the equivalent of the `describe` function in the form of a script looks like this (this assumes that *describe.xlsm* is open in Excel and that the function is applied to the range A3:F263):

```
import xlwings as xw
import pandas as pd


data_range = xw.Book("describe.xlsm").sheets[0]["A3:F263"]
df = data_range.options(pd.DataFrame, index=True, header=True).value
df.describe()
```

The options `index` and `header` wouldn't be required as they are using the default arguments, but I included them to show you how they are applied with UDFs. With *describe.xlsm* as your active workbook, click the Import Functions button, then type **=describe(A3:F263)** in a free cell, in H3, for example. What happens when you hit Enter depends on your version of Excel—more specifically if your version of Excel is recent enough to support *dynamic arrays*. If it does, you will see the situation as shown in Figure 12-5, i.e., the output of the `describe` function in cells H3:M11 is surrounded by a thin blue border. You will only be able to see the blue border if your cursor is within the array, and it is so subtle that you may have issues seeing it clearly if you look at the screenshot in a printed version of the book. We'll see how dynamic arrays behave in a moment and you can also learn more about them in the sidebar "Dynamic Arrays" on page 263.

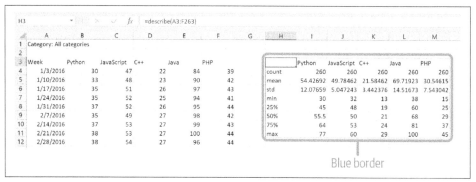

Figure 12-5. The describe function with dynamic arrays

If, however, you are using a version of Excel that doesn't support dynamic arrays, it will look as if nothing is happening: by default, the formula will only return the top-left cell in H3, which is empty. To fix this, use what Microsoft nowadays calls *legacy CSE arrays*. CSE Arrays need to be confirmed by typing the Ctrl+Shift+Enter key combination instead of hitting just Enter—hence their name. Let's see how they work in detail:

- Make sure that H3 is an empty cell by selecting it and hitting the Delete key.
- Select the output range by starting in cell H3, and then select all cells on the way to M11.
- With the range H3:M11 selected, type in the formula **=describe(A3:F263)**, and then confirm by hitting Ctrl+Shift+Enter.

You should now see almost the same picture as in Figure 12-5 with these differences:

- There is no blue border around the range H3:M11.
- The formula shows curly braces around it to mark it as a CSE array: {=describe(A3:F263)}.
- While you delete dynamic arrays by going to the top-left cell and hitting the Delete key, with CSE arrays, you always have to select the whole array first to be able to delete it.

Let's now make our function slightly more useful by introducing an optional parameter called selection that will allow us to specify which columns we want to include in our output. If you have a lot of columns and only want to include a subset in the describe function, this can become a useful feature. Change the function as follows:

```
@xw.func
@xw.arg("df", pd.DataFrame) ❶
def describe(df, selection=None): ❷
    if selection is not None:
        return df.loc[:, selection].describe() ❸
    else:
        return df.describe()
```

❶ I left off the `index` and `header` arguments, as they are using the defaults, but feel free to leave them in.

❷ Add the parameter `selection` and make it optional by assigning `None` as its default value.

❸ If `selection` is provided, filter the DataFrame's columns based on it.

Once you have changed the function, make sure to save it, and then hit the Import Functions button in the xlwings add-in—this is required since we have added a new parameter. Write **Selection** into cell A2 and **TRUE** into cells B2:F2 (note that you have to use your local version of TRUE if you are using an international version of Excel). Finally, adjust your formula in cell H3 depending on whether you have dynamic arrays or not:

With dynamic arrays
> Select H3, then change the formula to **=describe(A3:F263, B2:F2)** and hit Enter.

Without dynamic arrays
> Starting at cell H3, select H3:M11, and then hit F2 to activate the edit mode of cell H3 and change the formula to **=describe(A3:F263, B2:F2)**. To finalize, hit Ctrl+Shift+Enter.

To try out the enhanced function, let's change Java's TRUE in cell E2 to FALSE and see what happens: with dynamic arrays, you will see the table magically shrink by one column. With legacy CSE arrays, however, you will end up with an ugly column full of #N/A values, as shown in Figure 12-6.

To work around this issue, xlwings can resize legacy CSE arrays by making use of the return decorator. Add it by changing your function like this:

```
@xw.func
@xw.arg("df", pd.DataFrame)
@xw.ret(expand="table") ❶
def describe(df, selection=None):
    if selection is not None:
        return df.loc[:, selection].describe()
    else:
        return df.describe()
```

❶ By adding the return decorator with the option `expand="table"`, xlwings will resize the CSE array to match the dimensions of the returned DataFrame.

H3				fx	=describe(A3:F263, B2:F2)							
	A	B	C	D	E	F	G	H	I	J	K	L	M
1	Category: All categories											
2	Selection	TRUE	TRUE	TRUE	FALSE	TRUE						
3	Week	Python	JavaScript	C++	Java	PHP			Python	JavaScript	C++	PHP
4	1/3/2016	30	47	22	84	39		count	260	260	260	260
5	1/10/2016	33	48	23	90	42		mean	54.42692	49.78462	21.58462	30.54615
6	1/17/2016	35	51	26	97	43		std	12.07659	5.047243	3.442376	7.543042
7	1/24/2016	35	52	25	94	41		min	30	32	13	15
8	1/31/2016	37	52	26	95	44		25%	45	48	19	25
9	2/7/2016	35	49	27	98	42		50%	55.5	50	21	29
10	2/14/2016	37	53	27	99	43		75%	64	53	24	37
11	2/21/2016	38	53	27	100	44		max	77	60	29	45
12	2/28/2016	38	54	27	96	44						

H3				fx	{=describe(A3:F263, B2:F2)}							
	A	B	C	D	E	F	G	H	I	J	K	L	M
1	Category: All categories											
2	Selection	TRUE	TRUE	TRUE	FALSE	TRUE						
3	Week	Python	JavaScript	C++	Java	PHP			Python	JavaScript	C++	PHP	#N/A
4	1/3/2016	30	47	22	84	39		count	260	260	260	260	#N/A
5	1/10/2016	33	48	23	90	42		mean	54.42692	49.78462	21.58462	30.54615	#N/A
6	1/17/2016	35	51	26	97	43		std	12.07659	5.047243	3.442376	7.543042	#N/A
7	1/24/2016	35	52	25	94	41		min	30	32	13	15	#N/A
8	1/31/2016	37	52	26	95	44		25%	45	48	19	25	#N/A
9	2/7/2016	35	49	27	98	42		50%	55.5	50	21	29	#N/A
10	2/14/2016	37	53	27	99	43		75%	64	53	24	37	#N/A
11	2/21/2016	38	53	27	100	44		max	77	60	29	45	#N/A
12	2/28/2016	38	54	27	96	44							

Figure 12-6. Dynamic arrays (top) vs. CSE arrays (bottom) after excluding a column

After adding the return decorator, save the Python source file, switch over to Excel, and hit Ctrl+Alt+F9 to recalculate: this will resize the CSE array and remove the #N/A column. Since this is a workaround, I highly recommend you do whatever is in your power to get your hands on a version of Excel that supports dynamic arrays.

Order of Function Decorators

Make sure to place the `xw.func` decorator on top of the `xw.arg` and `xw.ret` decorators; note that the order of `xw.arg` and `xw.ret` doesn't matter.

The *return decorator* works conceptually the same way as the argument decorator, with the only difference that you don't have to specify the name of an argument. Formally, its syntax looks like this:

```
@xw.ret(convert=None, option1=value1, option2=value2, ...)
```

You usually don't have to provide an explicit `convert` argument as xlwings recognizes the type of the return value automatically—that's the same behavior we saw in Chapter 9 with the `options` method when writing values to Excel.

As an example, if you want to suppress the index of the DataFrame you return, use this decorator:

```
@xw.ret(index=False)
```

Dynamic Arrays

Having seen how dynamic arrays work in the context of the describe function, I am pretty sure you'd agree that they are one of the most fundamental and exciting additions to Excel that Microsoft has come up with in a long time. They were officially introduced in 2020 to Microsoft 365 subscribers who are using the most recent version of Excel. To see if your version is recent enough, check for the existence of the new UNIQUE function: start typing **=UNIQUE** in a cell and if Excel suggests the function name, dynamic arrays are supported. If you use Excel with a permanent license rather than as part of the Microsoft 365 subscription, you are likely to get it with the version that was announced for release in 2021 and that will presumably be called Office 2021. Here are a few technical notes about the behavior of dynamic arrays:

- If dynamic arrays overwrite a cell with a value, you will get a #SPILL! error. After making room for the dynamic array by deleting or moving the cell that is in the way, the array will be written out. Note that the xlwings return decorator with expand="table" is less smart and will overwrite existing cell values without warning!

- You can refer to the range of a dynamic array by using the top-left cell followed by a # sign. For example, if your dynamic array is in the range A1:B2 and you wanted to sum up all cells, write **=SUM(A1#)**.

- If you ever want your arrays to behave like the legacy CSE arrays again, start your formula with an @ sign, e.g., to have a matrix multiplication return a legacy CSE array, use **=@MMULT()**.

Downloading a CSV file and copy/pasting the values into an Excel file worked fine for this introductory DataFrame example, but copy/paste is such an error-prone process that you'll want to get rid of it whenever you can. With Google Trends, you can indeed, and the next section shows you how!

Fetching Data from Google Trends

The previous examples were all very simple, pretty much just wrapping a single pandas function. To get our hands on a more real-world case, let's create a UDF that downloads the data directly from Google Trends so you don't have to go online and download a CSV file manually anymore. Google Trends doesn't have an official API (application programming interface), but there is a Python package called pytrends (*https://oreil.ly/SvnLl*) that fills the gap. Not being an official API means that Google can change it anytime they want, so there is a risk that the examples in this section will stop working at some point. However, given that pytrends has been around for more than five years at the time of this writing, there's also a real chance that it will be updated to reflect the changes and make it work again. In any case, it serves as a good example to show you that *there's a Python package for just about anything*—a claim I made in Chapter 1. If you were restricted to using Power Query, you'd probably need to invest a lot more time to get something working—I, at least, wasn't able to find a plug-and-play solution that is available for free. Since pytrends isn't part of Anaconda and also doesn't have an official Conda package, let's install it with pip, if you haven't done this yet:

```
(base)> pip install pytrends
```

To replicate the exact case from the online version of Google Trends as shown in Figure 12-4, we'll need to find the correct identifiers for the search terms with the "Programming language" context. To do this, pytrends can print the different search contexts or *types* that Google Trends suggests in the dropdown. In the following code sample, mid stands for *Machine ID*, which is the ID we are looking for:

```
In [4]: from pytrends.request import TrendReq

In [5]: # First, let's instantiate a TrendRequest object
        trend = TrendReq()

In [6]: # Now we can print the suggestions as they would appear
        # online in the dropdown of Google Trends after typing in "Python"
        trend.suggestions("Python")

Out[6]: [{'mid': '/m/05z1_', 'title': 'Python', 'type': 'Programming language'},
         {'mid': '/m/05tb5', 'title': 'Python family', 'type': 'Snake'},
         {'mid': '/m/0cv6_m', 'title': 'Pythons', 'type': 'Snake'},
         {'mid': '/m/06bxxb', 'title': 'CPython', 'type': 'Topic'},
         {'mid': '/g/1q6j3gsvm', 'title': 'python', 'type': 'Topic'}]
```

Repeating this for the other programming languages allows us to retrieve the correct mid for all of them, and we can write the UDF as shown in Example 12-3. You'll find the source code in the *google_trends* directory within the *udfs* folder of the companion repository.

Example 12-3. The get_interest_over_time function in google_trends.py (excerpt with the relevant import statements)

```
import pandas as pd
from pytrends.request import TrendReq
import xlwings as xw


@xw.func(call_in_wizard=False) ❶
@xw.arg("mids", doc="Machine IDs: A range of max 5 cells") ❷
@xw.arg("start_date", doc="A date-formatted cell")
```

```
@xw.arg("end_date", doc="A date-formatted cell")
def get_interest_over_time(mids, start_date, end_date):
    """Query Google Trends - replaces the Machine ID (mid) of
    common programming languages with their human-readable
    equivalent in the return value, e.g., instead of "/m/05z1_"
    it returns "Python".
    """ ❸
    # Check and transform parameters
    assert len(mids) <= 5, "Too many mids (max: 5)" ❹
    start_date = start_date.date().isoformat() ❺
    end_date = end_date.date().isoformat()

    # Make the Google Trends request and return the DataFrame
    trend = TrendReq(timeout=10) ❻
    trend.build_payload(kw_list=mids,
                        timeframe=f"{start_date} {end_date}") ❼
    df = trend.interest_over_time() ❽

    # Replace Google's "mid" with a human-readable word
    mids = {"/m/05z1_": "Python", "/m/02p97": "JavaScript",
            "/m/0jgqg": "C++", "/m/07sbkfb": "Java", "/m/060kv": "PHP"}
    df = df.rename(columns=mids) ❾

    # Drop the isPartial column
    return df.drop(columns="isPartial") ❿
```

❶ By default, Excel calls the function when you open it in the Function Wizard. As this can make it slow, especially with API requests involved, we're switching this off.

❷ Optionally, add a docstring for the function argument, which will be shown in the Function Wizard when you edit the respective argument, as in Figure 12-8.

❸ The function's docstring is displayed in the Function Wizard, as in Figure 12-8.

❹ The assert statement is an easy way to raise an error in case the user provides too many mids. Google Trends allows a maximum of five mids per query.

❺ pytrends expects the start and end dates as a single string in the form YYYY-MM-DD YYYY-MM-DD. As we are providing the start and end dates as date-formatted cells, they will arrive as datetime objects. Calling the date and isoformat methods on them will format them properly.

❻ We're instantiating a pytrends request object. By setting the timeout to ten seconds, we reduce the risk of seeing a requests.exceptions.ReadTimeout error, which occasionally happens if Google Trends takes a bit longer to respond. If you still see this error, simply run the function again or increase the timeout.

❼ We provide the kw_list and timeframe arguments to the request object.

❽ We make the actual request by calling interest_over_time, which will return a pandas DataFrame.

❾ We rename the mids with their human-readable equivalent.

❿ The last column is called isPartial. True indicates that the current interval, e.g., a week, is still ongoing and therefore doesn't have all data yet. To keep things simple and to be in line with the online version, we're dropping this column when returning the DataFrame.

Now open *google_trends.xlsm* from the companion repository, click on Import Functions in the xlwings add-in, and then call the get_interest_over_time function from cell A4, as shown in Figure 12-7.

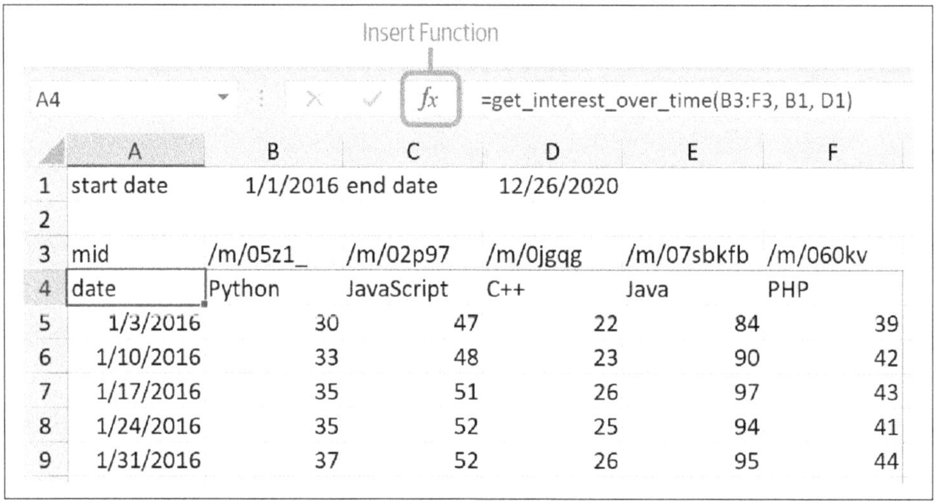

Figure 12-7. google_trends.xlsm

To get help with regard to the function arguments, click the Insert Function button to the left of the formula bar while cell A4 is selected: this will open the Function Wizard where you will find your UDFs under the xlwings category. After selecting get_interest_over_time, you'll see the name of the function arguments as well as the docstring as function description (restricted to the first 256 characters): see Figure 12-8. Alternatively, start typing **=get_interest_over_time(** into cell A4 (including the opening parenthesis) before hitting the Insert Function button—this will take you directly to the view shown in Figure 12-8. Note that UDFs return the dates unformatted. To fix this, right-click on the column with the dates, select Format Cells, and then select the format of your choice under the Date category.

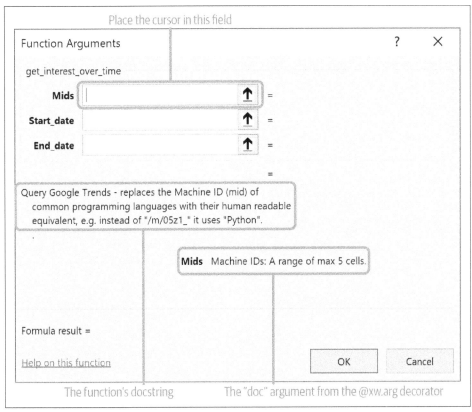

Figure 12-8. The Function Wizard

If you look closely at Figure 12-7, you can tell by the blue border around the result array that I am using dynamic arrays again. As the screenshot is cropped at the bottom and the array starts at the very left, you only see the top and right borders starting at cell A4, and even they might be hard to recognize on the screenshot. If your version of Excel doesn't support dynamic arrays, use the workaround by adding the following return decorator to the `get_interest_over_time` function (below the existing decorators):

```
@xw.ret(expand="table")
```

Now that you know how to work with more complicated UDFs, let's see how we can use plots with UDFs!

Plotting with UDFs

As you might remember from Chapter 5, calling a DataFrame's `plot` method returns a Matplotlib plot by default. In Chapters 9 and 11, we've already seen how you add such a plot as a picture to Excel. When working with UDFs, there's an easy way to produce plots: have a look at the second function in *google_trends.py*, shown in Example 12-4.

Example 12-4. The `plot` *function in google_trends.py (excerpt with the relevant import statements)*

```
import xlwings as xw
import pandas as pd
import matplotlib.pyplot as plt


@xw.func
@xw.arg("df", pd.DataFrame)
def plot(df, name, caller): ❶
    plt.style.use("seaborn") ❷
    if not df.empty: ❸
        caller.sheet.pictures.add(df.plot().get_figure(), ❹
                                  top=caller.offset(row_offset=1).top, ❺
                                  left=caller.left,
                                  name=name, update=True) ❻
    return f"<Plot: {name}>" ❼
```

❶ The `caller` argument is a special argument that is reserved by xlwings: this argument will not be exposed when you call the function from an Excel cell. Instead, `caller` will be provided by xlwings behind the scenes and corresponds to the cell from which you are calling the function (in the form of an xlwings `range` object). Having the `range` object of the calling cell makes it easy to place the plot by using the `top` and `left` arguments of `pictures.add`. The `name` argument will define the name of the picture in Excel.

❷ We set the `seaborn` style to make the plot visually more attractive.

❸ Only call the `plot` method if the DataFrame isn't empty. Calling the `plot` method on an empty DataFrame would raise an error.

❹ `get_figure()` returns the Matplotlib figure object from a DataFrame plot, which is what `pictures.add` expects.

❺ The arguments `top` and `left` are only used when you insert the plot for the first time. The provided arguments will place the plot in a convenient place—one cell below the one from where you call this function.

❻ The argument `update=True` makes sure that repeated function calls will update the existing picture with the provided name in Excel, without changing its position or size. Without this argument, xlwings would complain that there is already a picture with that name in Excel.

❼ While you don't strictly need to return anything, it makes your life much easier if you return a string: this allows you to recognize where in your sheet your plotting function sits.

In *google_trends.xlsm*, in cell H3, call the plot function like so:

```
=plot(A4:F263, "History")
```

If your version of Excel supports dynamic arrays, use A4# instead of A4:F263 to make the source dynamic as shown in Figure 12-9.

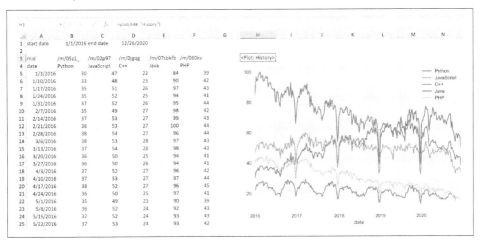

Figure 12-9. The plot function in action

Let's assume that you are slightly confused by how the get_interest_over_time function works. One option to get a better understanding is to debug the code—the next section shows you how this works with UDFs!

Debugging UDFs

A simple way to debug a UDF is to use the print function. If you have the Show Console setting enabled in the xlwings add-in, you will be able to print the value of a variable in the Command Prompt that shows up when you call your UDF. A slightly more comfortable option is to use the debugger of VS Code, which will allow you to pause at breakpoints and step through the code line by line. To use the VS Code debugger (or the debugger of any other IDE), you'll need to do two things:

1. In the Excel add-in, activate the checkbox Debug UDFs. This prevents Excel from automatically starting Python, which means you have to do it manually as explained under the next point.

2. The easiest way to run the Python UDF server manually is by adding the following lines at the very bottom of the file you're trying to debug. I have already added these lines at the bottom of the *google_trends.py* file in the companion repository:

```
if __name__ == "__main__":
    xw.serve()
```

As you may remember from Chapter 11, this `if` statement makes sure that the code only runs when you run the file as a script—it doesn't run when you import the code as a module. With the `serve` command added, run *google_trends.py* in VS Code in debug mode by pressing F5 and selecting "Python File"—make sure you don't run the file by clicking the Run File button as this would ignore breakpoints.

Let's set a breakpoint on line 29 by clicking to the left of the line number. If you are not familiar with using the debugger of VS Code, please have a look at Appendix B where I introduce it in more detail. When you now recalculate cell A4, your function call will stop at the breakpoint and you can inspect the variables. What's always helpful during debugging is to run `df.info()`. Activate the Debug Console tab, write **df.info()** in the prompt at the bottom, and confirm by hitting Enter, as shown in Figure 12-10.

Debugging with VS Code and Anaconda

This is the same warning as in Chapter 11: on Windows, when you run the VS Code debugger for the first time with code that uses pandas, you might be greeted by an error: "Exception has occurred: ImportError, Unable to import required dependencies: numpy." This happens because the debugger is up and running before the Conda environment has been activated properly. As a workaround, stop the debugger by clicking the stop icon and hit F5 again—it will work the second time.

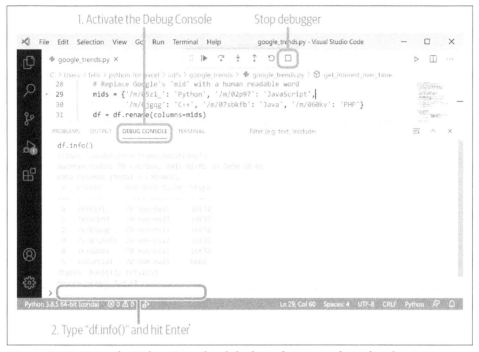

Figure 12-10. Using the Debug Console while the code is paused at a breakpoint

If you keep your program paused for more than ninety seconds on a breakpoint, Excel will show you a pop-up saying that "Microsoft Excel is waiting for another application to complete an OLE action." This shouldn't have an impact on your debugging experience other than having to confirm the pop-up to make it disappear once you're done with debugging. To finish this debugging session, click on the Stop button in VS Code (see Figure 12-10) and make sure to uncheck the Debug UDFs setting again in the xlwings ribbon add-in. If you forget to uncheck the Debug UDFs setting, your functions will return an error the next time you recalculate them.

This section showed you the most commonly used UDF functionality by working through the Google Trends case study. The next section will touch on a few advanced topics including UDF performance and the `xw.sub` decorator.

Advanced UDF Topics

If you use many UDFs in your workbook, performance can become an issue. This section starts by showing you the same basic performance optimizations as we've seen in Chapter 9, but applied to UDFs. The second part deals with caching, an additional performance optimization technique that we can use with UDFs. Along the way, we'll also learn how to have function arguments arrive as xlwings `range` objects rather than as values. At the end of this section, I will introduce you to the xw.sub decorator that you can use as an alternative to the RunPython call if you are exclusively working on Windows.

Basic Performance Optimization

This part looks at two performance optimization techniques: how to minimize cross-application calls and how to use the raw values converter.

Minimize cross-application calls

As you probably recall from Chapter 9, cross-application calls, i.e., calls between Excel and Python, are relatively slow, so the fewer UDFs you have, the better. You should therefore work with arrays whenever you can—having a version of Excel that supports dynamic arrays definitely makes this part easier. When you are working with pandas DataFrames, there isn't much that can go wrong, but there are certain formulas where you might not think of using arrays automatically. Consider the example of Figure 12-11 that calculates total revenues as the sum of a given Base Fee plus a variable fee determined by Users times Price.

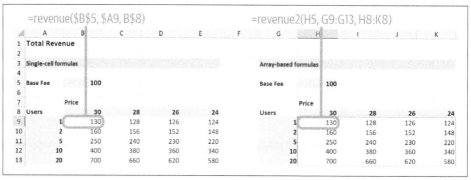

Figure 12-11. Single-cell formulas (left) vs. array-based formulas (right)

Single-cell formulas
> The left table in Figure 12-11 uses the formula =revenue($B$5, $A9, B$8) in cell B9. This formula is then applied to the whole range B9:E13. This means that you have 20 single-cell formulas that call the revenue function.

Array-based formulas
> The right table in Figure 12-11 uses the formula =revenue2(H5, G9:G13, H8:K8). If you don't have dynamic arrays in your version of Excel, you would need to add the decorator xw.ret(expand="table") to the revenue2 function or turn the array into a legacy CSE array by selecting H9:K13, pressing F2 to edit the formula, and confirming with Ctrl+Shift+Enter. Unlike the single-cell formula, this version only calls the revenue2 function once.

You can see the Python code for the two UDFs in Example 12-5, and you'll find the source file in the *revenues* folder within the *udfs* directory of the companion repository.

Example 12-5. revenues.py

```python
import numpy as np
import xlwings as xw


@xw.func
def revenue(base_fee, users, price):
    return base_fee + users * price


@xw.func
@xw.arg("users", np.array, ndim=2)
@xw.arg("price", np.array)
def revenue2(base_fee, users, price):
    return base_fee + users * price
```

When you change the base fee in cell B5 or H5 respectively, you will see that the right example will be much faster than the left one. The difference in the Python functions are minimal and only differ in the argument decorators: the array-based version reads in users and prices as NumPy array—the only caveat here is to read in users as a two-dimensional column vector by setting ndim=2 in the argument decorator. You probably remember that NumPy arrays are similar to DataFrames but without index or header and with only one data type, but if you want a more detailed refresher, have another look at Chapter 4.

Using raw values

Using raw values means that you are leaving out the data preparation and cleaning steps that xlwings does on top of pywin32, xlwings' dependency on Windows. This, for example, means that you can't work with DataFrames directly anymore as pywin32 doesn't understand them, but that may not be an issue if you work with lists or NumPy arrays. To use UDFs with raw values, use the string raw as the convert argument in the argument or return decorator. This is the equivalent of using the raw converter via the options method of an xlwings range object as we did in Chapter 9. In line with what we saw back then, you'll get the biggest speed up during write operations. For example, calling the following function without the return decorator would be about three times slower on my laptop:

```python
import numpy as np
import xlwings as xw
```

```
@xw.func
@xw.ret("raw")
def randn(i=1000, j=1000):
    """Returns an array with dimensions (i, j) with normally distributed
    pseudorandom numbers provided by NumPy's random.randn
    """
    return np.random.randn(i, j)
```

You'll find the respective sample in the companion repository in the *raw_values* folder within the *udfs* directory. When working with UDFs, you have another easy option to improve performance: prevent repeated calculations of slow functions by caching their results.

Caching

When you call a *deterministic* function, i.e., a function that given the same inputs, always returns the same output, you can store the result in a *cache*: repeated calls of the function don't have to wait for the slow calculation anymore but can take the result from the cache where it's already precalculated. This is best explained with a short example. A very basic caching mechanism can be programmed with a dictionary:

```
In [7]: import time

In [8]: cache = {}

        def slow_sum(a, b):
            key = (a, b)
            if key in cache:
                return cache[key]
            else:
                time.sleep(2)  # sleep for 2 seconds
                result = a + b
                cache[key] = result
                return result
```

When you call this function for the first time, the cache is empty. The code will therefore execute the else clause with the artificial two seconds pause that mimics a slow calculation. After performing the calculation, it will add the result to the cache dictionary before returning the result. When you now call this function a second time with the same arguments and during the same Python session, it will find it in the cache and return it right away, without having to perform the slow calculation again. Caching a result based on its arguments is also called *memoization*. Accordingly, you will see the time difference when you call the function for the first and second time:

```
In [9]: %%time
        slow_sum(1, 2)

Wall time: 2.01 s

Out[9]: 3
```

```
In [10]: %%time
         slow_sum(1, 2)

Wall time: 0 ns

Out[10]: 3
```

Python has a built-in decorator called lru_cache that can make your life really easy and that you import from the functools module that is part of the standard library. lru stands for *least recently used* cache and means that it holds a maximum number of results (by default 128) before it gets rid of the oldest ones. We can use this with our Google Trends example from the last section. As long as we're only querying historical values, we can safely cache the result. This will not only make multiple calls faster, but it will also decrease the amounts of requests that we send to Google, lowering the chance that Google blocks us—something that could happen if you send too many requests in a short time.

Here are the first few lines of the get_interest_over_time function with the required changes to apply caching:

```
from functools import lru_cache  ❶

import pandas as pd
from pytrends.request import TrendReq
import matplotlib.pyplot as plt
import xlwings as xw

@lru_cache  ❷
@xw.func(call_in_wizard=False)
@xw.arg("mids", xw.Range, doc="Machine IDs: A range of max 5 cells")  ❸
@xw.arg("start_date", doc="A date-formatted cell")
@xw.arg("end_date", doc="A date-formatted cell")
def get_interest_over_time(mids, start_date, end_date):
    """Query Google Trends - replaces the Machine ID (mid) of
    common programming languages with their human-readable
    equivalent in the return value, e.g., instead of "/m/05z1_"
    it returns "Python".
    """
    mids = mids.value  ❹
```

❶ Import the lru_cache decorator.

❷ Use the decorator. The decorator has to be on top of the xw.func decorator.

❸ By default, mids is a list. This creates a problem in this case as functions with lists as arguments can't be cached. The underlying issue is that lists are mutable objects that can't be used as keys in dictionaries; see Appendix C for more information about mutable vs. immutable objects. Using the xw.Range converter allows us to retrieve `mids` as xlwings `range` object rather than as list, which solves our problem.

❹ To make the rest of the code work again, we now need to get the values via the `value` property of the xlwings `range` object.

Caching with Different Versions of Python

If you are using a Python version below 3.8, you'll have to use the decorator with parentheses like so: `@lru_cache()`. If you are using Python 3.9 or later, replace `@lru_cache` with `@cache`, which is the same as `@lru_cache(maxsize=None)`, i.e., the cache never gets rid of older values. You also need to import the `cache` decorator from `functools`.

The `xw.Range` converter can also be useful in other circumstances, for example, if you need to access the cell formulas instead of the values in your UDF. In the previous example, you could write `mids.formula` to access the formulas of the cells. You'll find the complete example in the *google_trends_cache* folder within the *udfs* directory of the companion repository.

Now that you know how to tweak the performance of UDFs, let's wrap this section up by introducing the `xw.sub` decorator.

The Sub Decorator

In Chapter 10, I showed you how to speed up the `RunPython` call by activating the Use UDF Server setting. If you are living in a Windows-only world, there is an alternative to the `RunPython/Use UDF Server` combination in the form of the `xw.sub` decorator. This will allow you to import your Python functions as Sub procedures into Excel, without having to manually write any `RunPython` calls. In Excel, you will need a Sub procedure to be able to attach it to a button—an Excel function, as you get it when using the `xw.func` decorator, won't work. To try this out, create a new `quickstart` project called `importsub`. As usual, make sure to cd first into the directory where you want the project to be created:

```
(base)> xlwings quickstart importsub
```

In the File Explorer, navigate to the created *importsub* folder and open *importsub.xlsm* in Excel and *importsub.py* in VS Code, then decorate the main function with `@xw.sub` as shown in Example 12-6.

Example 12-6. importsub.py (excerpt)

```python
import xlwings as xw


@xw.sub
def main():
    wb = xw.Book.caller()
    sheet = wb.sheets[0]
    if sheet["A1"].value == "Hello xlwings!":
        sheet["A1"].value = "Bye xlwings!"
    else:
        sheet["A1"].value = "Hello xlwings!"
```

In the xlwings add-in, click on Import Functions before hitting Alt+F8 to see the available macros: in addition to the `SampleCall` that uses `RunPython`, you'll now also see a macro called `main`. Select it and click the Run button—you'll see the familiar greeting in cell A1. You could now go ahead and assign the `main` macro to a button as we did in Chapter 10. While the `xw.sub` decorator can make your life easier on Windows, bear in mind that by using it, you lose cross-platform compatibility. With `xw.sub`, we have met all xlwings decorators—I have summarized them again in Table 12-1.

Table 12-1. xlwings decorators

Decorator	Description
xw.func	Put this decorator on top of all functions that you want to import into Excel as an Excel function.
xw.sub	Put this decorator on top of all functions that you want to import into Excel as an Excel Sub procedure.
xw.arg	Apply converters and options to arguments, e.g., add a docstring via the doc argument or you can have a range arrive as DataFrame by providing pd.DataFrame as the first argument (this assumes that you have imported pandas as pd).
xw.ret	Apply converters and options to return values, e.g., suppress a DataFrame's index by providing index=False.

For more details on these decorators, have a look at the xlwings documentation (*https://oreil.ly/h-sT_*).

Conclusion

This chapter was about writing Python functions and importing them into Excel as UDFs, allowing you to call them via cell formulas. By working through the Google Trends case study, you learned how to influence the behavior of the function arguments and return values by using the `arg` and `ret` decorators, respectively. The last part showed you a few performance tricks and introduced the `xw.sub` decorator, which you can use as a `RunPython` replacement if you are exclusively working with Windows. The nice thing about writing UDFs in Python is that this allows you to replace long and complex cell formulas with Python code that will be easier to understand and maintain. My preferred way to work with UDFs is definitely to use pandas DataFrames with Excel's new dynamic arrays, a combination that makes it easy to work with the sort of data we get from Google Trends, i.e., DataFrames with a dynamic number of rows.

And that's it—we have reached the end of the book! Thanks so much for your interest in my interpretation of a modern automation and data analysis environment for Excel! My idea was to introduce you to the world of Python and its powerful open source packages, allowing you to write Python code for your next project instead of having to deal with Excel's own solutions like VBA or Power Query, thereby keeping a door open to easily move away from Excel if you need to. I hope I could give you a few hands-on examples to make the start easier. After reading this book, you now know how to:

- Replace an Excel workbook with a Jupyter notebook and pandas code
- Batch process Excel workbooks by reading them with OpenPyXL, xlrd, pyxlsb, or xlwings and then consolidate them with pandas
- Produce Excel reports with either OpenPyXL, XlsxWriter, xlwt, or xlwings
- Use Excel as a frontend and connect it to pretty much anything you want via xlwings, either by clicking a button or by writing a UDF

Soon enough, however, you'll want to move beyond the scope of this book. I invite you to check the book's home page (*https://xlwings.org/book*) from time to time for updates and additional material. In this spirit, here are a few ideas that you could explore on your own:

- Schedule the periodic run of a Python script using either the Task Scheduler on Windows or a cron job on macOS or Linux. You could, for example, create an Excel report every Friday based on data you consume from a REST API or a database.
- Write a Python script that sends email alerts whenever the values in your Excel files satisfy a certain condition. Maybe that is when your account balance, consolidated from multiple workbooks, falls below a certain value, or when it shows a different value from what you expect based on your internal database.
- Write code that finds errors in Excel workbooks: check for cell errors like #REF! or #VALUE! or logical errors like making sure that a formula is including all the cells it should. If you start tracking your mission-critical workbooks with a professional version control system like Git, you can even run these tests automatically whenever you commit a new version.

If this book inspires you to automate your daily or weekly routine of downloading data and copy/pasting it into Excel, I couldn't be any happier. Automation doesn't just give you back time, it also reduces the chance of committing errors dramatically. If you have any feedback, please let me know about it! You can contact me via O'Reilly, by opening an issue on the companion repository (*https://oreil.ly/vVHmR*) or on Twitter at @felixzumstein.

Conda Environments

In Chapter 2, I introduced Conda environments by explaining that (base) at the beginning of an Anaconda Prompt stands for the currently active Conda environment with the name base. Anaconda requires you to always work in an activated environment, but the activation is done automatically for the base environment when you start the Anaconda Prompt on Windows or the Terminal on macOS. Working with Conda environments allows you to properly separate the dependencies of your projects: if you want to try out a newer version of a package like pandas without changing your base environment, you can do so in a separate Conda environment. In the first part of this appendix, I will walk you through the process of creating a Conda environment called xl38 where we will install all packages in the version I used them to write this book. This will allow you to run the samples in this book as-is, even if some packages have released new versions with breaking changes in the meantime. In the second part, I will show you how to disable the auto activation of the base environment if you don't like the default behavior.

Create a New Conda Environment

Run the following command on your Anaconda Prompt to create a new environment with the name xl38 that uses Python 3.8:

```
(base)> conda create --name xl38 python=3.8
```

When hitting Enter, Conda will print what it is going to install into the new environment and asks you to confirm:

```
Proceed ([y]/n)?
```

Hit Enter to confirm or type **n** if you want to cancel. Once the installation is done, activate your new environment like this:

```
(base)> conda activate xl38
(xl38)>
```

The environment name changed from base to xl38 and you can now use Conda or pip to install packages into this new environment without impacting any of the other environments (as a reminder: only use pip if the package isn't available via Conda). Let's go ahead and install all packages from this book in the version I was using them. First, double-check that you are in the xl38 environment, i.e., the Anaconda Prompt is showing (xl38), then install the Conda packages like so (the following command should be typed in as a single command; the line breaks are only for display purposes):

```
(xl38)> conda install lxml=4.6.1 matplotlib=3.3.2 notebook=6.1.4 openpyxl=3.0.5
                      pandas=1.1.3 pillow=8.0.1 plotly=4.14.1 flake8=3.8.4
                      python-dateutil=2.8.1 requests=2.24.0 sqlalchemy=1.3.20
                      xlrd=1.2.0 xlsxwriter=1.3.7 xlutils=2.0.0 xlwings=0.20.8
                      xlwt=1.3.0
```

Confirm the installation plan and finalize the environment by installing the two remaining dependencies with pip:

```
(xl38)> pip install pyxlsb==1.0.7 pytrends==4.7.3
(xl38)>
```

 How to Use the xl38 Environment

If you would like to use the xl38 environment rather than the base environment to work through the examples in this book, make sure to always have your xl38 environment activated by running:

```
(base)> conda activate xl38
```

That is, wherever I show the Anaconda Prompt as (base)>, you will want it to show (xl38)> instead.

To deactivate the environment again and get back to the base environment, type:

```
(xl38)> conda deactivate
(base)>
```

If you want to delete the environment completely, run the following command:

```
(base)> conda env remove --name xl38
```

Instead of going through the steps manually to create the xl38 environment, you can also take advantage of the environment file *xl38.yml* that I included in the *conda* folder of the companion repository. Running the following commands takes care of everything:

```
(base)> cd C:\Users\username\python-for-excel\conda
(base)> conda env create -f xl38.yml
(base)> conda activate xl38
(xl38)>
```

By default, Anaconda always activates the base environment when you open a Terminal on macOS or the Anaconda Prompt on Windows. If you don't like this, you could disable auto activation as I'll show you next.

Disable Auto Activation

If you don't want the base environment to be activated automatically whenever you fire up an Anaconda Prompt, you can disable it: this will require you to type **conda activate base** manually on a Command Prompt (Windows) or Terminal (macOS) before you are able to use Python.

Windows

On Windows, you will need to use the regular Command Prompt instead of the Anaconda Prompt. The following steps will enable the conda command in a normal Command Prompt. Make sure to replace the path in the first line with the path where Anaconda is installed on your system:

```
> cd C:\Users\username\Anaconda3\condabin
> conda init cmd.exe
```

Your regular Command Prompt is now set up with Conda, so going forward you can activate the base environment like this:

```
> conda activate base
(base)>
```

macOS

On macOS, simply run the following command in your Terminal to disable auto activation:

```
(base)> conda config --set auto_activate_base false
```

If you ever want to revert, run the same command again with true instead of false. Changes will come into effect after restarting the Terminal. Going forward, you will need to activate the base environment like this before you can use the python command again:

```
> conda activate base
(base)>
```

Advanced VS Code Functionality

This appendix shows you how the debugger works in VS Code and how you can run Jupyter notebooks directly from within VS Code. The topics are independent of each other, so you may read them in any order.

Debugger

If you've ever used the VBA debugger in Excel, I have good news for you: debugging with VS Code is a very similar experience. Let's start by opening the file *debugging.py* from the companion repository in VS Code. Click into the margin to the left of line number 4 so that a red dot appears—this is your breakpoint where code execution will be paused. Now hit F5 to start debugging: the Command Panel will appear with a selection of debug configurations. Choose "Python File" to debug the active file and run the code until it hits the breakpoint. The line will be highlighted and code execution pauses, see Figure B-1. While you debug, the status bar turns orange.

If the Variables section doesn't show up automatically on the left, make sure to click on the Run menu to see the values of the variables. Alternatively, you can also hover over a variable in the source code and get a tooltip with its value. At the top, you will see the Debug Toolbar that gives you access to the following buttons from left to right): Continue, Step Over, Step Into, Step Out, Restart, and Stop. When you hover over them, you will also see the keyboard shortcuts.

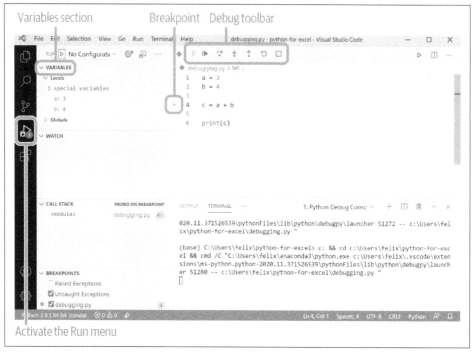

Figure B-1. VS Code with the debugger stopped at the breakpoint

Let's see what each of these buttons does:

Continue

This continues to run the program until it either hits the next breakpoint or the end of the program. If it reaches the end of the program, the debugging process will stop.

Step Over

The debugger will advance one line. *Step Over* means that the debugger will not visually step through lines of code that are not part of your current scope. For example, it will not step into the code of a function that you call line by line—but the function will still be called!

Step Into

If you have code that calls a function or class, etc., *Step Into* will cause the debugger to step into that function or class. If the function or class is in a different file, the debugger will open this file for you.

Step Out

If you stepped into a function with Step Into, *Step Out* causes the debugger to return to the next higher level until eventually, you will be back on the highest level from where you called Step Into initially.

Restart

This will stop the current debug process and start a new one from the beginning.

Stop

This will stop the current debug process.

Now that you know what each button does, click on Step Over to advance one line and see how variable c appears in the Variables section, then finish this debugging exercise by clicking on Continue.

If you save the debugging configuration, the Command Panel will not show up and ask you about the configuration every time you hit F5: click on the Run icon in the Activity Bar, then click on "create a launch.json file." This will cause the Command Panel to show up again and when you select "Python File," it creates the *launch.json* file under a directory called *.vscode*. When you now hit F5, the debugger will start right away. If you need to change the configuration or want to get the Command Panel pop-up again, edit or delete the *launch.json* file in the *.vscode* directory.

Jupyter Notebooks in VS Code

Instead of running your Jupyter notebooks in a web browser, you can also run them with VS Code directly. On top of that, VS Code offers a convenient Variable explorer as well as options to transform the notebook into standard Python files without losing the cell functionality. This makes it easier to use the debugger or to copy/paste cells between different notebooks. Let's get started by running a notebook in VS Code!

Run Jupyter Notebooks

Click the Explorer icon on the Activity Bar and open *ch05.ipynb* from the companion repository. To continue, you may need to make the notebook a trusted one by clicking on Trust in the notification that pops up. The layout of the notebook looks a bit different from the one in the browser to match the rest of VS Code, but otherwise, it's the same experience including all the keyboard shortcuts. Let's run the first three cells via Shift+Enter. This will start the Jupyter notebook server if it isn't running yet (you will see the status at the top right of the notebook). After running the cells, click on the Variables button in the menu at the top of the notebook: this will open the Variable explorer, in which you can see the values of all variables that currently exist, as in Figure B-2. That is, you will only find variables from cells that have been run.

Saving Jupyter Notebooks in VS Code

To save notebooks in VS Code, you need to use the Save button at the top of the notebook or hit Ctrl+S on Windows or Command-S on macOS. File > Save won't work.

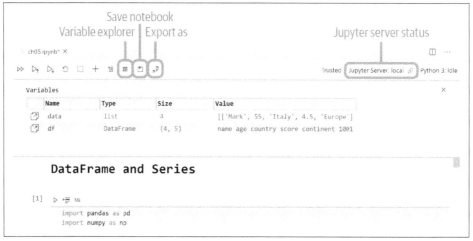

Figure B-2. Jupyter notebook Variable explorer

If you use data structures like nested lists, NumPy arrays, or DataFrames, you can double-click the variable: this will open the Data Viewer and give you a familiar spreadsheet-like view. Figure B-3 shows the Data Viewer after double-clicking the df variable.

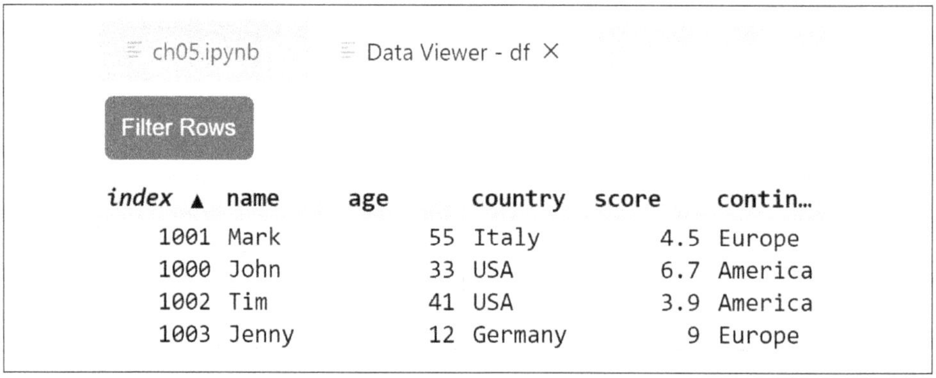

Figure B-3. Jupyter notebook Data Viewer

While VS Code allows you to run standard Jupyter notebook files, it also allows you to transform the notebooks into normal Python files—without losing your cells. Let's see how it works!

Python Scripts with Code Cells

To use Jupyter notebook cells in standard Python files, VS Code uses a special comment to denote cells: # %%. To convert an existing Jupyter notebook, open it and hit the Export As button in the menu at the top of the notebook; see Figure B-2. This will allow you to select "Python File" from the command palette. However, instead of converting an existing file, let's create a new file that we call *cells.py* with the following content:

```
# %%
3 + 4
# %% [markdown]
# # This is a Title
#
# Some markdown content
```

Markdown cells need to start with # %% [markdown] and require the whole cell to be marked as comment. If you want to run such a file as notebook, click on the "Run Below" link that appears when you hover over the first cell. This will open up the *Python Interactive Window* to the right, as shown in Figure B-4.

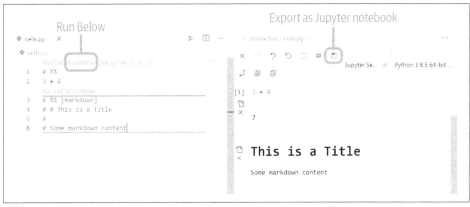

Figure B-4. Python Interactive Window

The Python Interactive Window is again shown as notebook. To export your file in the *ipynb* format, click the Save icon (Export as Jupyter notebook) at the top of the Python Interactive Window. The Python Interactive Window also offers you a cell at the bottom from where you can execute code interactively. Using regular Python files as opposed to Jupyter notebooks allows you to use the VS Code debugger and makes working with version control easier as output cells, which typically add a lot of noise between versions, are ignored.

Advanced Python Concepts

In this appendix, we're taking a closer look at the following three topics: classes and objects, time-zone-aware datetime objects, and mutable vs. immutable objects. The topics are independent of each other, so you may read them in any order.

Classes and Objects

In this section, we will write our own class to get a better understanding of how classes and objects are related. Classes define new types of objects: a class behaves like a springform you use to bake a cake. Depending on the ingredients you use, you get a different cake, for example, a chocolate cake or a cheesecake. The process of getting a cake (the object) out of the springform (the class) is called *instantiation*, which is why objects are also called *class instances*. Whether chocolate or cheesecake, they are both a *type* of cake: classes allow you to define new data types that keep related data (*attributes*) and functions (*methods*) together and therefore help you to structure and organize your code. Let me now return to the car racing game example from Chapter 3 to define our own class:

```
In [1]: class Car:
            def __init__(self, color, speed=0):
                self.color = color
                self.speed = speed

            def accelerate(self, mph):
                self.speed += mph
```

This is a simple car class with two methods. Methods are functions that are part of a class definition. This class has one regular method called `accelerate`. This method will change the data (`speed`) of an instance of this class. It also has a special method that starts and ends with double underscores called `__init__`. It will be called automatically by Python when an object is *initialized* to attach some initial data to the object. The first argument of every method represents the instance of the class and is called self by convention. This will get clearer when you see how you use the Car class. First, let's instantiate two cars. You are doing this in the same way as you are calling a function: call the class by adding parentheses and by providing the arguments of the __init__ method. You never provide anything for self, as Python will take care of that. In this sample, self will be car1 or car2, respectively:

```
In [2]: # Let's instantiate two car objects
        car1 = Car("red")
        car2 = Car(color="blue")
```

When you call a class, you are really calling the __init__ function, which is why everything with regard to function arguments applies here as well: for car1, we provide the argument as positional argument, while for car2, we are using keyword arguments. After instantiating the two car objects from the Car class, we'll have a look at their attributes and call their methods. As we will see, after accelerating car1, the speed of car1 is changed, but it is unchanged for car2 as the two objects are independent of each other:

```
In [3]: # By default, an object prints its memory location
        car1
```

```
Out[3]: <__main__.Car at 0x7fea812e3890>
```

```
In [4]: # Attributes give you access to the data of an object
        car1.color
```

```
Out[4]: 'red'
```

```
In [5]: car1.speed
```

```
Out[5]: 0
```

```
In [6]: # Calling the accelerate method on car1
        car1.accelerate(20)
```

```
In [7]: # The speed attribute of car1 changed
        car1.speed
```

```
Out[7]: 20
```

```
In [8]: # The speed attribute of car2 remained the same
        car2.speed
```

```
Out[8]: 0
```

Python also allows you to change attributes directly without having to use methods:

```
In [9]: car1.color = "green"
```

```
In [10]: car1.color
```

```
Out[10]: 'green'
```

```
In [11]: car2.color  # unchanged
```

```
Out[11]: 'blue'
```

To summarize: classes define the attributes and methods of objects. Classes allow you to group related functions ("methods") and data ("attributes") together so that they can conveniently be accessed via dot notation: `myobject.attribute` or `myobject.method()`.

Working with Time-Zone-Aware datetime Objects

In Chapter 3, we briefly looked at time-zone-naive `datetime` objects. If time zone is of importance, you usually work in the *UTC* time zone and only transform to local time zones for display purposes. UTC stands for *Coordinated Universal Time* and is the successor of Greenwich Mean Time (GMT). When you work with Excel and Python, you may want to turn naive timestamps, as delivered by Excel, into time-zone-aware `datetime` objects. For time-zone support in Python, you can use the dateutil package, which isn't part of the standard library but comes preinstalled with Anaconda. The following samples show a few common operations when working with `datetime` objects and time zones:

```
In [12]: import datetime as dt
         from dateutil import tz

In [13]: # Time-zone-naive datetime object
         timestamp = dt.datetime(2020, 1, 31, 14, 30)
         timestamp.isoformat()

Out[13]: '2020-01-31T14:30:00'

In [14]: # Time-zone-aware datetime object
         timestamp_eastern = dt.datetime(2020, 1, 31, 14, 30,
                                         tzinfo=tz.gettz("US/Eastern"))
         # Printing in isoformat makes it easy to
         # see the offset from UTC
         timestamp_eastern.isoformat()

Out[14]: '2020-01-31T14:30:00-05:00'

In [15]: # Assign a time zone to a naive datetime object
         timestamp_eastern = timestamp.replace(tzinfo=tz.gettz("US/Eastern"))
         timestamp_eastern.isoformat()

Out[15]: '2020-01-31T14:30:00-05:00'

In [16]: # Convert from one time zone to another.
         # Since the UTC time zone is so common,
         # there is a shortcut: tz.UTC
         timestamp_utc = timestamp_eastern.astimezone(tz.UTC)
         timestamp_utc.isoformat()

Out[16]: '2020-01-31T19:30:00+00:00'

In [17]: # From time-zone-aware to naive
         timestamp_eastern.replace(tzinfo=None)
```

```
Out[17]: datetime.datetime(2020, 1, 31, 14, 30)

In [18]: # Current time without time zone
         dt.datetime.now()

Out[18]: datetime.datetime(2021, 1, 3, 11, 18, 37, 172170)

In [19]: # Current time in UTC time zone
         dt.datetime.now(tz.UTC)

Out[19]: datetime.datetime(2021, 1, 3, 10, 18, 37, 176299, tzinfo=tzutc())
```

Time Zones with Python 3.9

Python 3.9 added proper time zone support to the standard library in the form of the `timezone` module. Use it to replace the `tz.gettz` calls from `dateutil`:

```
from zoneinfo import ZoneInfo
timestamp_eastern = dt.datetime(2020, 1, 31, 14, 30,
                                tzinfo=ZoneInfo("US/Eastern"))
```

Mutable vs. Immutable Python Objects

In Python, objects that can change their values are called *mutable* and those that can't are called *immutable*. Table C-1 shows how the different data types qualify.

Table C-1. Mutable and immutable data types

Mutability	Data Types
mutable	lists, dictionaries, sets
immutable	integers, floats, booleans, strings, datetime, tuples

Knowing about the difference is important as mutable objects may behave differently from what you are used to from other languages, including VBA. Have a look at the following VBA snippet:

```
Dim a As Variant, b As Variant
a = Array(1, 2, 3)
b = a
a(1) = 22
Debug.Print a(0) & ", " & a(1) & ", " & a(2)
Debug.Print b(0) & ", " & b(1) & ", " & b(2)
```

This prints the following:

```
1, 22, 3
1, 2, 3
```

Now let's do the same example in Python with a list:

```
In [20]: a = [1, 2, 3]
         b = a
         a[1] = 22
         print(a)
         print(b)

[1, 22, 3]
[1, 22, 3]
```

What happened here? In Python, variables are names that you "attach" to an object. By doing b = a, you attach both names to the same object, the list [1, 2, 3]. All variables attached to that object will, therefore, show the changes to the list. This only happens with mutable objects, though: if you would replace the list with an immutable object like a tuple, changing a would not change b. If you want a mutable object like b to be independent of changes in a, you have to explicitly copy the list:

```
In [21]: a = [1, 2, 3]
         b = a.copy()

In [22]: a

Out[22]: [1, 2, 3]

In [23]: b

Out[23]: [1, 2, 3]

In [24]: a[1] = 22  # Changing "a"...

In [25]: a

Out[25]: [1, 22, 3]

In [26]: b  # ...doesn't affect "b"

Out[26]: [1, 2, 3]
```

By using a list's copy method, you are creating a *shallow copy*: you will get a copy of the list, but if the list contains mutable elements, these will still be shared. If you want to copy all elements recursively, you need to make a *deep copy* by using the copy module from the standard library:

```
In [27]: import copy
         b = copy.deepcopy(a)
```

Let's now look at what happens when you use mutable objects as function arguments.

Calling Functions with Mutable Objects as Arguments

If you come from VBA, you are probably used to marking function arguments as pass-by-reference (ByRef) or pass-by-value (ByVal): when you pass a variable to a function as argument, the function will have the ability to change it (ByRef) or will work on a copy of the values (ByVal), thus leaving the original variable untouched. ByRef is the default in VBA. Consider the following function in VBA:

```
Function increment(ByRef x As Integer) As Integer
    x = x + 1
    increment = x
End Function
```

Then, call the function like this:

```
Sub call_increment()
    Dim a As Integer
    a = 1
    Debug.Print increment(a)
    Debug.Print a
End Sub
```

This will print the following:

```
2
2
```

However, if you change ByRef in the increment function to ByVal, it will print:

```
2
1
```

How does this work in Python? When you pass around variables, you pass around names that point to objects. This means that the behavior depends on whether the object is mutable or not. Let's first use an immutable object:

```
In [28]: def increment(x):
             x = x + 1
             return x

In [29]: a = 1
         print(increment(a))
         print(a)

2
1
```

Now let's repeat the sample with a mutable object:

```
In [30]: def increment(x):
             x[0] = x[0] + 1
             return x

In [31]: a = [1]
         print(increment(a))
         print(a)

[2]
[2]
```

If the object is mutable and you would like to leave the original object unchanged, you will need to pass in a copy of the object:

```
In [32]: a = [1]
         print(increment(a.copy()))
         print(a)

[2]
[1]
```

Another case to watch out for is the use of mutable objects as default arguments in function definitions—let's see why!

Functions with Mutable Objects as Default Arguments

When you write functions, you normally shouldn't use mutable objects as default arguments. The reason is that the value of default arguments is evaluated only once as part of the function definition, not every time when the function is called. Therefore, using mutable objects as default arguments can lead to unexpected behavior:

```
In [33]: # Don't do this:
         def add_one(x=[]):
             x.append(1)
             return x

In [34]: add_one()

Out[34]: [1]

In [35]: add_one()

Out[35]: [1, 1]
```

If you want to use an empty list as a default argument, do this instead:

```
In [36]: def add_one(x=None):
             if x is None:
                 x = []
             x.append(1)
             return x

In [37]: add_one()

Out[37]: [1]

In [38]: add_one()

Out[38]: [1]
```

Index

array-based formulas (xlwings), 272
arrays (NumPy)
    broadcasting, 79-80
    constructors, 83
    data analysis issues in, 84
    data types, 78-79
    getting and setting elements, 82-83
    operational overview, 77-79
    universal functions (ufuncs), 80-81
    vectorization, 79-80
    views versus copies, 83-84
asfreq method (pandas), 137
attributes
    help documentation, 50
    purpose of, 45, 291-293
augmented assignment notation, 63
auto activation of Conda environments, disabling, 283
autocomplete, 34
autofit method (xlwings), 203
automation in Excel (see xlwings)

B

backends
    purpose of, 241
    in Python Package Tracker, 245-248
best practices for programming
    DRY principle, 8
    separation of concerns, 6-7
    testing, 8
    version control, 9-11
big data, xi, 138, 169-173
Binder, 33
Bokeh, 119
Book class (xlwings), 188
book object (xlwings), 188
books collection (xlwings), 193
bool constructor, 48
boolean data type, 47-49, 148
boolean indexing (pandas)
    selecting data by, 95-96
    setting data by, 98-99
boolean operators, 47, 95
break statement, 62
breakpoints (VS Code), setting, 270
broadcasting, 79-80, 104
built-in converters (xlwings), 196
built-in options for range object (xlwings), 196
business intelligence (see Power BI)

business layer, 6
ByRef function arguments (VBA), 295-296
ByVal function arguments (VBA), 295-296

C

cache decorator, 276
caching, 274-276
calculations, separate layer for, 7
calling functions, 44, 66, 295-297
capitalize method (pandas), 105
Cascading Style Sheets (CSS), 177
Case statement (VBA), 56
case studies
    Excel reporting, 143-147, 178, 202-203
    Google Trends case study
        DataFrames and dynamic arrays, 258-263
        debugging UDFs, 269-271
        explanation of Google Trends, 257-258
        fetching data, 263-267
        plotting data, 267-269
    Python Package Tracker
        adding packages, 223-225
        application structure, 240
        backend, 245-248
        databases, 229-237
        debugging, 248-249
        error handling, 238-240
        frontend, 241-245
        web APIs, 226-229
cd command, 23
cell formatting (xlwings), clearing, 207-208
cell looping, 158
cells (Jupyter notebooks)
    edit mode versus command mode, 31-32
    in Python scripts, 289
    operational overview, 29-31
    output, 30
    run order, 32
chaining indexing and slicing operations, 52, 82
changing
    cell types (Jupyter notebooks), 30
    directories, 23
    list separators (Excel), 187-188
    to parent directory, 23
charts (Excel), 114
    (see also plots)
    creating in OpenPyXL, 160-162
    creating in XlsxWriter, 163-165

About the Author

Felix Zumstein is creator and maintainer of xlwings, a popular open source package that allows the automation of Excel with Python on Windows and macOS. He also organizes the xlwings meetups in London and NYC to promote a broad range of innovative solutions for Excel.

As CEO of xltrail, a version control system for Excel files, he has talked to hundreds of users who use Excel for business critical tasks and has therefore gained deep insight into the typical uses cases and issues with Excel across various industries.

Colophon

The animal on the cover of *Python for Excel* is a false coral snake (*Anilius scytale*). This brightly colored snake, also known as the American pipe snake, is found in the Guianas region of South America, the Amazon rainforest, and Trinidad and Tobago.

The false coral snake grows up to around 70 cm in length and has bright red and black bands. Its banded appearance is similar to that of the coral snake, from whom it derives one of its common names; however, the false coral snake is missing the distinctive yellow bands of the "true" coral snake. Its body has roughly the same diameter for most of its length with a very short tail, giving it a tube-like appearance. It small eyes are covered by large head scales.

This burrowing snake has been observed to be ovoviviparous. It feeds on beetles, amphibians, lizards, fish, and other small snakes. The false coral snake also retains spurs, or small protruding bits of bone near its vent, which are vestigial traces of hips and occasionally upper leg bones. This feature, along with the thick bones and distinctive shape of its skull, makes the false coral snake closely resemble snakes' ancestral, lizard-like condition.

The conservation status of the false coral snake is "Data Deficient," meaning that there is not yet enough information to judge the threat of its extinction. Many of the animals on O'Reilly covers are endangered; all of them are important to the world.

The cover illustration is by Karen Montgomery, based on a black and white engraving from *English Cyclopedia Natural History*. The cover fonts are Gilroy Semibold and Guardian Sans. The text font is Adobe Minion Pro; the heading font is Adobe Myriad Condensed; and the code font is Dalton Maag's Ubuntu Mono.

O'REILLY®

Learn from experts.
Become one yourself.

Books | Live online courses
Instant Answers | Virtual events
Videos | Interactive learning

Get started at oreilly.com.

Milton Keynes UK
Ingram Content Group UK Ltd.
UKHW031835031224
451932UK00002B/4